THE KENNEDY CURSE

THE
KENNEDY CURSE

WHY AMERICA'S FIRST FAMILY HAS BEEN
HAUNTED BY TRAGEDY FOR 150 YEARS

EDWARD KLEIN

ST. MARTIN'S PRESS ❧ NEW YORK

www.stmartins.com

Book design by Gretchen Achilles

Library of Congress Cataloging-in-Publication Data

Klein, Edward.
    The Kennedy curse : why America's first family has been haunted by
tragedy for 150 years / Edward Klein.—1st ed.
        p.   cm.
    Includes bibliographical references (p. 229) and index (p. 253).
    ISBN 0-312-31292-X
    1. Kennedy family.   2. Politicians—United States—Family
relationships.   3. Politicians—United States—Biography.
4. Politicians' spouses—United States—Biography.   5. Children of
presidents—United States—Biography.   I. Title.

E843.K58 2003
929.7'0973—dc21

                                                                2003041400

10   9   8

IN MEMORY OF MY PARENTS,
MEYER AND GERTRUDE KLEIN

CONTENTS

CONTENTS

THE KENNEDY CURSE

AN ILL-FATED HOUSE

It was an ill-fated house. . . . A curse seemed to hang over the family, making men sin in spite of themselves and bringing suffering and death down upon the innocent as well as the guilty.

—EDITH HAMILTON, *Mythology*

"I WANT TO HAVE KIDS, but whenever I raise the subject with Carolyn, she turns away and refuses to have sex with me."

The speaker was John F. Kennedy Jr., and he was sitting on the edge of a king-size bed, a phone cradled in the crook of his shoulder, pouring his heart out to a friend. It was late on the afternoon of July 14, 1999—two days before John's fatal plane crash—and the last rays of sunlight were flooding his room at the Stanhope, a fashionable New York hotel located across Fifth Avenue from the Metropolitan Museum of Art.

"It's not just about sex," John told his friend, who recalled the conversation for me several days later, while it was still fresh in his memory. "It's impossible to talk to Carolyn about *anything*. We've become like total strangers. . . ."

For a moment, the words choked in John's throat, and his friend could sense his struggle to regain his composure. Then all of John's pent-up bitterness and frustration exploded over the phone line.

"I've *had* it with her!" he said. "It's got to stop. Otherwise, we're headed for divorce."

A thousand days had passed since John exchanged wedding vows with Carolyn Bessette on a wild, unspoiled island off the coast of Georgia, and during that time the truth about their troubled marriage had been kept a well-guarded secret. Now John and Carolyn were living apart—he at the Stanhope, she in their downtown loft in TriBeCa—and John was on the verge of calling it quits.

For the life of him, John could not understand why his marriage had soured, especially since it had begun with so much sweetness and hope. An inveterate prankster, John eagerly endorsed Carolyn's wish to keep their wedding plans secret. "This is one thing *I'm* in control of, not John," Carolyn told a close friend. "No one's going to know where or when we're getting married."

From the start, Carolyn was in a quandary over who would make her wedding dress. Should she ask Calvin Klein, who until recently had employed her as a mid-level publicist? Should she choose her old roommate, the talented black fashion designer Gordon Henderson? Or should she turn to Narciso Rodriguez, a former Calvin Klein staffer who now worked for the Paris couturier Nino Cerruti? Carolyn knew that her choice would have major repercussions, for her wedding dress and its designer were certain to garner worldwide publicity.

It was not until fifteen days before the wedding that Carolyn finally made a decision. She picked the relatively unknown Narciso Rodriguez to design both her rehearsal dinner dress and wedding dress, as well as Caroline Kennedy Schlossberg's matron-of-honor dress.

Gordon Henderson, who was Carolyn's closest friend, was devastated. He had dreamed of designing Carolyn's dress—and becoming a bigger fashion star.

As a consolation, Carolyn asked Henderson to make John's suit and orchestrate the details of the wedding. Preparations were conducted with all the secrecy of a military operation. Only a few close friends and family members were invited. Everything seemed to go smoothly until Carolyn attempted to put on her wedding dress and found that she could not manage to get the $40,000 pearl-colored silk crepe floor-length gown over her head. It was cut on the bias without a zipper, and like many such dresses, it was difficult to put on. Try as hard as she might, she could not squeeze herself into it.

Under mounting pressure, Carolyn grew hysterical and began yelling at everyone around her. Henderson gently led her into a bathroom, put a scarf over her head, and managed to get her into the dress. Then, still in a state of high anxiety, she sat while her makeup and hair were redone.

Carolyn's stiletto heels drilled holes in the sandy beach on the way to Cumberland Island's tiny wood-frame First African Baptist Church. A stunning six-foot-tall, size-six, corn-silk blond bride, she was two hours late for her own wedding.

The one-room church was illuminated by candlelight, and it was so dim inside that the young Jesuit priest, the Reverend Charles J. O'Byrne of Manhattan's Church of St. Ignatius Loyola, where Jacqueline Kennedy Onassis's funeral Mass was held in 1994, had to read the service by flashlight. John's cousin and closest friend, Anthony Radziwill, served as best man (as John had served as best man at Tony's wedding), and at the end of the ceremony John turned to Tony and told him that he had never been happier in his life.

The marriage made front-page news everywhere, and a new Kennedy myth was born. The man who could have had any woman in the world had chosen as his bride one who was not rich or famous or ennobled by family background or distinguished by any professional accomplishment. What Carolyn had were certain charismatic qualities—exceptional beauty, a unique sense of style, and a shrewd, sharp, hard intelligence.

The media played the marriage as a Cinderella story, casting Carolyn as the commoner who had found true love with Prince Charming. But it turned out to be a doomed fairy tale, a nightmare of escalating domestic violence, sexual infidelity, and drugs—a union that seemed destined to end in one kind of disaster or another.

When John and Carolyn returned from their honeymoon in the fall of 1996, they found a swarm of journalists camped outside their front door at 20 North Moore Street in the heart of Manhattan's chic TriBeCa district. The rowdy media mob terrified Carolyn, and in a gallant effort to protect his wife, John pleaded with the reporters and cameramen to back off and give her a chance to adjust to her new role as a celebrity.

His pleas fell on deaf ears. Over the course of the next few weeks, the siege of North Moore Street got only worse. Reporters foraged through the newlyweds' garbage, searching for clues to their sex life. Paparazzi pursued John and Carolyn wherever they went, pounding on the sides of their automobile to make them turn toward the cameras, then blinding them with flashbulbs.

Normally, only supernovas of the magnitude of Madonna had to suffer through this kind of public ordeal. But Carolyn was suddenly thrust into their celestial company. Photos of her appeared everywhere. She drove the fashion world mad with excitement. The editor of *Women's Wear Daily,* Patrick McCarthy, crowned Carolyn a modern style icon, heir to Jackie O, her deceased mother-in-law. Anna Wintour at *Vogue* and Liz Tilberis at *Harper's Bazaar* were eager to get Carolyn to pose for their covers. And Ralph Lauren tried to hire Carolyn as his personal muse. "Every time you design something, or create something," Ralph instructed one of his top aides, "think of Carolyn Bessette. "

John was accustomed to this kind of treatment. The narcissist in him thrived on it. To get attention, he often indulged in exhibitionist stunts, such as appearing shirtless in Central Park or having his picture taken while sailing with a thong-clad Carolyn Bessette. As someone who had grown up in the klieg lights of public scrutiny, John equated celebrity with power. And like most megastars, he dreaded the emptiness that came with being ignored.

But Carolyn was a different story. As the months wore on, she could not handle the relentless personal scrutiny and exploitation that went with public glorification. When a photographer approached her on the street, she cast her eyes to the ground and hunched her shoulders. "She makes herself look like the Hunchback of Notre Dame," complained Calvin Klein. And indeed, in many photos, she looked like a hunted creature.

To avoid the paparazzi, Carolyn sought refuge in the West Village apartment of Gordon Henderson. "She didn't feel at home in the North Moore Street apartment," said a friend. "She hated it. She didn't like where it was located. And John had decorated it—badly. It was very cold, like a young man's first loft."

It was clear to friends that Carolyn was cracking under the pressure. She displayed the classic signs of clinical depression. A few months after the marriage, she began spending more and more time locked inside her apartment, convulsed by crying jags and, as gossip columnist Liz Smith observed, "bemoaning her fate as the wife of the most famous man in the world."

"John's life was huge—with dozens of friendships and involvements—but Carolyn couldn't handle that," one of her closest friends told me. "She didn't want to go out. She would ditch John's friends, not show up for dinner, refuse go to people's houses or events. She burned a lot of bridges."

As a child of divorce who had long been estranged from her father, Carolyn was sensitive to any sign of male desertion. In her view, John had forsaken her to work on *George,* his political lifestyle magazine. One time she faxed him at his office: "Please come home now, I need you." In addition, she resented that John had reverted to his old bachelor ways—pumping iron at the gym late into the night, going off on kayak trips with the boys, and (Carolyn suspected) playing around behind her back with the girls.

One time, when John returned in the evening to their loft, he found Carolyn sprawled on the floor in front of a sofa, disheveled and hollow-eyed, snorting cocaine with a gaggle of gay fashionistas—clothing designers, stylists, male models, and one or two publicists. Without asking John's permission, Carolyn gave keys to their loft to some of her friends so they could come and go as they pleased.

"You're a cokehead!" John screamed at her, according to one of the people who was present that night.

Her friends in the fashion industry were aware that Carolyn was a heavy user of street drugs.

"She and I went to dinner one night when John was sick at home with the flu," recalled a close acquaintance who worked at *George* magazine. "She made at least a half dozen trips to the bathroom, and came back to the table with white rings around her nostrils. We went from bar to bar, and she wanted to come over to my apartment, but I said no because I knew it would be an all-nighter. I finally dropped her off at three A.M. The next morning, John came into the office and asked, 'Why did you keep my wife out so late?' And I said, 'A better question, John, is why your wife didn't want to go home.'

"Carolyn was like a wild horse," this person continued. "She had a trash mouth and loved being irreverent. She used to call John a fag all the time. Once, there was a party at Mar-a-Lago, Donald Trump's private club in Florida, and Carolyn announced to a roomful of people, 'I had to take a Puerto Rican bath on the way down in the airplane.'"

Their fights frequently turned violent, and John told friends that he felt trapped in an abusive relationship. One time he had to be rushed to the emergency room for an operation to repair a severed nerve in his right wrist. He tried to dismiss the injury as the result of a stupid household accident. But his friends knew better: they were certain that Carolyn was the culprit.

Both Carolyn and John had fiery tempers, but it was always she who seemed to get the better of their arguments. When she heard rumors that John was seeing his old flame Daryl Hannah behind her back, Carolyn flew into a rage.

People who knew Carolyn doubted she would ever let John go. Her insecurity fueled a need to control and manipulate; her addiction to cocaine made her paranoid. She was jealous of John's sister, Caroline Kennedy Schlossberg, and his business partner at *George,* Michael Berman— in fact, of anyone who challenged her for undisputed control over John.

"Carolyn didn't like Michael Berman," said one of her friends. "She thought Michael wasn't on the up-and-up, and that he had a vested interest in her husband. She poisoned John's relationship with Michael. I heard her tell John, 'I don't believe Michael's your real friend. The only reason he's close to you is because you're John F. Kennedy Jr.' "

But it was Carolyn's constant meddling in the editorial operations of *George* that finally wrecked John's relationship with Michael Berman and was one of the factors that led to Berman's departure. Partly as a result, the magazine, which had been Berman's idea in the first place, was teetering on the brink of disaster.

"The divorce between Michael Berman and JFK Jr. was fateful for *George*," said Jean-Louis Ginibre, the former editorial director of the U.S. division of Hachette Filipacchi Magazines, the Paris-based publisher that bankrolled and distributed *George*. "When Berman left, something was lost in the mix."

Carolyn had also engineered a bitter falling-out with Caroline Kennedy Schlossberg after hearing that John's sister had made snide remarks about the Cumberland Island wedding. A stickler for punctuality, Caroline had criticized the bride for being late to her own wedding and for insisting on wearing four-inch heels as she trudged down the sandy beach to the church. Now Carolyn and Caroline were barely on speaking terms, and John was caught in the middle between his wife and his adored sister.

When he married, John dreamed of having a son. He had even picked out a name: Flynn. But Carolyn was never willing to start a family.

"I hate living in a fishbowl," she confided to a friend. "John may be comfortable living like this, but I'm not. How could I bring a child into this kind of world?"

What attracted John to this ill-fated relationship?

Several explanations were making the rounds in the months before his violent death. Many of his friends told me that they suspected he had married Carolyn Bessette because he was looking for someone to take the place of his dead mother, on whom he had depended all his life.

At first I tended to dismiss this explanation as psychobabble. But after I had a chance to think it over, I decided that John's friends were probably right. As they pointed out, John was still as needy as the little boy who had saluted his father's coffin after the presidential assassination. And John himself admitted to his friend on the phone, "I'm attracted to strong-willed women like my mother."

But Carolyn was not just a strong-willed woman. She could be demanding, domineering, and, according to even her best friends, downright bitchy. Some people felt that John overlooked her faults because he was blinded by Carolyn's glamorous Jackie O style. In her own edgy, modern way, Carolyn was as chic as Jackie; she dressed with the simple elegance that John adored. Like the ethereal Jackie, Carolyn affected an air of mystery and unavailability, which drove the media crazy and sustained the public frenzy that John found exciting and fun. And like Jackie, Carolyn was very controlling, which made John feel protected and cared for.

From the moment John laid eyes on Carolyn, he became obsessed with her. "He lived and breathed Carolyn," one of his friends told me, echoing the sentiments of many. "He could not keep his hands off her. He constantly stroked her hair, which she had dyed white blond."

Carolyn accepted John's worshipful attention as though it was her due—as though *he* was lucky to have *her*, rather than the other way around. Carolyn's aloof attitude set her apart from other women John had dated in the past—Madonna, Sarah Jessica Parker, Sharon Stone, Daryl Hannah, and many lesser-known names. Many of those women had thrown themselves at John, which made him suspicious of their motives. Carolyn, on the other hand, appeared to be unimpressed by his fame, and in the end it was probably her posture of cool indifference, as much as her beauty, that captivated him and held him spellbound.

Carolyn possessed another quality that attracted John, who hated to be thought of as square.

"She is the hippest person I ever met," said Hachette's Jean-Louis Ginibre. "She is totally au courant. Very bright. There is nothing she doesn't know. She can focus on one person for ten to twenty minutes and be totally involved with this person. She is very intense, very touchy-feely, and can mesmerize a person."

Jacqueline Kennedy Onassis, who managed to mesmerize more than a few men in her time, died of cancer of the lymphatic system before she had the opportunity to meet her son's future wife. However, that did not stop people from asking, "What would Jackie have thought of John's marriage to Carolyn?"

As a friend of Jackie's for more than a dozen years, I had many opportunities to talk with her about her children. My conversations with Jackie lead me to believe that had she lived, she would have disapproved of John's choice of Carolyn. Furthermore, I feel certain that Jackie would have done everything in her power to prevent their marriage.

Jackie was a shrewd judge of character and would have seen Carolyn Bessette for what she was—a flirtatious, seductive, and psychologically unstable young woman who had set her cap for the Prince of Camelot. Jackie would have been gravely alarmed that in a marriage to such a woman, John would inevitably come to harm.

Jackie had an almost pathological obsession with the safety of her children. She worried that John and Caroline were in constant danger of losing their lives. Her anxiety was understandable: she had lost three other children (a stillbirth, a miscarriage, and her two-day-old son, Patrick), two husbands (John Kennedy and Aristotle Onassis), a stepson (Onassis's son, Alexander), and a brother-in-law (Robert Kennedy). She had come to the conclusion that in some mystical way she was personally responsible for these tragedies.

"I sometimes feel as though I'm a kind of Typhoid Mary," Jackie once told me. Another time she said, "If I had known Jack was going to be killed, I would never have named our son John F. Kennedy Jr."

I never knew how to respond to these jaw-dropping remarks.

"Surely," I would tell Jackie, "you don't believe in a family jinx or curse."

But she was deadly serious about her premonitions of disaster.

It was clear to me that although Jackie loved both her children, she reserved her deepest feelings—and concern—for John. Though John looked like a Bouvier, he had the Kennedy daredevil encoded in his DNA, which naturally gave Jackie cause for concern. She believed that John was immature and did not have a clue about how the real world worked. He was absentminded, always late, and constantly misplacing his wallet and credit cards. He was also clumsy and accident-prone. Because he lost things, he kept his keys on a chain, but when he played with the key chain, he often hit himself in the eye.

Caroline, on the other hand, was the spitting image of her father: she had his hair, eyes, smile, and complexion. But she possessed her mother's cautious temperament, desire for privacy, and drive to excel. When Jackie talked about Caroline, it was always in terms of her achievements.

Caroline made her proud; John made her light up.

"My daughter is so analytical," she would tell me. "She's doing this book on privacy. Caroline is so focused and dedicated compared with John, who is spread out. He's a good boy, but he's always getting into a jam. Compared with Caroline, John has a more open personality. But that also means he's more open to stimulation and being led in the wrong directions. I always tell him he's got to be careful never to do anything that could darken the family name. But I'm not sure he's listening. You never know what he'll do next, or what terrible thing might happen to him."

Jackie feared that when she was no longer around, John would get into serious trouble. Which, of course, is exactly what happened.

Death was merciful to Jackie; it spared her a parent's worst nightmare—the loss of a child. If Jackie had lived to see her only son perish in a plane crash while on his way to his cousin Rory's wedding, I believe the news would have killed her.

However, if she had somehow managed to survive the staggering blow, she would have been doubly horrified by the familiar pattern. For once again, at a moment that should have been filled with joy and celebration, a member of America's most famous family was struck by tragedy.

As Jackie knew, Robert F. Kennedy had raised the notion of a family curse. Following Jack's assassination in 1963, Bobby—who could never shake the suspicion that his enemies had retaliated against him by killing his brother—began reading ancient Greek tragedies for consolation.

"In the plays of Aeschylus and Sophocles," writes RFK's biographer Evan Thomas, "Kennedy discovered fate and hubris. He began to wonder if the Kennedy family had somehow overreached, dared too greatly. In his copy of Edith Hamilton's *The Greek Way,* he had underlined Herodotus: 'All arrogance will reap a harvest rich in tears. God calls men to a heavy reckoning for overweening pride.' . . . The Kennedys *were* the House of Atreus, noble and doomed, and RFK began to see himself as Agamemnon."

After his brother Ted's plane crashed in 1964, Bobby said, "Somebody up there doesn't like us." And in 1968, after Bobby himself was murdered, his son Michael commented, "It was as if fate had turned against us. There was now a pattern that could not be ignored."

A year after *that,* Senator Edward Kennedy became the first member of the family to use the word *curse* in public. He told a TV audience that among the "irrational thoughts" that had occurred to him after Chappaquiddick was the question of "whether some awful curse did actually hang over all the Kennedys."

It turned out that Senator Kennedy's irrational thoughts came from a notably sane source—Theodore Sorensen, the Kennedy clan's greatest wordsmith and the former chief speechwriter for President John F. Kennedy. Sorensen and other writers crafted Teddy Kennedy's Chappaquiddick speech, with its reference to "some awful curse," and it was approved by several members of the Kennedy family as well as their closest advisers.

And so it was the Kennedys themselves—not their detractors—who were the first true believers in the curse.

Exactly thirty years elapsed between Mary Jo Kopechne's drowning at Chappaquiddick and John F. Kennedy Jr.'s fatal accident off Martha's Vineyard. During that time, the public's curiosity about the Kennedy

Curse was roused now and then by what appeared to be isolated events—Joe Kennedy II's 1973 Jeep accident, which left one of his teenage girlfriends, Pamela Kelly, paralyzed; David Kennedy's 1984 drug death; Willy Smith's 1991 rape trial; Michael Kennedy's 1997 affair with his children's baby-sitter, and his subsequent death on a ski slope in Aspen, Colorado.

It was not until the 1999 crash of JFK Jr.'s private plane, with the loss of three vibrant young lives, that many people were finally shocked into thinking seriously about the nature of the curse and its origins.

"When John and Robert Kennedy were assassinated, their death seemed, if nothing else, at least commensurate with the drama and weight of their public life," *Time* magazine noted at the time. "When their children die prematurely, it can seem almost as if fate were picking them off for sport."

The shock of JFK Jr.'s death in the summer of 1999 set me to thinking about my conversations with Jackie during the last dozen years of her life. And as I reviewed my reporter's diaries, I was struck all over again by Jackie's unshakable conviction that John and Caroline—indeed, all the Kennedys—were the hapless victims of some inexplicable and malignant fate.

Like many others, I had always found it difficult to embrace the notion that the Kennedys lived at the receiving end of a *supernatural* curse. Perhaps because I am a journalist, I prefer to focus on definable facts—things that can be explained by the known forces or laws of nature. By definition, the supernatural does not fall into that category; it can be neither proved nor disproved.

But after John F. Kennedy Jr.'s death, it was no longer possible for even the most dedicated rationalist to believe that all this suffering has been a matter of chance. When a family has a history of repeated self-destructiveness going back many decades, common sense tells us that a certain pattern—something more profound than bad luck or coincidence—must be at work.

It seems that virtually every time a Kennedy was on the verge of achieving a goal or ambition, he was doomed to pay a tragic price. Take the case of Joseph Kennedy, who spent a lifetime trying to elect one of his sons President; as soon as he succeeded, he was struck dumb by a stroke. Then there is the example of his son, John F. Kennedy, who struggled for three years to master the role of President; just as he showed signs of becoming a skillful commander-in-chief and chief executive, he was felled by an assassin's bullet. And *his* son, JFK Jr., married the woman of his dreams, only to be the one who was responsible for both their deaths.

Of course, all families suffer adversity, and some suffer far more than their "fair share." Perhaps the most dramatic example of a family tragedy occurred during World War II, when five Sullivan brothers went down with their ship, the USS *Juneau*—an event that became the inspiration half a century later for Steven Spielberg's film *Saving Private Ryan*.

Members of rich families, who have the resources and opportunity to do things that are denied others, seem to suffer more misfortune than poor people. In Italy, the late automobile magnate Gianni Agnelli, a member of one of the largest and wealthiest families in Europe, lost his father in a plane crash when he was fourteen; a decade later he himself narrowly escaped death in a car accident; he saw his brother Giorgio die at the age of thirty-five; he lost an aunt, Ancieta Nasi, who died while giving birth, leaving her five children motherless; he consoled his brother Umberto when Umberto's eldest son, Giovanni, died of cancer; he was shattered when his son, Edoardo, a drug addict, committed suicide.

But the heartbreaking record of the Agnelli family pales by comparison with the tragic history of the Kennedy clan. In the savage and unrelenting ferocity of its afflictions, no other modern family has come even close. As Bobby Kennedy discovered after the assassination of his brother, one must go back to the ancient Greeks and the House of Atreus—to such legendary figures as Agamemnon, Clytemnestra, Orestes, and Electra—to find a family that has been subjected to such a mind-boggling chain of calamities.

Destiny—as in circumstances beyond one's control—has traditionally been the most popular explanation for a curse.

According to ancient custom, a curse can be caused by either human or supernatural forces. "As an example of the first," writes Joe Nickell in *Skeptical Inquirer*, "in the Old Testament, when Noah became displeased by his son Ham, he placed a curse on him (Genesis 9:21–27); and, as a supernatural example, Jehovah dealt with an intransigent pharaoh by visiting upon him ten plagues (Exodus 7–12)." There are similar stories in the New Testament: Jesus cursed a fig tree for not bearing fruit, and Paul the Apostle struck a sorcerer blind.

Millions of people the world over believe in the supernatural power of curses. According to a Gallup poll on the prayer habits of Americans, 5 percent of Americans—about 14 million people—are willing to admit that they have prayed for harm to come to others. "The actual prevalence of using prayer to hurt others is undoubtedly much greater," Larry Dossey, M.D., writes in *Be Careful What You Pray For . . . You Just Might Get It*. "Some of these prayers appeared indistinguishable from curses and hexes—attempts to control the thought and behavior of a victim against his or her will."

To this day, many Greeks believe that Jackie Kennedy brought the Kennedy Curse with her when she married Greek shipping tycoon Aristotle Onassis. They point out that when the young American widow first met Onassis, he and his only son, Alexander, were healthy and money was pouring into the Onassis coffers. However, "in the year after his marriage to Jackie, four of his vessels suffered major mishaps," notes Onassis biographer Nicholas Gage. "Those closest to Onassis, including his intimate friends and top executives, whispered among themselves that the old man was losing his touch, and many of them were quick to blame it on the 'Jackie jinx.'" Seven years later, both Onassis and Alexander were dead and the family business had suffered a grievous blow.

The unspoken assumption behind the notion of the Kennedy Curse is that the Kennedys are being punished for their ill-gotten wealth and abuse of power. "What goes around, comes around" is the way many people put it. In this view, Joseph P. Kennedy, the ruthless patriarch of the family, made a Faustian pact with the devil, and the Kennedys have been paying for it ever since.

"Nothing in the universe is coincidence," Rabbi Meir Yeshurun of the Kabbalah Center in Boca Raton, Florida, told a reporter for the *Palm Beach Post*. "Somebody in the [Kennedy] family did something to open the family to this negative energy, and that has been plaguing the Kennedys for decades."

According to a story that is told in mystical Jewish circles, shortly before the outbreak of World War II, Joseph Kennedy, who was then ambassador to the Court of St. James's in London, returned to the United States aboard an ocean liner that was also carrying Israel Jacobson, a poor Lubavitcher rabbi, and six of his yeshiva students, who were fleeing the Nazis.

A notorious anti-Semite, Kennedy complained to the captain that the bearded, black-clad Jews were upsetting the first-class passengers by praying on the Jewish high holy day of Rosh Hashanah. Kennedy demanded that the captain stop the Jews from conducting their services in front of the other passengers. In retaliation, or so the story goes, Rabbi Jacobson put a curse on Kennedy, damning him and all his male offspring to tragic fates.

"I don't believe in curses or any other form of predestination," *New York Times* columnist William Safire wrote on the occasion of John F. Kennedy Jr.'s death. "Owning the Hope diamond or opening King Tut's tomb brought nobody bad luck. Allowing for genetic breaks, we are free to make much of our own fate."

Most people would agree with Safire. And yet it is a curious fact that the very same people who scoff at the concept of kismet, or fate, find it difficult to dismiss the concept of curses. After Robert Kennedy's son Bobby Jr. was sentenced to two years' probation on a felony drug charge, his cousin Christopher Lawford noted, "If you think of it as one movement from Grandfather's early days to what has happened to Bobby right now, you realize that the Kennedy story is really about karma, about people who broke the rules and were ultimately broken by them."

The belief in curses has deep roots in human psychology. As children, most of us are taught by our parents that we live in a just world governed by immutable moral laws and that we shall be punished if we do something wrong. This belief becomes so embedded in our consciousness that in our mature years, we find it nearly impossible to accept the idea of an amoral and random universe.

"A dynastic curse represents proof that nothing is random," *The Guardian* of London editorialized after John F. Kennedy Jr.'s plane crash. "If the Kennedys' tragedy is part of the natural order, then so too their entitlement to power and money is a supernatural given. Every word that is uttered or written about the 'curse' of the dynasty confirms the belief that the family is divinely ordained to be different from the rest of us."

Of course, the Kennedys have never been satisfied with being merely *different* from the rest of us. In their take-no-prisoners approach to life, they must always be *the best*.

"Daddy was always very competitive," said Eunice Kennedy Shriver, the fifth of Joseph Kennedy's nine children. "The thing he always kept telling us was that coming in second was just no good."

"He didn't like anyone to be second best, and he expected you to prepare yourself better than the other fellow and then try harder than he did," said Jack Kennedy's friend K. LeMoyne Billings. "Any other course of action in his mind suggested stupidity."

When one of the Kennedy children failed to come in first, he or she was sent to the kitchen to eat alone. And it did not matter how many times a child won a contest; victory—and parental acceptance—had to be won over and over again.

Joe Kennedy not only expected his children to win at any cost, he also demanded that they deny any feelings that contradicted the image of invincibility he sought to project.

16

"Kennedys don't cry," he instructed his brood.

"He wanted us to be able to smile no matter how tough things were," Ted Kennedy remarked. " 'I don't want any sourpusses around here,' he would say."

It did not matter if his children *felt* sad or fearful. They had to *act* as though they were brave, courageous, and fearless, which frequently translated into impulsive and reckless behavior—and the inevitable tragic collisions with reality.

This need to project an image at the expense of one's true feelings is characteristic of narcissistic personalities.* Contrary to popular belief, narcissists do not love themselves. They are full of self-loathing and self-destructive impulses. Because they are obsessed with enhancing their grandiose image at the expense of their true self, they are more concerned with how they *appear* than with how they *feel*. What's more, since narcissists are deadened to their own feelings, they are incapable of loving others.

"Listen," Kathleen Kennedy told one of her boyfriends when he complained of her emotional frigidity, "the thing about me you ought to know is that I am like Jack—incapable of deep affection."

And once when a friend showed Jack a teary letter that he had received from a girlfriend, Jack shocked him with his response.

"It may be romantic to you," said Jack, "but it's shit to me!"

Narcissists such as the Kennedys have an overwhelming need to foster fantasies of omnipotence and other godlike qualities—to believe that they are *entitled* to get away with things that others cannot—in order to compensate for deep feelings of vulnerabilty.

We can trace these feelings back to the Kennedys' early history,

---

*In Greek mythology, Narcissus was a handsome youth with whom the nymph Echo fell in love. But since Echo could repeat only the last syllable of words that she heard, she was unable to express her love for Narcissus. When he spurned Echo's advances, she died of a broken heart, and the gods punished Narcissus for being incapable of loving others by making him fall in love with his own reflection in a pool. He pined away for his own image until he died and was turned into the flower that bears his name.

which left an indelible scar on their psyche. Among America's immigrant groups in the nineteenth century, the Irish were the only people who suffered the soul-searing experience of colonialism. Before coming to America, they lived under the heel of cruel English oppressors for several centuries. That experience left them with feelings of humiliation and powerlessness.

Life did not improve much for the Irish after they arrived in America. The poor, powerless, dispossessed Irish souls who came over on "coffin ships" wore themselves out in America "digging, shoveling, lifting, hauling and dragging, laboring for ten, twelve, fourteen hours a day with seldom a break and never a vacation." The sons of these immigrants were often treated worse than Negro slaves; they were despised as brutish, simian creatures; they were excluded from living in good neighborhoods, from sending their children to decent schools, and from joining WASP clubs.

Although the Kennedys achieved financial security early in their American sojourn, they were denied social acceptance and status by the Protestant establishment. Decades after arriving in this country, Irish Catholics such as the Kennedys remained, in the words of sociologist Oscar Handlin, "a massive lump in the community, undigested and undigestible."

The presence of loving parents might have helped assuage the pain inflicted on the Kennedys by a hostile world. But such loving figures were absent from their childhood. The home of Joseph and Rose Kennedy—with its harsh, authoritarian father and cold, rejecting mother—was the perfect hothouse for nurturing narcissists.

"As children, narcissists suffer what analysts describe as severe narcissistic injury, a blow to self-esteem that scars and shapes their personalities," writes Alexander Lowen, M.D., in *Narcissism: Denial of the True Self*. "This injury entails humiliation, specifically the experience of being powerless while another person enjoys the exercise of power and control over one."

The dictatorial Joseph Kennedy was a textbook example of the successful psychopathic narcissist. Alan Harrington, who made a study of such personalities, describes them as "brilliant, remorseless people with icy intelligence, incapable of love or guilt, with aggressive designs on the rest of the world."

"Joe ran the family like a football team," the author Ronald Kessler notes in his definitive biography of Joseph Kennedy, *The Sins of the Father*. "He was the coach, the manager, and the referee. Rose was the water boy, constantly filling the children's mind with trivia. The aim was to win at everything, no matter what."

The Kennedy children lived in terror of their father's disapproval and his towering rage.

"When Joe spoke, everyone hopped to," said Edward F. Mc-Laughlin Jr., a friend of Jack's who later became lieutenant governor of Massachusetts. "We were lolling around on the porch one day. The word came that he [Joe] was landing at the airport. Everyone had to get a new activity. Everyone hopped to, playing football. He didn't want to see you sitting on your fanny. He drilled that into people."

Joe employed sarcasm, mockery, and derision to keep his brood in line.

"I don't know what is going to happen to this family when I die," he once remarked to his grown children in Palm Beach, according to author Ronald Kessler. "There is no one in the entire family . . . who is living within their means. No one appears to have the slightest concern for how much they spend."

He then turned to one of his daughters and said that she was "the worst." She burst into tears and fled from the room.

Rose Kennedy, on the other hand, was a religious fanatic who exhibited an almost complete lack of human feeling and empathy.

"Mrs. Kennedy didn't say she loved her children," recalled Luella R. Hennessey, the children's nurse. "It just wasn't said. It was all about respect."

Otto Kernberg, considered by many to be the world's leading authority on narcissism, writes about chronically cold parental figures such as Rose Kennedy in his classic study, *Borderline Conditions and Pathological Narcissism*. In all cases of narcissism, he notes, there is "a parental figure, usually the mother or a mother surrogate, who functions well on the surface in a superficially well-organized home, but with a degree of callousness, indifference, and nonverbalized, spiteful aggression. . . . Sometimes it was . . . the cold hostile mother's narcissistic use of the child which made him 'special,' set him off on the road in search for compensatory admiration and greatness."

These traumatic childhood experiences help explain why the men in the Kennedy family were left with a sense of worthlessness and suffered from a strong urge to punish themselves to the point of self-destruction.

"This is not to claim that the Kennedy accidents and murders were in any way planned by the victims, which in light of the known facts would be absurd," writes Nancy Gager Clinch in *The Kennedy Neurosis*. "But, very definitely when a person is driven by unconscious emotional conflicts toward self-suffering, he will tend to bring about the circumstances that may eventually cause this suffering.

"The evidence of recurrent Kennedy recklessness, indifference to danger, and bodily self-injury is too clear to be ignored," Clinch continues. "Disaster may come whether we wish it or not. But if part of us is unconsciously drawn to the pain or destruction of the disliked self, sooner or later disaster will almost certainly be ours."

Joe Jr., Jack, Bobby, and Teddy were full of longing for a warm and tender mother. They had an overpowering craving to be close to a woman, and yet they hated this feeling because they feared it meant that they were weak as men. As a result, they put on a tremendous show of Don Juanish behavior to demonstrate that they were in actuality strong, powerful men. But this was a compensatory image. Deep down, they felt like tiny, powerless boys.

The physical and emotional absence of a loving mother was keenly felt by these powerless boy-men.

"My mother was either at some Paris fashion house or else on her knees in some church," John F. Kennedy famously complained. "She was never there when we really needed her. . . . My mother never really held me and hugged me. *Never! Never!*"

Restless and bored, the Kennedys were always in search of new thrills. In 1993, the year before Jacqueline Kennedy Onassis's death, molecular geneticists reported a major scientific breakthrough regarding thrill-seeking behavior that made headlines and captured Jackie's attention. The scientists announced that they had discovered a variant of the gene that makes the protein receptor for dopamine, the brain's chemical messenger, in that portion of the brain controlling the personality.

Jackie told me that several things interested her about the discovery. Fifty percent of people with attention deficit disorder, like her son John, were found to have the rare variant of the DRD4 7R gene. People who abuse alcohol and drugs, of whom the Kennedy family has had more than its share, are also more likely to possess the gene than those who are not addicted to alcohol and drugs. Most important of all, Jackie was fascinated by the nickname the scientists gave to the gene. They called it the "thrill-seeking gene."

For forty years, scientists had known that certain personality traits are at least partly inherited, or genetically predisposed. They had done extensive studies on identical and fraternal twins who had been separated at birth and raised by different families. The separated twins displayed a striking similarity in their personalities and behavior, especially in their propensity for risk taking. Now the researchers had identified a variant of a gene, DRD4 7R, that they thought was directly linked to that kind of behavior.

"The best evidence that the gene DRD4 7R probably runs in the Kennedy family is in the consistent thrill-seeking behavior of its members," said Dr. Robert Moyzis, professor of molecular genetics at the University of California at Irvine. "Individuals with this gene are always out on the edge, taking more chances than most other people. And being out there, they've had some spectacular successes. But risk taking obviously has its downside, too. When a calamity befalls a Kennedy, people wonder, 'Why did this terrible thing happen to them?' But it's just the other side of the same coin.

"Like all thrill seekers, the Kennedys take risks because the payoffs are big," he continued. "And since, over the years, they've enjoyed uncommon success, that behavior has become reinforced and part of their family culture. That is why so many spectacular things happen to them. But it's also why they are always setting themselves up for a big fall."

Geneticists such as Dr. Moyzis do not suggest that a single gene is the last word on the subject of the Kennedy Curse. Obviously, something as complicated as human behavior is the result of many factors, including how a person learns from his experience and then passes that experience on to future generations.

"In every family, there is a certain myth that penetrates from generation to generation and explains what they are and what is expected of them," Peter Neubauer, an eminent psychoanalyst, told me in an interview for this book. "That is certainly true of the Kennedys, whose need for power and achievement overrides all standards. It is a pathological myth, because it is based on the fantasy of omnipotence.

"In the case of many Kennedys," Neubauer continued, "their drive for power is often supported by good deeds, by a desire to help the poor and disenfranchised, by humanitarian goals. They describe what they do not merely as 'politics' but as the much more lofty-sounding 'public service.' All this reduces the need for them to feel guilty about their single-minded pursuit of power. But it doesn't solve their substantive problem, because they still have to contend with the consequences of reality. Thus, there are these destructive collisions between their fantasy of omnipotence and reality, and the inevitable and repeated disasters."

This book is a detective story.

It is an investigation of one of the great mysteries of our time—

the Kennedy Curse. It explores the underlying pattern that governs the curse and examines the many influences—historical, psychological, and genetic—that have shaped the Kennedys' character and led to their self-defeating behavior.

The stories in this book illustrate how the Kennedy Curse began in the common Irish immigrant experience of poverty and humiliation, and developed into an obsessive lust for power and dominance over others at the expense of all ethical behavior. Each of the seven people who is profiled demonstrates in his and her own way the basic premise of this book:

> The Kennedy Curse is the result of the destructive collision between the Kennedys' fantasy of omnipotence—their need to get away with things that others cannot—and the cold, hard realities of life.

The people in this book were, for the most part, on a fatal collision course with reality. They felt immune to mortal laws and somehow divinely protected from the inevitable consequences of their deeds and misdeeds. In their hunger for unlimited power, they saw themselves as superior beings who resided above the common herd. They felt *special*—omnipotent and worthy of being worshiped.

"These, of course, are the attributes of a god," writes Dr. Alexander Lowen, a psychiatrist who specializes in narcissism. "On some deep level, narcissists . . . see themselves as little gods. Too often, unfortunately, their followers look up to them in that light too."

Our inclination to idolize the Kennedys has obscured their human attributes. And so, finally, this book is an attempt to demystify the Kennedys by telling the story of how the descendants of Patrick Kennedy, a poor Irish immigrant who came to the shores of the New World in 1849, pulled, tore, scratched, scraped, clutched, and clawed their way to the top of American society—and, in the process, made the fatal mistake of thinking of themselves as divine.

A CHRONICLE OF
THE KENNEDY CURSE

In the forty years since the assassination of President John F. Kennedy, tragedy has struck the Kennedys and those associated with the family on an average of nearly once every two years. But this sad American saga did not begin with JFK and his ambitious father, Joe. The chronology:

1858 Less than ten years after emigrating from Ireland, thirty-five-year-old Patrick Kennedy dies of consumption on November 22. The cause of death is common in the nineteenth century, but the date is seen by some as significant: it is exactly 105 years to the day before John. F. Kennedy's assassination. In any case, Patrick leaves a legacy of humiliation that encourages recklessness and risky behavior by his descendants.

1873 Eight-year-old Josie Hannon, who will grow up to become Rose Fitzgerald Kennedy's mother, is responsible for the drowning of her sister Elizabeth, four, and Elizabeth's friend. Overcome by guilt and self-reproach, Josie retreats into religious mysticism, which will have a profound influence on Rose Kennedy and her children.

1881 Michael Hannon Jr., twenty-one, Rose Kennedy's uncle, dies of alcoholism, a self-destructive disease that is known in his family as "the curse of the Irish."

1885 Thomas Fitzgerald, sixty-two, dies, leaving John Francis "Honey Fitz" Fitzgerald, age twenty-two, the future father of Rose Fitzgerald Kennedy, with the responsibility of raising his eight brothers. A full-blown narcissist, Honey Fitz becomes the flamboyant mayor of Boston, opening the way for future Kennedys to enter politics.

1888 Jimmy Hannon, twenty-five, another of Rose Kennedy's uncles, and a notorious ne'er-do-well who was fired from a postmaster job in disgrace, dies of alcoholism.

1890 John Edmond Hannon, thirteen, yet another of Rose Kennedy's uncles, has his leg badly mangled in a train accident. During an operation without ether, his leg is amputated below the knee.

1905 According to a front-page story in the *Boston Post*, Lawrence Kane, a close Kennedy relative, is "Killed by Fierce Rays of the July Sun." His reckless disregard for his own safety results in death by heat exhaustion.

1928 Another Kennedy relative, Humphrey Charles Mahoney, dies when he and his grandson are struck by an automobile while vacationing in Saratoga Springs.

1936 Rose Kennedy's sister, Mary Agnes (Fitzgerald) Gargan, forty-three, is found dead by her son, six-year-old Joseph Gargan Jr. Mary Agnes's three children—Joe Jr.; Mary Jo, three; and Ann, two—are raised and educated by Rose and Joe Kennedy. In the aftermath of the Chappaquiddick scandal thirty-three years later, Senator Edward Kennedy asks his "brother" Joe Gargan to take the rap and say that he was at the wheel of the car that killed Mary Jo Kopechne.

1941 With his sights set on seeing one of his sons enter the White House, Joe Kennedy orders a lobotomy on his daughter

Rosemary, who is an embarrassment to the family because she suffers from mild mental illness. For twenty years, Joe keeps the lobotomy a secret from his wife, Rose.

1944 Joseph P. Kennedy Jr., the future standard-bearer of the family, fails to heed warnings and perishes at the age of twenty-nine in a plane explosion while on a secret mission during World War II.

1948 Joseph P. Kennedy Sr.'s favorite daughter, Kathleen "Kick" Kennedy, also disregards warnings and dies in a plane crash at the age of twenty-eight. Her lover, Peter Fitzwilliam, a thirty-seven-year-old married British peer, and the pilot and copilot of the plane die along with her.

1955 Ethel Kennedy's parents are killed in a small plane crash in Oklahoma while on vacation.

1961 After years of planning and engineering his son's election as President of the United States, Joseph P. Kennedy suffers a massive stroke in the first year of John Kennedy's administration. The stroke robs Joe of the ability to speak and to participate in his son's political decision making.

1962 Marilyn Monroe, a lover of both John and Robert Kennedy, dies at age thirty-five of an overdose of sleeping pills. Suspicions linger that the Kennedy brothers are somehow implicated in her death.

1963 Jacqueline Bouvier Kennedy gives birth to a son, Patrick, six weeks premature. The baby dies two days later. Some biographers suggest that President Kennedy's chronic venereal disease may have been responsible for his wife's problems conceiving full-term babies.

1963 On a political trip to Texas, John F. Kennedy recklessly rejects safety measures proposed by the Secret Service and is assassinated at age forty-six in Dallas.

1964 Edward M. Kennedy imprudently insists on flying to a political event during a major storm. He is seriously injured in a plane crash. An aide, Edward Moss, and the pilot, Edwin J. Zimny, are both killed.

1964 Mary Pinchot Meyer, one of President Kennedy's lovers, is murdered under mysterious circumstances on a towpath along the Potomac River in Washington, D.C. Her diary is destroyed by James Jesus Angleton, chief of the CIA's counterintelligence branch, because it presumably contains intimate details of her illicit relationship with the slain President.

1967 Ethel Kennedy's brother George Skakel, a scion of the star-crossed Skakel family, is killed in a plane crash.

1967 George Skakel's widow, Joan Patricia Skakel, chokes to death on a piece of meat at a dinner party at her home in Greenwich, Connecticut.

1968 Robert F. Kennedy is assassinated at age forty-three in Los Angeles.

1969 Edward M. Kennedy, thirty-seven, drives a car off a bridge on Massachusetts' Chappaquiddick Island; the body of

Mary Jo Kopechne is discovered dead in the submerged car. Teddy flees the scene of the accident and tries to cover it up.

1973 Joseph P. Kennedy II, a son of Robert and Ethel Kennedy, who later becomes a congressman, runs his Jeep off the road on Nantucket Island. It overturns and leaves Pamela Kelly paralyzed.

1975 After fifteen-year-old Martha Elizabeth Moxley is brutally slain in Greenwich, Connecticut, suspicion for her murder falls on Ethel Kennedy's nephews Thomas and Michael Skakel. Thomas was later cleared.

1982 Joan Bennett Kennedy, who could never keep up with her hypercompetitive Kennedy in-laws, divorces Senator Edward Kennedy and is admitted to an alcohol rehabilitation center.

1984 David Kennedy, the son of Robert and Ethel Kennedy, dies of a drug overdose in the Brazilian Court Hotel in Palm Beach.

1985 Patrick Kennedy, the eighteen-year-old son of Edward and Joan Kennedy, seeks treatment for cocaine addiction.

1991 William Kennedy Smith, the son of Stephen and Jean Kennedy Smith, is accused of raping a woman at the family's Palm Beach estate. Though he is acquitted of the crime by a jury, many people refuse to believe that he is innocent.

1994 Jacqueline Kennedy Onassis, a health and fitness enthusiast, dies of cancer at age sixty-four.

1997 Michael Kennedy, the son of Robert and Ethel Kennedy, is accused of having an affair with his children's fourteen-year-old baby-sitter. He dies that same year on a ski slope in Aspen, Colorado, while skiing backward and playing a Kennedy family game of catch with a water bottle filled with snow.

1998 Robert Kennedy Jr. reveals that no fewer than nine members of the Kennedy clan are members of Alcoholics Anonymous.

1999 After being warned by his orthopedic surgeon not to fly solo, John F. Kennedy Jr., who is still recovering from a broken ankle, takes off after dark in his Piper Saratoga high-performance plane. John; his wife, Carolyn Bessette Kennedy; and her sister Lauren Bessette die in a crash off the coast of Martha's Vineyard.

1999 Anthony Radziwill, John Kennedy Jr.'s cousin and best friend, dies of testicular cancer.

2001 The tormented mother of the teenage baby-sitter seduced by Michael Kennedy is driven to drink by the humiliating scandal. She dies of complications from alcoholism.

2001 Robert Speisman, a son-in-law of Maurice Tempelsman, the longtime companion of the late Jacqueline Kennedy Onassis, is among the passengers who die aboard American

Airlines Flight 77 when it crashes into the Pentagon after being hijacked by terrorists.

2002 Michael Skakel, Ethel Kennedy's nephew, is convicted by a Greenwich, Connecticut, jury of the twenty-seven-year-old murder of Martha Moxley.

2003 Kara Kennedy, daughter of Edward and Joan Kennedy, is treated for lung cancer.

PART ONE

SCOURGE

CHAPTER ONE

PATRICK KENNEDY

THE UNINTENTIONAL CRIME

IN THE FAINT PEWTER LIGHT of an Irish dawn, a young man riding bareback on an old gray draft horse emerged from a fogbank on the outskirts of New Ross, a river port south of Dublin. A cold, hard rain pelted the sides of his horse, and the fog roiled up above the treetops, concealing the road ahead. A stranger might have hesitated to proceed any farther for fear of getting lost, but the young man knew the countryside like the back of his hand. He was a local lad, and the sum total of his life's experience, along with the memory and bones of his ancestors, was encompassed within a fifteen-mile radius of the town.

He made his way through the maze of fogbound alleys, and when he came to the stone wharf, he dismounted and tethered his horse to a post. His large hands were cut and calloused, a sign that he worked at a trade requiring sharp instruments. Beneath an untidy shock of reddish brown hair, his pale blue eyes looked upon the world with an odd mixture of fear and defiance.

Because he was Roman Catholic, no baptism certificate existed to fix the precise date of his birth (at the time, only Protestants were considered deserving of that privilege), but according to family tradition, he was born in Dunganstown, County Wexford, in 1823, which made him twenty-six years old. Though we possess only the barest scraps of information about this young man, it is important for the purposes of our inquiry into the Kennedy Curse that we try to piece together his story from the accounts of family members, written and oral histories, and Irish folklorists.

His name was Patrick Kennedy, and on this foggy February morning, he was about to leave his family and the tangled web of personal relationships in Ireland that had sustained him and given his life meaning, and take his chances in America. Once in Boston, Patrick would marry, have children, then die of consumption—all within the space of nine years. In that brief period of time, he became the founding father of the greatest political dynasty in American history. Through his bloodline, he gave America its first Catholic President, three U.S. senators, a U.S. attorney general, two members of the House of Representatives, two additional presidential contenders, and the dream of a golden age called Camelot.

In years to come, people would assume that Old Joe Kennedy— "the ruthless tycoon, with his film star mistress Gloria Swanson, his fortune carved from bootlegged booze, and his purchased political respectability"—was responsible for the Kennedy Curse. However, as we shall see, the seeds of the family's destruction were planted long ago in the unforgiving soil of famine-stricken Ireland.

That fateful morning Patrick Kennedy made a very odd sight indeed.

He was dressed in a cocked hat with the brim folded up against the crown and a swallow-tailed coat with long, tapering tails at the back. The coat was too narrow for his broad shoulders and the sleeves too short for his arms. He probably had no idea that his outfit, the height of fashion during the time of Napoleon, had gone out of style more than thirty years before. These shabby discards, which he had bought from an itinerant peddler for a few pennies, were all he could afford for the journey he intended to take far beyond the tidewater of New Ross.

In preparation for his trip, he had been visiting friends and family to bid them farewell. His first stop had been at the chapel, as the local Catholic church was called, where he received a blessing from the parish priest, Father Michael Mitten, who no doubt quoted from 2 Corinthians: "Weep sore for him that goeth away: for he shall return no more, nor see his native country."

He paid a parting call on the Glascotts, the Protestant family that held Whitechurch Parish and much of the surrounding land and were landlords of the Kennedys and other Catholic tenants. The Glascotts were themselves tenants of an even larger estate owned by the Tottenhams. But Patrick did not have to remove his cocked hat and bow his head to the Tottenhams, for they lived in England and did not deign to dirty their boots with the soil of Ireland.

Patrick had come to New Ross this day to say good-bye to his fellow workers at the Cherry Brothers Brewery, where he had been apprenticed for the past several years as a cooper, learning to carve casks and barrels. While he waited in the fog for the brewery to open, he could hear the creaking timber of sailing ships on the River Barrow and a distant watch bell striking the half hour.

At some point he became aware of a rustling sound on the cobblestones near where he stood. At first, he mistook the noise for a flock of seagulls. Then he realized that the entire street was stirring with homeless people, awakening from a night's sleep.

He watched them stand and stretch. "The barely human shapes," reported one observer, "were so emaciated, bones seemed to be held together by nothing more than skin." A few shrunken things that resembled children huddled near the entrance of the New Ross workhouse, their mouths stained green from eating grass.

The year was 1849, and it was the fourth consecutive winter of a mysterious blight that had destroyed the potato crop of Ireland. Without potatoes, the staple of their diet, people could not survive, and Ireland was in the grip of a great hunger.

An estimated million people had died of starvation and disease, although no one knew the precise number. Perhaps another 2 million had emigrated to England, Australia, Canada, and the United States. Columns of weary refugees, evicted from their homes by landlords, wandered the roads without aim or purpose. Looking back from the perspective of our era, a writer noted that the Irish Famine represented "the greatest concentration of civilian suffering and death in Western Europe between the Thirty Years' War and World War II."

Patrick Kennedy had witnessed sights of such unimaginable horror that he and his descendants would be haunted for generations by the memory. He had seen desperate people fighting with rats over the half-eaten flesh of decomposing corpses. He had watched as emaciated bodies were dumped into mass graves from reusable coffins with trapdoors. He had been present when a starving mob besieged the New Ross workhouse while nearby a convoy of English soldiers guarded the loading of surplus butter, eggs, wheat, barley, pork, and beef earmarked for shipment to the dining tables of England.

With Ireland transformed into a vast charnel house, Patrick had decided to join the exodus to America. Unlike those who chose to uproot themselves from other European countries for the promise of the New World, he did not view himself as a voluntary emigrant. In Irish mythology, being cast adrift on the ocean was punishment for a crime committed unintentionally. Patrick believed that he was being punished by the deceitful and treacherous English for the unintentional crime of being Irish.

Ireland's English overlords did not see it that way, of course. Conveniently enough, they believed that the Famine was God's punishment for Irish sins. "Ireland," declared a Protestant landlord, "is under the curse of God and will be till she is delivered from the curse of Popery."

In London all funds for Irish famine relief were controlled by one man, Assistant Secretary of the Treasury Charles Edward Trevelyan. He was a typical Victorian Englishman: self-righteous, devoutly religious, "and not noted for his admiration of the Irish." Trevelyan excused his failure to take bold action in Ireland on the grounds that "government should not meddle" with the natural laws of supply and demand, "for the market [is] nothing less than a reflection of God's will."

Some Catholics agreed that the Famine was a well-deserved scourge—"a calamity with which God wishes to purify . . . the Irish people," as the archbishop of Armagh put it. But most concurred with a band of young Catholic professionals, journalists, and poets who called themselves Young Ireland and scoffed at the idea that the Famine was a visitation of Providence.

"The Almighty, indeed, sent the potato blight, but the English created the Famine," thundered the celebrated Irish firebrand John Mitchel.

In his newspaper, the *United Irishman,* and in his bestselling books, *Jail Journal* and *The Last Conquest of Ireland (Perhaps),* Mitchel framed the context of the Famine for Patrick Kennedy and countless other Irishmen, both at home and abroad. Mitchel portrayed Ireland as a virtuous nation locked in mortal combat with an evil empire hell-bent on genocide. Every Irish generation since the Great Rebellion of 1798 had risen up against the English, wrote Mitchel, and it was the responsibility of succeeding generations to pay a debt to the patriot dead until Ireland was rid of its oppressors.

This unquenchable desire for revenge would fuel the Kennedys' ambition for the next century and a half.

The Famine was a direct assault on Irish masculinity, for it undermined the Irishman's confidence in his *manly* responsibility to feed and protect his family. Along with other Irishmen, Patrick Kennedy embraced Mitchel's romantic myth, for it helped relieve him of an overpowering sense of guilt.

Guilt found fertile soil in Patrick's Irish soul. For as long as he could remember, he had been afflicted by an overabundance of it, as though he personally bore the blame for Christ's Passion and Crucifixion. Irish boys like Patrick were taught from childhood that they owed God an *eineaclann,* or blood fine, because they were born in

Original Sin. When Patrick used the Lord's name as an oath, Jesus suffered, and when he succumbed to the weakness of the flesh and did something bad, "Jesus's wounds were reopened and bled anew."

Patrick paid dearly for his guilt. Like oppressed people everywhere, he internalized the worst prejudices of his oppressors. Without being aware of it, he accepted the English caricature of the Irishman as an apelike creature, "a slouched simian brute." One Irish writer declared that the Famine wrought "the most dismal change in the people themselves," leaving "a new race of beggars, bearing only a distant and hideous resemblance to humanity," who were "mutilated" and emasculated by their English masters.

In the words of the eminent Irish historian Kevin Whelan, the Famine would eventually "melt like the snows in the Northern Sea." But the memory of his humiliation and powerlessness during the Great Famine flowed in the veins of Patrick Kennedy.

Out of Patrick's suffering came a distinct breed of Kennedy men, ones who buried their feelings of self-loathing and indulged in compensatory fantasies of omnipotence. They masked their melancholy and cynicism with maudlin poetry, sentimental songs, and cruel wit; they employed charm and cool detachment as a way of exerting power over others; they tested themselves, pushed themselves beyond the limit, often risked their very lives—all in an effort to prove that they were special and could get away with things that others could not.

Though not as dirt-poor as most of his neighbors, Patrick Kennedy was painfully aware of his limited prospects in Ireland. His father was dead; his eldest brother, John, had passed away long before the potato crop failed; and the middle brother, James, was in line to inherit the family's entire thirty-five acres. As the youngest son, Patrick would receive nothing to support himself and a family. That was why he had become an apprentice cooper.

According to a story that has been handed down, Patrick was long on ambition and short on scruples—personality traits that would skip a generation and reappear with a vengeance in Patrick's ruthless grandson, Joseph Kennedy. Not long before he left Ireland, Patrick agreed to a "made match," or arranged marriage, to a woman he was not in love with. She was the daughter of a family named Welch, who were reputed to be quite prosperous. When Patrick visited them, he was pleased to note that their farm was teeming with animals of every kind, including numerous horses and cattle.

The wedding took place in due course, and the marriage was consummated on the first night. But when Patrick woke up the next day, he discovered that all the animals were gone. It turned out that the Welches were as poor as the Kennedys and had borrowed the animals from a rich neighbor to impress Patrick and trick him into marrying their daughter.

No record of this marriage can be found. Civil registration of Roman Catholic marriages did not take place in Ireland until 1864, fifteen years after Patrick left. Catholic marriage registers were notoriously slipshod and unreliable. Some historians suspect that the union between Patrick and the Welches' daughter was annulled. Others wonder if it ever took place.

Nor can anyone vouch for the authenticity of another popular tale concerning Patrick—that he borrowed a large sum of money, using as collateral the handsome dowry he expected to receive from his wife. By the time he realized the truth about his in-laws' pitiful financial condition, Patrick had already spent a portion of the borrowed money and was unable to repay the loan.

Facing the prospect of debtor's prison, Patrick returned home to Dunganstown. He found the cottage walls covered with posters from Her Majesty's Colonial Land and Emigration Commissioners. English landlords were eager to rid themselves of tenants in order to convert inefficient small farms and potato plots into profitable pastures for cattle. A quarter of a million copies of the *Emigrants' Guide* were distributed to the Irish peasants, and it is quite likely that Patrick read this pamphlet, with its description of the wonders awaiting emigrants in America.

As luck would have it, one of Patrick's best friends, Patrick Barron, his cousin, had gone to America and settled in Boston. Barron sent back letters praising America as a land of "golden opportunity." Such emigrant letters, along with generous cash remittances from America, were flooding Ireland in the middle of the nineteenth century, and they helped persuade Patrick that emigration was the best way for him to avoid going to prison for his delinquent debt.

Before Patrick Barron left for America, he introduced his friend Patrick Kennedy to his cousin Bridget Murphy. Bridget's family, who were poorer than the Kennedys, lived on the south side of the legendary hill Slieve Coillte in the townland of Cloonagh. Patrick lived on the north side of the hill in Dunganstown, fifteen miles away—the so-called marriage field within which most of the local matches were made.

Bridget was a highly intelligent woman whose ambition burned as brightly as Patrick's. However, without a suitable dowry, she had no hope of attracting an eligible husband. Once her family was evicted by the landlord, which seemed to grow more likely with each passing day of the Famine, Bridget would be forced to join thousands of other semiliterate, unmarriageable Irish girls who crossed the Irish Sea to Britain and sought employment as factory workers in bleak Dickensian sweatshops or as maids with English families.

When Patrick told Bridget that he was planning to flee Ireland and emigrate to America, she saw her chance to escape a dreadful fate. But first she had to convince him to take her along. Though it was customary in Ireland for girls to guard their reputations as zealously as their chastity, Bridget took the lead in courting Patrick.

On fair days, she walked the fifteen miles from Cloonagh to Dunganstown to be alone with Patrick on the Lookout, the highest point on Slieve Coillte. There, they were safe from Father Michael Mitten, the parish priest who stalked the countryside with a large blackthorn shillelagh, hunting for unchaperoned couples.

As Patrick talked about his dream of starting life over in America, he and Bridget could look down from Slieve Coillte and see most of County Wexford and beyond: the Saltee Islands in the east, the brooding blue Comeragh Mountains to the west, and in between, the patchwork of fields in countless shades of green partitioned by hedgerows. It was a landscape of heartbreaking beauty, and as Bridget had hoped, Patrick fell in love with her.

Patrick kept his feelings secret from his mother and brother, who surely would have disapproved of a union between cousins, however distant. When Patrick completed his apprenticeship at the Cherry Brothers Brewery, he bought four tickets for passage to Liverpool, one for himself and three for the Murphys—Bridget, her mother, and her father. To conceal Patrick's plan, it was agreed that the Murphys would travel separately from him. He would meet them in Liverpool, and together they would board a packet liner and cross the Atlantic to Boston, where Patrick would marry Bridget.

The shipping office where Patrick booked their passage is still standing in New Ross along the banks of the River Barrow, a wide, deep stream that in days past could handle the 500-tonners that came up from the sea. The four tickets to Liverpool cost about eighty dollars, a considerable sum of money back then, and certainly more than a poorly paid apprentice was likely to have saved. The second leg of the trip—from Liverpool to Boston—would be even more expensive.

Where did Patrick get the money?

A story persists to this day in New Ross, not far from where Patrick's descendants still tend the fields of the original Kennedy homestead, that he bought the tickets with the money he had borrowed against his first wife's dowry. Had that marriage been annulled by the Church? Or was Patrick on his way to becoming a bigamist?

History is unable to answer these questions.

What seems certain, however, is that Patrick grubstaked his new life in America with embezzled funds.

———

After he had said his farewells to the lads at the Cherry Brothers Brewery, Patrick returned home to help his mother and brother James prepare for a party in his honor. The next morning he would sail for Liverpool and board a ship there for America. But that night, the entire village would share his last hours on Irish soil in a ritual known as an American Wake.

The allusion to a burial ceremony is not coincidental. Emigration is regarded by the Irish as a kind of death. There is no word in Irish for *emigrant*. Instead, the Irish use *deorai,* which means "exile" and comes from the Old Irish word *deoraid,* a person without a family, an outsider, a stranger, an outlaw.

At about four o'clock, neighboring families began arriving at the cottage. The men stuffed their caps into their jacket pockets and headed for the bedroom to the left of the kitchen, where there was a table laid with refreshments, including a barrel of stout and some homemade "mountain dew," as the illegal alcohol was called. The women crowded into the kitchen. They squeezed onto benches and chairs and, in some places, piled three-deep on one another's laps, the flesh of their thighs pressed together.

After they were settled, an old woman began to keen.

"O choneh! . . . O choneh! Ohhh!"

Before long, she was joined by a chorus of other female voices.

"O CHONEH! . . . O CHONEH! OHHH!"

No matter how many times Father Michael Mitten had heard the shrill, piercing wail of the Irish keen, it made his blood run cold. He had been ordered by his bishop to discourage the heathen practice of keening and had specifically admonished Patrick's mother, Mary Johanna Kennedy, that the Holy Father in Rome, Pius IX, preferred "prayers to keens and kneeling to mourning."

Father Michael put down his plate, which he had heaped with buttered raisin cake and stiff Wexford Bay herring, and went into the kitchen. A bright fire, made of turf, beanstalks, and sticks, crackled in the fireplace at the gable end of the house. He approached Mary Johanna and told her to stop her bawling.

Now, didn't she have a fine voice? he asked. Well, then, she should use the voice God gave her, and give them a song.

Mary Johanna looked across the room at Patrick. He was standing next to the fireplace. His cheeks had turned apple red from the heat of the fire and the half-empty cup of *poteen* (moonshine) in his callused hand. In the pocket of his swallow-tailed jacket, he carried a little sack of salt that had been given to him by his mother as a talisman against evil. Sewn into the lining of his tapered breeches was a small piece of linen soaked in menstrual blood, a love charm placed there by Bridget Murphy before she left for Liverpool, to ensure that he would remain faithful to her.

A fiddler played a tune, and Patrick's mother sang. Silence followed her mournful song. Then someone said, "Did you hear the story of the woman who had a husband who was very fond of the drink?"

There was general agreement that no one had ever heard such a story, which of course was not true, since jokes of that nature were well known, as Diarmaid O'Muirithe and Deirdre Nuttall note in their book, *Folklore of County Wexford.*

"Well, then," said the storyteller, "nearly every night he'd come home drunk. At last, his wife went to the priest to complain and ask his advice. The priest told her to get a sheet and put it over her head and wait for the husband and he coming home drunk some night. So she went to a lonely part of the road and waited for the husband and he coming home. The priest told her to say she was the devil, if her husband spoke to her.

"The husband came along the road and he well oiled. When he saw the white figure and heard it groaning, he said, 'Who are you?' 'I'm the devil,' she cried. 'Well,' says he, 'I'm married to your sister.'"

As laughter filled the room, Patrick's friends dragged an unhinged door across the yellow clay floor and placed it in front of the fireplace. The fiddler struck up a lively tune, perhaps "The Kilrane Boys," and soon young couples were step-dancing on the door, making an unholy racket.

Patrick watched the dancers for a few minutes, then slipped out of the cabin and went into the yard. It was growing dark, and the hired man was hustling the animals into the shelter provided by one of the rough-hewn outhouses. The horse and pig had little bits of red thread tied around their tails to ward off the evil eye—a tradition that has been recorded in the archives of the Irish Folklore Commission. The other outhouse contained sacks of malting barley that the Kennedys grew for the brewery in New Ross, where a bark named the *Dunbrody* weighed at anchor, ready to take Patrick away from Dunganstown.

As a child, Patrick had wrestled with his elder brothers, John and James, in the soft earth of the farmyard and had learned not to cry when they hurt him. When he was seven or eight, his parents had been compelled by a newly enacted British law to send him to a nearby primary school, where the teachers refused to speak to the children in their native language. Only English was permitted.

Patrick's father, who died when his son was eleven, had been a florid character who had an opinion on every subject under the sun. His proudest boast was that the Kennedys were descended from kings. All Irishmen embraced the grandiose notion that they were heirs to a throne, but Patrick's father claimed that he could actually trace the Kennedy lineage back more than eight hundred years to Brian Boru, who was born Brian Mac Cennedi (pronounced "Kennedy"). Brian was the high king of Ireland who defeated the Norsemen at the Battle of Clontarf in 1014.

The original seat of the O'Kennedy clan was in East County Clare at a place called Glen Ora, the name President John F. Kennedy would one day bestow on the home he rented in the horse country of Virginia. Brian Boru's reign in Glen Ora was a period of unparalleled peace and prosperity, a kind of Irish Camelot. Patrick's father said that whenever a cow lay down in a field in Ireland, she sighed for the good life in the time of Brian.

According to Patrick's father, the O'Kennedys were conspicuous for their height, the splendor of their dress, and their willingness to take risks. Brian Boru's brothers, Mahon and Donnchuan, died during raids on neighboring landholders, which were regarded in ancient times as nothing more than "a violent form of sport." Hotheaded Kennedys did not spare their own relatives. In 1194 Murough O'Kennedy was slain by Loughlain O'Kennedy. And in 1599 an O'Kennedy of Ballingarry seduced a sister of an O'Kennedy in Lorrha, who slew his cousin in revenge.

Back in those days, it was believed that the murder of a near relative was a *fionghal,* or fratricide. Anyone who violated this taboo risked bringing *geasa,* or curses, upon himself and his family. "The more eminent a person was, the more *geasa* he had," notes Peter O'Connor, an expert on Irish mythology, in *Beyond the Mist.* Too many *geasa* brought about an untimely death. Later some people came to the conclusion that the Kennedy Curse stemmed from an excess of these *geasa.*

Patrick's father was as superstitious as the next man. He believed in the miraculous curative powers of saints, holy wells, and certain priests—especially those who had "a taste for the wee drop" or who had been removed from their pulpit and "silenced" by their bishops. He believed there were dangerous places all over the landscape, lonely sites that were portals to the world of fairies, banshees, and leprechauns. And he believed in curses, a notion that he passed on to Patrick, who in turn would pass it on to generations of Kennedy descendants down to the present day.

Standing in the farmyard, Patrick noticed that the fog was beginning to lift. A few weak rays of the setting sun filtered through the mist, casting a dull glow over Slieve Coillte. Patrick decided to climb to the top one last time.

It was here that he had listened to his father's stories and had come to view his family's sad history as synonymous with that of Ireland. In 1691 the Protestant Parliament in London passed the infamous Penal Laws, history's first recorded example of government-sponsored ethnic cleansing. The Penal Laws, which remained in effect with some modifications for more than 150 years, made it illegal for Catholics to exercise their religion, receive an education, enter a profession, hold public office, engage in trade or commerce, own a horse of greater value than five pounds, purchase land, lease land, vote, or keep any arms for protection.

By the beginning of the eighteenth century, royal rank was a distant memory for the Kennedys. Distant or not, however, the memory was kept alive by Kennedy men, who believed that their bloodline was inextinguishable and that the Kennedys would someday be restored to their rightful place in the scheme of things.

Patrick's eyes were adjusting to the darkness that had descended on Slieve Coillte. The top of the hill had been sheared off eons ago by a glacier, leaving a broad grassy plateau. It was on this hallowed ground that Patrick's grandfather John Kennedy and his father, who was also named Patrick, joined the army of United Irishmen during the Rebellion of 1798.

On June 4 of that year, five thousand Irishmen under the command of Bagenal Harvey had gathered on Slieve Coillte for the Battle of New Ross. Among them, Patrick's father and grandfather stood shoulder to shoulder in close file, wielding twelve-foot-long pikes to fight off cavalry charges by the British Crown garrison.

At one point, the Wexfordmen broke through the British lines, driving the enemy back to the center of New Ross. But after twelve hours of fierce hand-to-hand combat in New Ross, the Irish lost the day. Among the wounded was John Kennedy, Patrick's grandfather (and President John F. Kennedy's great-great-great grandfather), who was cut down by an English musket ball on the quay near the New Ross Bridge. He was rescued by his thirteen-year-old son, Patrick's father, who bound up his wound with a handkerchief, hauled him into a rowboat, and brought him down the River Barrow six miles to Dunganstown.

In the aftermath of the Battle of New Ross, terrible atrocities were committed by both sides. The Irish burned a barn in which a hundred defenseless English prisoners were housed. In some of the worst offenses, English soldiers herded Irish families into churches throughout County Wexford, barred the doors, then burned the buildings to the ground. One out of every two adult males in Wexford lost his life, twenty thousand in all.

Patrick's father had the true Irish gift for storytelling. His words stirred Patrick's imagination and left him with a lifelong love of history and a habit of quoting poetry. But then Patrick's father died, leaving him nothing but the bloodstained handkerchief that he had used to bind *his* father's wound. And as he came of age as a man, Patrick was left in the care of his mother.

To her neighbors, Mary Johanna Kennedy appeared to be a good mother who knew how to keep a well-ordered home. But to Patrick, there was always something feigned and unauthentic about her emotional responses. One moment she was hugging and kissing him and calling him by endearing names; the next she was off doing something else and acting as though he hardly existed.

Patrick felt emotionally cheated by his mother. Yet despite this, he was aware of the intense, clutching relationship that existed between them. He could not explain this paradox, but he knew that he had an urgent need to break the bond. He had to purge himself of any trace of degrading femininity and become a man among men.

In his adult years, Patrick lost no opportunity to praise physical prowess and condemn weakness—a preoccupation he shared with his future great-grandson President John F. Kennedy, who proclaimed that America's "growing softness, our increasing lack of physical fitness, is a menace to our security." Like JFK, Patrick projected an image of independence, courage, and strength that effectively hid his vulnerability from himself and others. His physical posture—straight, stiff, proud—proclaimed "I am in control."

"For narcissists," writes Alexander Lowen, "control serves the same function as power—it protects them from possible humiliation. First, they control themselves by denying those feelings which might make them vulnerable. But they also have to control situations in which they find themselves; they have to make sure that there is no possibility that some other person will have power over them. Power and control are two sides of the same coin."

With first light, it was time for Patrick to leave for his ship. Family and friends assembled on the muddy road that ran by the Kennedy farm and led down the tree-lined boreen to the port of New Ross. Patrick helped his mother climb into the horse-drawn Mass cart that she used on Sundays to go to chapel. His belongings were loaded on a handcart along with the youngest children. Father Michael Mitten bestowed one last blessing, then everyone set off down the hill. They passed by acres of rotting potatoes that gave off a terrible sulfurous stench.

When they arrived at New Ross, four ships were lined up along the quay, including the *Dunbrody,* a 176-foot-long, three-masted bark owned by a prominent merchant family named Graves. The *Dunbrody,* which was named after the Cistercian abbey down river from the town, plied between Liverpool and New Ross, carrying cargo and a complement of passengers. On the deck, Captain John W. Williams supervised the loading of passengers and provisions.

The dock was aswarm with sailors, stevedores, emigrants, friends, families, and hawkers of food and trinkets. But it was remarkably quiet. "Never before could you have been in an Irish crowd like this and not been greeted and shouted at," Walter Macken wrote of a similar scene in his novel *The Silent People.* "There would be jokes and obscenities flying. Calling and shouting." For once, words seemed to fail the Irish.

Patrick lifted his mother from the Mass cart and set her down on the stone quay. He knelt before her, threw his arms around her voluminous skirt, and asked for her blessing.

As before, Mary Johanna Kennedy's face betrayed no emotion. She placed Patrick's head between her hands and bent to kiss his forehead. Then, all at once, she let out a low moan and collapsed, dragging Patrick with her to the ground. They lay on the cold, wet cobblestones, sobbing and whimpering, rocking back and forth in each other's arms.

"*O choneh!* . . . *O choneh! Ohhh!*"

The women standing nearby had taken up their keening again. This time, Father Michael made no effort to stop them. He waited several minutes, then stepped forward and helped Patrick and his mother to their feet. The priest was carrying a little bottle of holy water, and he sprinkled a few drops over Patrick.

Patrick crossed himself and wiped away his tears. He shook hands all around and kissed his mother one last time. She began to collapse again, and one of the men caught her in his arms.

Patrick gathered up his two battered old cardboard suitcases and climbed up the gangplank of the *Dunbrody*. At the top, he stopped, took out his father's bloodstained handkerchief, and wiped his brow. Then, without looking back, he disappeared into the crowd of silent strangers.

The *Dunbrody* sailed up the mouth of the Mersey River on the morning tide. Perched on the topgallant forecastle, Patrick Kennedy observed dozens of tall-masted ships and steamers sailing in and out of the harbor of Liverpool, the second-largest city in England and, next to London, the commercial capital of the British Empire.

To a country lad like Patrick, who had never seen a town larger than New Ross, Liverpool was the most spectacular sight of his life. We can picture him standing in the frigid February wind on the deck of the *Dunbrody,* dressed in his threadbare clothes, shivering with fear and defiance as he entered the belly of the British beast.

While Ireland starved, Liverpool had gorged on profits from cotton, tobacco, sugar, and human cargo. The city's merchants had dominated the world's slave trade in the eighteenth century, and when slaving was abolished by Britain in the early nineteenth century, the ship-owners filled their empty slave holds with emigrants. By 1849, the year Patrick Kennedy arrived, the *Illustrated London News* reported that ships embarking from Liverpool's docks transported more than 150,000 emigrants to the New World, a record number.

As the *Dunbrody* approached the Clarence Dock, where Irish emigrants disembarked, Patrick Kennedy watched the dockmaster mount the poop of a nearby vessel and hail the surrounding ships to make room for the newcomer.

Drawing closer, Patrick could smell the odor of "brine, bilgewater, and pungent tar of hundreds of wooden ships" in their berths, writes the historian Robert James Scally in *The End of Hidden Ireland*. Mingling with these aromas was the powerful stench of sewage and human waste that gave Liverpool its nickname, "The Black Spot on the Mersey."

No sooner had the *Dunbrody* docked than a contingent of uniformed constables trooped aboard with orders to clear the ship as quickly as possible so that she could be prepared for her return trip. The policemen shouted obscenities at the dazed emigrants and chased them off the deck with nightsticks. Patrick Kennedy tumbled down the gangplank into a scene of chaos and confusion.

He was instantly set upon by an army of disreputable dock runners, who acted as agents for passenger brokers, shopkeepers, and boardinghouse proprietors. Known as "crimps," "touts," and "mancatchers," the runners were for the most part Irishmen who had come to Liverpool on earlier ships. Because new arrivals such as Patrick found it hard to believe that men from the auld sod would cheat them, they made easy prey.

The runner who snagged Patrick led him to a boardinghouse in the neighborhood of the Waterloo Dock. For fourpence a night, Patrick rented a tiny space in a smelly, dank cellar that was crowded with a dozen other emigrants. At the time, there were 7,700 such cellars in Liverpool, occupied by 27,000 people. Patrick was given a board to sleep on because, as one landlord explained, "if we gave [the Irish] a bed, we should be obliged to throw it away the next day . . . they are so dreadfully dirty."

Patrick had never seen a woman without her clothes on, but in his new underground den, some of the women disrobed, washed, urinated, and defecated in full view of the men. At night they kept him awake with the uninhibited moans and cries of their lovemaking.

Years later, after Patrick settled in Boston and could be persuaded to tell his "crossing story"—how he became an American—he avoided talking about the month or so he had spent in Liverpool. The Black Spot on the Mersey was his introduction to the savage world of Victorian capitalism and urban poverty that had so horrified Charles Dickens and Karl Marx. The experience left an impression on Patrick's soul that was passed on to his descendants and found expression in President Kennedy's famous remark, "My father told me that all businessmen were SOBs."

Finding Bridget Murphy in the teeming metropolis of Liverpool proved to be a far harder task than Patrick had anticipated. She was not at the lodging house where they had agreed she and her parents would stay. For several days Patrick wandered the streets of Whitechapel and Sailor Town, passing crowded public houses, brothels, and gambling dens, visiting one filthy lodging house after another until he had all but given up hope of finding Bridget. Then one day on Vulcan Street, he stumbled by chance upon the Catholic-run Emigrant Home, and there in this clean, orderly, well-lit place, he found Bridget and her parents patiently awaiting his arrival.

To purchase a ticket for their passage, Patrick was advised to go to Goree Piazza, which was named after the notorious island off the coast of Senegal, where Liverpool ship captains had once taken on their cargoes of slaves. The walls of Goree Piazza were plastered with notices of Atlantic packet ships that sailed on regular timetables. There were no fewer than twenty-two brokers who sold space on these ships and received a commission for each berth they filled. One of the ship brokers was Daniel P. Wichell, agent for the White Diamond Line.

"The reputation of this line is very well known in the New England states," Wichell informed Patrick, quoting from a recent newspaper advertisement. "The ships have been built expressly for packets. They sail fast, have spacious berths between decks that are well ventilated, and are commanded by masters of long experience in the trade."

Patrick had some reservations about the White Diamond Line. Only the year before, one of its ships, the *Ocean Monarch,* had caught fire while at sea, with the loss of 176 lives out of 350 passengers. With limited navigational aids and notoriously incompetent crews, accidents were bound to happen. Between 1847 and 1853, fifty-nine emigrant ships went down, with the loss of thousands of lives.

Disease was an even greater problem. Dysentery, cholera, and typhus decimated the ranks of passengers on the North Atlantic crossing. As a result, before Patrick could board a ship, he had to submit to a medical examination. It took place at a dockside shack called the doctor's shop, where MOs, or medical officers, were paid by the head—usually one pound for every hundred passengers examined.

"Are you quite well?" an MO shouted at Patrick from behind a little window. "Show your tongue."

Before Patrick had a chance to comply with this order, the doctor had stamped his ticket.

"If an emigrant could stand, he was deemed healthy," noted a historian. "There were reports of Medical Officers not even looking at the people as they filed past, simply barking out questions without waiting for answers before declaring the examinee fit."

The stamped ticket in Patrick's hand was for steerage class on the SS *Washington Irving,* a White Diamond Line ship that had been built by Donald McKay, one of the most famous shipbuilders of the time. She was a relatively new ship (her keel had been laid in 1845), and Patrick had chosen her because she was said to be heavily sparred and sturdy. Under the command of Captain Eben Caldwell, the *Washing-*

ton Irving was scheduled to sail for Boston on the seventeenth of March, Saint Patrick's Day.

When Patrick and the Murphys arrived at the Waterloo Dock at seven o'clock in the morning on sailing day, they found a large crowd waiting impatiently at the gate. Captain Caldwell would not allow the steerage passengers to board the ship until the cargo was stowed away. Finally, the captain gave the signal, and the emigrants rushed forward, pushing and shoving one another to get on the gangplank. They were joined by scores of peddlers—orange girls, cap merchants, and dealers in toffee, ribbons, lace, pocket mirrors, gingerbread nuts, and sweetmeats. In the mad scramble, the crew yanked people on board and tossed them like bales of cotton onto the deck.

Captain Caldwell gave orders for the ship to cast off. Those who had not yet made it on board rushed round to the dock entrance, where it was narrow and ships were usually detained for a few minutes. There, the late arrivals climbed up the side of the ship. Many of them fell into the murky waters of the Mersey and had to be fished out. Some drowned.

A steam tug took the *Washington Irving* to the mouth of the bay. At the bell buoy, the pilot transferred to the tug, along with the stowaways and peddlers, and the tug turned back to port.

The ship's sails were set. And as the crew hauled on the ropes, they sang a halyard chantey.

Far away, oh far away,
We seek a world o'er the ocean spray!
We seek a land across the sea,
Where bread is plenty and men are free.

When he bought the tickets, Patrick Kennedy imagined that he had purchased separate berths for himself and each of the Murphys. But that was not the way steerage passengers were treated.

Four emigrants were stuffed into a dark, boxlike bunk that was six feet long and six feet wide, leaving each person with just eighteen inches of shoulder room. Sometimes men and women were berthed together. Sir George Stephen, a well-known philanthropist, once asked a ship's mate how he managed sleeping arrangements for married couples at sea. To which the mate replied, "There is no difficulty as to that; there is plenty of that work going on every night to keep them all countenanced [calm and composed]."

Under a heavy press of canvas, the *Washington Irving* rounded the Tuskar Rock and then Cape Clear. Soon she was leaving the choppy waters of the Irish Sea for the big rollers of the Atlantic Ocean. What Herman Melville, in his novel *Redburn, His First Voyage,* called the "irresistible wrestler" of seasickness forced many passengers to remain in steerage. That, "compounded by the lack of sanitation, made conditions on board such vessels horrific," notes Jim Rees in *Surplus People*. "No doubt, there were those who just lay in their six-by-one-and-a-half-feet space neither knowing nor caring if they would ever reach their destination."

The "well ventilated" accommodations that ship broker Wichell had promised Patrick turned out to be a cramped, dirty space between decks. The living quarters would not be cleaned during the entire voyage. Nor was it possible for passengers to change their clothes or bedding, and the spread of lice soon became a problem.

According to Terry Coleman's chronicle of the North Atlantic passage, *Going to America,* food rations were stingy and often consisted of a coarse concoction of wheat, barley, rye, molasses, and peas. Some passengers had thought to bring along their own food, but the water they were given for cooking was often contaminated. People did not have enough to eat, creating, in the phrase of historian Robert James Scally, "an almost famine."

The one item that never seemed to be in short supply was grog— rum diluted with water—which was sold twice a week at an exorbitant profit by Captain Caldwell himself. Many of the sailors got drunk and abused the passengers, especially the women, who were constantly at their mercy.

In bad weather, the hatches were closed, and the air in steerage became pestilential. It was not long before dysentery spread among the emigrants, then cholera and other forms of "ship fever." Each morning, writes a Kennedy biographer, sailors would "call out for the dead bodies and the garbage, haul both up through the hatches, and throw the combined refuse overboard to the sharks that constantly trailed the ship."

For Patrick Kennedy, the agonizing weeks in steerage amounted to a form of bondage. The experience was branded on his memory and would become a permanent part of the Kennedy family mythology. Indeed, in the years ahead, the "coffin ship" on which Patrick and Bridget came to America would be compared by their descendants to the slaves' "middle passage" and the boxcars of the Holocaust.

The comparison to these crimes against humanity is not as extreme as it may appear. Within a period of five short years, the Irish nation had lost more than half its population—3 million people—to starvation, disease, and emigration. Future Kennedys would never allow themselves to feel so powerless again.

Patrick and Bridget stood on deck, staring out to sea. Any minute now, they expected to see America looming over the horizon. Patrick had been told by Daniel Wichell, the Goree Piazza ship broker, that the crossing would take only twenty days, when in fact it could take anywhere from five to twelve weeks, depending on the wind and the weather. No one but Captain Caldwell and his first mate knew the position of the *Washington Irving*, and they kept that information to themselves.

Then one day the ocean became noticeably calmer and the deck did not heave as much. For the first time, Captain Caldwell ordered the ship to be cleaned from stem to stern. The emigrants scrubbed the steerage and dried the timbers with pans of hot coals from the galley. The captain was determined that his ship should look as though she had made "a safe, clean, and comfortable voyage" when she passed through customs in America.

Late in the afternoon of April 17, nearly five weeks out of Liverpool, one of the lookouts shouted, *"Land!"* and a speck of coastline
appeared on the distant horizon. Patrick and Bridget stayed on deck
long past sunset, when a thick haze spread over the ocean and blotted
out the moon and the stars. That night they passed the spot off the
coast of Martha's Vineyard where, 150 years later, John F. Kennedy
Jr.—Patrick's great-great-grandson—would become disoriented in his
Piper Saratoga and crash into the sea.

In Boston, Patrick soon found that he had substituted one killing field
for another. Within three months of his arrival, a virulent strain of
Asiatic cholera swept through Boston's squalid slums, claiming the
lives of seven hundred people, most of them Irish. In 1849, the year
of Patrick's arrival, Boston's Committee of Internal Health on the Asiatic Cholera inspected one of the city's Irish quarters and observed:

> This whole district is a perfect hive of human beings, without
> comforts and mostly without common necessaries; in many
> cases, huddled together like brutes without regard to sex, or
> age . . . grown men and women sleeping together in the same
> apartment, and sometimes wife and husband, brothers and
> sisters in the same bed. Under such circumstances, self-
> respect, forethought, all high and noble virtues soon die out,
> and sullen indifference and despair, or disorder, intemperance
> and utter degradation reign supreme.

Patrick moved into the coldwater flat of his old friend Patrick Barron, where the two men shared a table, a couple of chairs, a bed, and
a black cast-iron stove that supplied heat in the winter and fire for
cooking. On Saturday nights Barron poured hot water from a large
kettle into a galvanized-iron tub for his once-a-week bath. When he
stepped out of the tub, Patrick stepped in and bathed in the same
water.

The only indoor toilet for the tenement's thirty families was located in the dirt-floor basement. "No one was responsible for the care of these communal instruments," the sociologist Oscar Handlin has observed, "and as a result they were normally out of repair. Abominably foul and feculent, perpetually gushing over into the surrounding yards, they were mighty carriers of disease."

Unlike most of his countrymen, Patrick had come to America with a trade, and he found work at Daniel Francis's cooperage and brass foundry on Summer Street, not far from Donald McKay's shipyard and the Cunard wharves on Border Street.

"Mr. Francis made beer and water barrels and ship castings," notes a biographer, "and when he saw Patrick's ability with the adze and the croze, he gave the young man a job. The work was twelve hours a day, seven days a week. . . . By starting off making beer barrels, Patrick unwittingly began a Kennedy family tradition of being connected with the beer and liquor business that would last for almost a century."

"Of all the immigrant nationalities in Boston, the Irish fared the least well, beginning at a lower rung and rising more slowly on the economic and social ladder than any other group," the historian Doris Kearns Goodwin writes.

They were despised by Boston Brahmins for their ignorance, rural customs, poverty, and Roman Catholicism. They were thought fit only for manual labor. "Even the Negro," writes Richard J. Whalen, "faced less discrimination than the Irishman." "The Negroes," added the Reverend John F. Brennan, "held jobs closed to the Irish, such as cooking and barbering."

Many want ads in the Boston papers read "None need apply but Americans." When Irish men and women showed up for jobs, they encountered notices that read NO IRISH NEED APPLY, which eventually became shortened to NINA. The only jobs available were the most menial and the cheapest. Live-in Irish maids, called "potwhallopers," "biddies," and "kitchen canaries," were paid two dollars a week. Unskilled Irish laborers made about the same wage and were called "clod-hoppers," "Micks," and "Paddies."

Constant humiliation only deepened Patrick Kennedy's view of the world as a dangerous place that had to be kept at arm's length. "If anything," wrote Terry Golway in *The Irish in America,* "America could be worse than Ireland, for here Catholics were a distinct minority in a nation that increasingly took the view that democracy and Protestantism were inseparable."

Even skilled workers like Patrick could not avoid the virulent anti-Catholic nativism that was fomented by the infamous Know-Nothing Party. In 1854, five years after Patrick's arrival, the Know-Nothing Party captured the governor's office and virtually every seat in the Massachusetts General Court. The party harassed Catholic schools, disbanded Irish militia companies, and tried to pass legislation mandating a twenty-one-year wait before a naturalized citizen could vote. All this struck Patrick like a replay of the notorious British Penal Laws in Ireland.

But Patrick Kennedy never regretted leaving his blighted homeland. Within weeks of his arrival in Boston, he married Bridget Murphy. And over the next several years, they had five children—a son who died in infancy; three daughters; and a second son, who lived and was named after his father.

"Nurtured from birth with the doctrine that they have a lien on greatness, the Irish are unable to come to terms with their own powerlessness," notes the historian Thomas J. O'Hanlon.

In America, this outlook created two distinct strains in the Irish character. One type was the compliant, loyal, God-fearing Irishman, an easy-go-lucky people-pleaser who got along by playing by the rules; went to Mass on Sunday and was deeply moved by the depiction of Christ bleeding under his bloody crown of thorns; readily confessed his sins; accepted suffering in silence; and often ended up as a priest or a day laborer, train conductor, garbage collector, policeman, fireman, or some other kind of civil servant who counted the days to retirement on a secure government pension.

The other type was the defiant, unruly, rebellious Irishman, a dark, brooding, frequently manic-depressive character who nurtured a sense of resentment against all established authority; did not show up at church very often, if at all; could not deal with the humiliations of the past and rarely if ever talked about the Great Famine because he did not want it reported that he had not been able to feed his family; considered his primary loyalty to be to his wife and children, not his country; and often became a journalist, scholar, pub keeper, politician, gangster, lawyer, businessman, or secret sympathizer of outlawed Irish rebels such as the Fenians.

Patrick Kennedy was the rebellious sort. Though he eked out a meager existence as a barrel maker and had a wife and four children to support, he contributed his pennies to the cause of Irish independence and was an ardent supporter of the Irish Republican Brotherhood, or Fenians, who used modern methods of terrorism in their fight against the British.

"The British," said Patrick, "understand one thing—force. The only way to get them out of Ireland is to bomb them out."

Patrick was a popular figure in the Irish pubs along Summer Street. Like his father, he was a born storyteller. With an actor's flair for impersonation, he could keep his drinking companions entertained for hours with rousing tales of heroism during the Great Rebellion of 1798.

Everyone said that Patrick Kennedy had a way with words, which was a high compliment indeed, for language was the Irishman's most potent weapon. Patrick kept his weapon honed with sarcasm; he liked to quote John Mitchel, who was a master of mockery and ridicule.

"Now, my dear surplus brethren," Patrick would say, quoting one of Mitchel's most famous passages in "To the 'Surplus' Population of Ireland," "I have a simple, a sublime, a patriotic project to suggest. It must be plain to you that you *are* surplus, and must somehow be got rid of. Do not wait ingloriously for famine to sweep you off—if you must die, die gloriously; serve your country by your death, and shed around your name the halo of a patriot's fame. Go; choose out in all the island two million trees, and thereupon *go and hang yourselves.*"

"[Sarcasm] was used for offense and defense," writes Peter Quinn, one of the most astute observers of the Irish in America. "It was a weapon to cut down anyone in the community who might think or act like he was better than his peers. . . . Such ambition was regarded as a form of treason. Sarcasm was equally a means for dismissing those realms [of WASP culture] as the preserve of frauds and pompous lightweights. . . . Sarcasm was a form of subversion, a defensive mechanism of colonized people like the Irish."

In the fall of 1858, Patrick, now thirty-five years of age, fell ill with tuberculosis. His complexion became pale and he lost a good deal of weight, experienced pains in his chest, and began spitting up blood. Bridget insisted that they call a doctor.

By the time the doctor arrived, Patrick had hemorrhaged several pints of blood and was delirious with a high fever. His voice was almost entirely lost, and he could make himself heard only in a whisper when the doctor asked him to describe his symptoms.

"I can't swallow," he said. "I'm starving to death."

Bridget stood in the door, holding their ten-month-old son, who had been named after her husband, Patrick Joseph, and was nicknamed P.J. Peeking from behind her skirts were her three young daughters.

"Please, can you do something for him, Doctor?" Bridget said.

The doctor took Patrick's pulse. It was 124. He gave him some creasote and nitromuriatic acid with cod-liver oil.

Under this course of treatment, Patrick's pulse fell to 100, and he was able to take a few spoonfuls of clear soup. However, over the next few days he continued to lose weight, and soon he was but a shadow of the handsome, muscular man with bright blue eyes who had come to America.

On November 22—exactly 105 years to the day before John. F. Kennedy's assassination—Patrick, much emaciated and profusely sweating, emitted one last loud gurgling noise and died.

"He had survived in Boston for nine years, only five less than the life expectancy for an Irishman in America at mid-century," Peter Collier and David Horowitz write. "The first Kennedy to arrive in the New World, he was the last to die in anonymity."

But not the last to die before his time.

As Patrick lay dying, the next pivotal event in the Kennedy story was taking place across the harbor in Boston. There, in the North End, an Irish immigrant by the name of Thomas Fitzgerald was welcoming his first son into the family fold. Most of Thomas's offspring lived and died in obscurity. But one—John Francis Fitzgerald, his fourth and most brilliant son—became famous as a two-term mayor of Boston, the grandfather of President Kennedy, and a principal architect of the Kennedy Curse.

CHAPTER TWO

JOHN FRANCIS FITZGERALD

FAVORITE SON

JOHN FRANCIS FITZGERALD MADE HIS WAY down Causeway Street in Boston. He was a cocky bantam of a man, barely five feet two inches tall, as light on his feet as a leprechaun. On this sunny spring day in 1892, he was decked out in a high stiff collar, a morning coat with a boutonniere, and salt-and-pepper trousers. A black derby sat on his head at a rakish angle, framing a pair of bright blue eyes, a mouthful of prominent teeth, and a big, square jaw—all features that would be stamped indelibly on the countenances of his daughter Rose, grandson Teddy, great-grandson JFK Jr., and countless other Kennedy descendants.

Among the Boston Irish, Fitzgerald was known by an assortment of nicknames, including Johnny Fitz, Fitzie, and, most memorably, Honey Fitz (derived, it was said, from a boyhood habit of dipping his fingers into the sugar barrel in his father's grocery-and-grog shop). The diminutive Honey Fitz had a giant ego; he loved to hear the sound of his own voice, and his excessive talkativeness had come to merit its own name: Fitzblarney.

He was a natural politician who never passed an acquaintance on the street without stopping for a hearty handshake, a pat on the back, or—in the case of a pretty young woman—a breast-crushing hug. Like all full-blooded narcissists, Honey Fitz could not live without an admiring audience. Politics furnished him with the opportunity to use his charm, wit, and good looks to seduce admirers. It also offered him the kind of power that the Irish American community often associated with status and sexual potency.

Honey Fitz embodied the rebellious strain in the Irish American character. He had no sense of limits or self-restraint and felt free to ignore society's rules and create his own lifestyle. It was these traits, along with the distinctive features he passed on to his Kennedy descendants, that made Honey Fitz one of the great architects of the Kennedy Curse.

His gregarious nature endeared Honey Fitz to the sociable Irish, but it made him chronically tardy. This morning was no exception: one glance at his pocket watch told Honey Fitz that he was late for an important meeting—one that would have a profound impact not only on his life but on the future course of the Kennedy political dynasty.

When he came to Bowdoin Square, he ducked into the Hendricks Club, headquarters of the Democratic Party machine in Boston's West End. Taking the stairs two at a time, he reached the second-floor landing and burst into the office of Martin Lomasney, the legendary boss of Ward Eight.

"Sorry I'm late," Honey Fitz said.

He had a slight lisp, and the word *sorry* came out sounding like "sharry."

Seated in a chair, his legs outstretched, and surrounded by half a dozen loyal aides, the Mahatma, as Lomasney was called, projected an air of awesome power. He was a large-boned, heavily muscled man with a massive dome, a small mustache, and a prominent jaw that stuck out, as one biographer has noted, "at a pugnacious angle."

From his office on Bowdoin Square, the Mahatma worked round

the clock running a kind of shadow government, a combination welfare and employment agency. He satisfied the needs of the immigrant poor, earning their gratitude and loyalty and, more important, their votes.

"Behind his gold-rimmed spectacles," writes historian Doris Kearns Goodwin, "Lomasney's piercing gray-blue eyes must have seen in young Fitzgerald the towering ambition that would eventually bring the two of them into bitter conflict, giving Lomasney, as he himself later put it, 'more sleepless nights than any other individual.' But at their first meeting, Fitzgerald greatly impressed Lomasney as 'a pink-cheeked youngster' with a remarkable personality."

The Mahatma was known to have a wicked temper and to take cruel pleasure in wounding people with his sarcastic humor. But Honey Fitz, who did not seem at all intimidated by him, announced that he wanted to run for George McGahey's state senate seat in neighboring Ward Seven.

"Gettin' a bit above yourself, aren't you, boy-o?" the Mahatma said.

The caustic remark was greeted by a round of laughter from his aides.

Honey Fitz had expected this reaction, and he was ready with his rebuttal. His speech—for that is what it was, a prepared speech— turned out to be part family history, part political calculation, and part pure Fitzblarney.

More than ten years earlier, when Honey Fitz was still a teenager, his father, Thomas Fitzgerald, had marked him for greatness.

As Honey Fitz told the story, the turning point in his life occurred one afternoon in 1879 when he was sixteen years old and his father, a tough, wily saloonkeeper, took the family for a picnic at Caledonian Grove. His mother, Rosanna, was pregnant with her thirteenth child (three children had died in infancy) and did not feel well enough to attend the outing, so she was left alone in the family's tenement apartment.

Later that day a man on horseback came riding through the neighborhood yelling out the news (inaccurate, as it turned out) that there had been a terrible accident on the train carrying the picnickers to Caledonian Grove. The shocking report triggered an attack of what Rosanna's doctor later called "cerebral apoplexy," or a stroke, and she collapsed on the floor and died.

Thomas Fitzgerald could not forgive himself for leaving his exhausted and pregnant wife unattended, and he devised a scheme to redeem himself. He would send Honey Fitz to medical school so that his son could learn how to prevent the kind of misfortune that had killed Rosanna.

Thomas Fitzgerald did not ask his son if he wanted to become a doctor. As in the case of Joseph Kennedy, who would one day draft *his* son John into politics, Thomas Fitzgerald presented his son with a fait accompli—Honey Fitz would go into medicine and atone for his father's sins.

In his role as the family's great hope, Honey Fitz was treated by his father and brothers like a prince. And under their constant stroking, he developed a sense of confidence and entitlement that remained with him for the rest of his days.

Considerable sacrifices were required of Thomas Fitzgerald and his other sons to pay for Honey Fitz's education. As the owner of a small grocery store/saloon, Thomas made a decent income but still dwelled near the bottom of the social ladder. We know where he stood in the pecking order thanks to the habit of status-conscious Irish Americans for inventing a vivid vocabulary to describe their rank and station.

At the foot of the ladder, according to a history of the Kennedys assembled by the editors of the Associated Press, were "shanty Irish" (*shanty* being the word for a wood shack); then, in ascending order of prominence, were so-called lace curtain Irish; two-bathroom Irish; wall-to-wall Irish; and, at the very pinnacle, Irish who "had fruit in the home when no one was sick."

The Fitzgeralds were lace curtain. And proud of it.

———

Thomas Fitzgerald's saloon, like other grog shops in the densely populated waterfront slums of Boston, was the hub of neighborhood activity. The pub functioned as a political club, bail-bond agency, lending bureau, charity, secret Irish revolutionary cell, and union hall all rolled into one. It was a sanctuary for confirmed bachelors, widowers, misogynists, storytellers, and thirsty workingmen. An alarming number of them were alcoholics.

In "The Fixation Factor," a study of Irish American alcoholism, the author Robert F. Bales suggests that the Irish substituted drinking for eating because of a sense of guilt about eating brought on by poverty, famine, and the Catholic Church's encouragement of fasting. What's more, Bales goes on, "it was always comparatively easy for an Irish patriot, sincere or otherwise, to gain an audience at the gathering of the boys, or men, at some hidden 'shibbeen' and stir up a minor rebellion."

In Irish culture, alcohol played a major role in male bonding. "Only Ireland . . . preserved a culturally demanded link between drinking and male identity," writes Richard Stivers in *Hair of the Dog: Irish Drinking and Its American Stereotype.* "One's ability to drink hard demonstrated great powers of manliness, just as athletic prowess or expertise in storytelling did."

Others have traced Irish American alcoholism to psychological roots. "There is a tremendous anger in the alcoholic, which is turned against the self through guilt," writes Alexander Lowen. "Guilt about sexual feelings and rage is probably the psychological basis for recourse to alcohol. The alcoholic, however, is not unique in this guilt. Other neurotics suffer from it, too. Moreover, the suppression of these feelings is not complete; they threaten constantly to break through. When the effort to contain these feelings reaches the point where the individual senses that he or she can no longer hold on, the person turns to drink."

Alcohol—its uses and abuses—would become a major factor in the Fitzgeralds' rise to power, as it would in the case of the Kennedys.

Of Thomas's nine sons who survived infancy, three eventually followed their father into the liquor business, while three others became alcoholics and died young from the disease.

"Whenever anything happened in the family," a Fitzgerald relative would recall, "my mother would sigh deeply and then with fear and bitterness in her voice she would say, 'It's the curse of the liquor money, I know it.'"

When Honey Fitz was a first-year medical student at Harvard, his father died, leaving $150 in cash and $12 worth of furniture. The local parish priest tried to persuade him to break up the family and send his brothers to live with their three aunts. But Honey Fitz would not hear of it. Instead, he turned to Matthew Keany, the political boss of the North End, for advice on how to support his orphaned brothers.

In the minds of Irish Americans, the political ward boss—with his street smarts, bravado, and power over people's daily lives—was the epitome of a man of the world. Matthew Keany was a husky Irishman with a walrus mustache and a keen appreciation of human nature. He sized up Honey Fitz as a young man with an exceptional combination of brains, drive, and ambition and offered him a job as his apprentice.

Honey Fitz dropped out of medical school, and over the course of the next few years, he learned everything there was to learn from Matthew Keany about ward politics—from how to deliver assistance to desperately needy people to how to deliver (or forge) votes on election day.

By the late 1880s, ward bosses such as Keany were replacing Catholic bishops in matters of Irish American politics, and an unofficial concordat had been reached between the clergymen and the bosses. The political leaders defended the Church's unquestioned prerogatives in family matters such as birth control, premarital sex, and the sacredness of the matrimonial bond. In return, the bishops instructed the members of their flock to vote as the bosses told them.

Money played a vital role in this arrangement. It cost a lot to run the dozens of different Catholic lay societies, schools, and charities.

Though the Church raised substantial sums through Sunday donations, a significant source of wealth came in the form of under-the-table cash delivered by the ward bosses.

Just how crooked was the Irish machine, which nurtured and shaped the Kennedy political dynasty? An answer of sorts, in the form of an amusing soliloquy, is provided by one of the characters in *Roscoe*, a novel by Irish American writer William Kennedy (no relation), the gist of which is worth quoting.

"How do you get the money, boy?" a crusty old ward boss says.

> If you run 'em for office and they win, you charge 'em a year's wages. Keep taxes low, but if they have to raise 'em, call it something else. The city can't do without vice, so pinch the pimps and milk the madams. Anybody that sells the flesh, tax 'em. If . . . they play craps, poker or blackjack, cut the game. If they play faro or roulette, cut it double. Opium is the opiate of the depraved, but if they want it, see that they get it, and tax those lowlife bastards. If they keep their dance halls open 24 hours, tax 'em twice. If they run a gyp joint, tax 'em triple. If they send prisoners to our jail, charge 'em rent, at hotel prices. Keep the cops happy and let 'em have a piece of the pie. A small piece. . . . If you pave a street, a 3-cent brick should be worth 30 cents to the city. Pave every street with a church on it. Cultivate priests and acquire the bishop.

When Honey Fitz had completed his apprenticeship, Matthew Keany made him a vote checker at precinct headquarters. In the election of 1888, Honey Fitz spotted one of his friends voting for the "wrong" candidate. Should he turn in his friend, or look the other way?

Loyalty to Keany won out over friendship, and Honey Fitz signaled the boss's waiting crew of ward heelers, who swarmed over the unfortunate man and informed him that he was being fired from his job and would never work in the North End again.

In 1892, when Honey Fitz was twenty-nine years old, Matthew Keany died, and his young protégé took over as the boss of the North End. Honey Fitz "was viewed as a boy by some of the old-timers," a biographer writes, "but, with favored access to all the index cards and secret lists that Keany had kept in his safe for decades, he knew exactly whom to approach for support and how best to make that approach."

In the world that Honey Fitz inhabited, victories were achieved, as Thomas H. O'Connor writes, "through the prosaic techniques of bribery, extortion, blackmail, physical intimidation . . . or just plain dirty tricks. . . . Carefully placed reports that a rival candidate was planning to divorce his wife, had run away with a young girl, had converted to Protestantism, or had been seen eating meat on Friday were always good for damaging a reputation in Catholic Boston."

Nineteenth-century urban politics was red in tooth and claw. But Honey Fitz's value system, in which the pursuit of power and achievement took precedence over ethical standards, was kept alive by his Kennedy descendants all through the twentieth century.

Honey Fitz had been talking without a break for more than twenty minutes when the Mahatma finally held up a hand as a signal for him to stop. He had heard enough, the Mahatma said. His mind was made up. Honey Fitz could count on the support of the Hendricks Club.

For a moment, Honey Fitz was speechless. Then, breaking into a toothy grin, he allowed his grandiosity to get the better of him.

"Ah," he told Lomasney, with a twinkle in his eye, "I knew you couldn't reshisht my pershuashive charms."

But it wasn't Fitzblarney that had swayed Lomasney. It was the Mahatma's thirst for revenge. He hated George McGahey with a passion, because McGahey had once dared cast his vote at a party convention against the boss's closest friend, Ned Donovan. Now the Mahatma saw his chance to pay McGahey back. He would take the coveted senate seat away from that bastard McGahey and give it to this pain-in-the-ass young upstart Fitzgerald.

The strategy worked, and Honey Fitz defeated George McGahey in the 1892 election. At the age of twenty-nine, he became one of the youngest senators in Massachusetts' history. But his victory only whetted his appetite. Two years later Honey Fitz made a bid for a seat in the U.S. House of Representatives from the same district from which his grandson John Fitzgerald Kennedy would launch *his* political career almost fifty years later.

Campaigning for the Democratic nomination on the slogan "Give Youth a Chance," Honey Fitz organized street rallies, torchlight parades, fireworks displays, and marching bands. He charmed reporters and attracted reams of positive coverage in Boston newspapers.

Still, his chance of winning the nomination did not look promising. Some of the city's most influential pols—including Patrick Kennedy's son, P. J. Kennedy, the undisputed boss of East Boston—were backing a different candidate. But once again, Honey Fitz was rescued by the Mahatma, who saw an opportunity to show everyone that *he* was the real boss of the city.

To almost universal surprise, Honey Fitz won his party's nomination, humiliating the bosses who had supported his rival. On the morning after his primary victory, Honey Fitz set out to mend fences with his onetime adversaries.

He met with P. J. Kennedy in his Brockton mansion. After the two men shook hands, Honey Fitz was introduced to P.J.'s six-year-old son, Joseph P. Kennedy. He lifted the little lad onto his lap and gave him a lollipop. It was the first meeting with his four-year-old daughter Rose's future husband.

If Honey Fitz had three people to thank for his boost in life—his father, Matthew Keany, and Martin Lomasney—P. J. Kennedy had only one: his mother.

Bridget Kennedy was a remarkable woman. Her courage and tenacity were all the more amazing because, at the time of her husband's death, she was nearly destitute, a woman worn out by years of child-bearing, barely able to read and write, and utterly lacking in the skills to make her way in the world. To put bread on the table, Bridget was forced to join the legions of Irish immigrant women who cooked, sewed, and cleaned for wealthy Brahmin families in Boston.

Before she turned forty, however, Bridget had managed to regain much of the spunk she had exhibited back in County Wexford, where she had walked the fifteen miles from Cloonagh to Dunganstown to be alone with Patrick Kennedy on the Lookout. Bridget got a job in a notions shop at 25 Border Street in East Boston, a block from the ferry to Boston, and eventually bought the shop, expanded it into a grocery and variety store that sold whiskey, and moved her family into an apartment over the store. In addition, she worked as a hairdresser at Jordan Marsh, the elegant department store across the harbor in Boston, where she came into contact with Brahmin women, whose fine clothes and genteel manners she envied and tried to emulate.

Inspired by his mother's entrepreneurial example, P.J. dropped out of school in his early teens and went to work as a stevedore on the East Boston docks. By the time he was in his early twenties, he had saved enough money to open his own business just down the street from his home. He established a Kennedy tradition by making his living from the liquor trade, eventually opening several saloons that catered to impoverished Irish workingmen.

P.J. made a deep and lasting impression on all who met him.

"A handsome, well-built young man with fair skin and light brown hair flecked with red, sporting the handlebar moustache which was fashionable at the time, P.J. dressed in a big white apron and sleeve garters from behind the bar of his saloon, made friends with everybody, heard everybody's problems, gave out free drinks to people he thought could be useful to him, and gradually built up a constituency of his own," writes John H. Davis. "Between his and Bridget's customers, the Kennedys . . . acquired a following. So much so that in 1885, when P.J. was only twenty-seven, the young saloon keeper ran as a representative from East Boston to the Massachusetts state legislature and won."

P.J. served five consecutive terms in the Massachusetts House of Representatives, and two terms in the state senate. He also held a number of important patronage positions and was appointed as a delegate to three of his party's national conventions.

"One of Joe Kennedy's earliest memories," writes Thomas C. Reeves, "was the visit of two ward heelers who proudly told his election-commissioner father, 'Pat, we voted 128 times today.' 'Win at all costs' was the iron law of P.J.'s world, a dictum that would be passed on to generations of Kennedys."

P.J. established yet another family tradition by marrying up. He chose as his bride an attractive young woman named Mary Augusta Hickey, who was the daughter of a prosperous saloonkeeper and the sister of a doctor, a police captain, and the mayor of Brockton.

Snobbish and vain, Mary Augusta was the polar opposite of her mother-in-law, Bridget. However, the two women had one attribute in common: a consuming desire to gain acceptance in WASP society. Such an aspiration was sometimes mocked by Irish Americans as "getting above yourself." But Mary Augusta did not care what less-ambitious people thought.

Her husband was just as resolved as she was to unlatch the door of opportunity and grab a share of the America Dream. And in time, P. J. Kennedy grew rich; he bought a whiskey-distributing business, a coal business, and a share of a bank. With the profits from his businesses, and his illicit take from municipal spoils, he purchased the mansion in Brockton.

Now Mary Augusta was able to hire her own Irish household help. By the time their first child, Joseph Patrick (President Kennedy's father), came along in 1888, the Kennedys were firmly established as one of those Irish families that had "fruit in the home when no one was sick."

P. J. Kennedy and Honey Fitz—President Kennedy's grandfathers—were among the handful of Irish ward bosses who met as the unofficial Board of Strategy, which ran the Democratic machine in Boston. Their secret meetings, which took place in the old Quincy House hotel near Scollay Square, began promptly at noon in Room Eight. There, over a lavish lunch followed by cigars, the members decided who was going to be superintendent of streets, police commissioner, and mayor.

For years the board had backed one of the party's most respected figures, Patrick A. Collins, in his campaigns for mayor of Boston—a post that Honey Fitz yearned to fill himself. In the fall of 1905—just eight weeks before that year's Democratic mayoral primary—Collins died of pneumonia while on vacation in Hot Springs, Virginia, and his sudden death set off a scramble to find a successor.

"Fitzgerald did not have my verbal promise," Lomasney later recalled, "but he didn't need it the way we felt early in that year and of course, he had every right to think I would be with him."

The other ward bosses felt menaced by the Lomasney-Fitzgerald alliance and, prodded by P. J. Kennedy, the chairman of the Board of Strategy, came up with a Machiavellian scheme. They persuaded City Clerk Ned Donovan—the Mahatma's dearest friend—to run for the nomination against Honey Fitz. Knowing that Lomasney could not disappoint his friend, the bosses sent the guileless Donovan to tell the Mahatma of his decision.

"I want it, I want the honor," Donovan said, according to author Doris Kearns Goodwin. "Are you going to stand in my way?"

"I knew they were working on you," Lomasney said, "but I'd hoped they would not get anywhere with it. . . . But don't say another word, old sport . . . if it means that much to you, I'll go the limit."

Stunned by Lomasney's betrayal, Honey Fitz responded to the news with characteristic vigor. He gathered all the disaffected politicians who had been excluded from the regular Democratic organization and launched a campaign against the system of bossism of which he had been a part.

"I am making my contest single-handedly against the machine, the bosses, and the corporations," he told campaign crowds with a straight face.

Honey Fitz went on to win an easy primary victory over Ned Donovan, and all but one of the Democratic leaders pledged their support for him in the general election. But the Mahatma felt that he and Donovan had been badly used, and he declared war on Honey Fitz.

He gathered his followers at the Hendricks Club on the eve of the mayoral election. "I am not going to support Fitzgerald," he told them, leaving the impression that he wanted them to support the Republican candidate. "I don't think [Fitzgerald] can be beaten, but I'm not going to lay down and be with the gang that has done such a job on us."

On election day, Ward Eight followed the Mahatma's wishes and voted Republican. But Honey Fitz swept to victory anyway. At forty-four years of age, he was viewed by Bostonians as a youthful visionary. His soaring promises of a brighter, better day would echo half a century later in John F. Kennedy's Inaugural Address.

As a reform candidate, Honey Fitz had promised to clean up city hall and run a spotless administration. But in his first term as mayor, he was rocked by a series of sensational scandals involving extortion, embezzlement, and bribery.

Public revulsion was strong. Thrown on the defensive, the mayor hunkered down and turned for help to his brothers, whom he made his closest advisers (just as a beleaguered President Kennedy, after the Bay of Pigs fiasco, would turn to *his* brother Robert). One writer referred to the Fitzgeralds as the city's "royal family."

A cry for reform went up, and when election time rolled around, Honey Fitz was soundly defeated. His brother James was accused of fraud, and the mayor himself was hauled before a grand jury, where he sought to heap blame for his corrupt administration on one of his oldest friends, Michael Mitchell, an undertaker who ran the Supply Department, which was in charge of city purchases. The hapless Mitchell, who had merely been following orders from Honey Fitz and his crooked brothers, was subsequently indicted, tried, and sentenced to a year of hard labor.

Honey Fitz may have thought that the customarily pliable grand jury would never indict Mitchell. If he believed that, "Fitzgerald displayed a certain hubris which we will see again and again in his life story and in the story of his family," his biographer writes. "It seemed as though the very courage and defiance that had lifted Fitzgerald from the slums of the North End to the mayor's seat in Boston carried with it a disregard of ordinary restraints which allowed him to take wanton risks with others."

His indifference to the welfare of others earned Honey Fitz powerful enemies, including Michael Mitchell's attorney, Daniel Coakley, who vowed to take revenge on the former mayor. In fact, it was possible to see in Honey Fitz's self-destructive behavior evidence of what a later generation would call the Kennedy Curse. For no sooner had Honey Fitz achieved the greatest ambition of his life and become mayor of Boston than fate (in the form of his character defects) crushed him and those around him.

Until then, William O'Connell, the aristocratic archbishop of Boston, had been willing to overlook Honey Fitz's shortcomings and vices, even his well-known fondness for spending evenings in dance halls, where he was seen kissing women and snuggling with them on his lap. But after Honey Fitz's public disgrace, Archbishop O'Connell began to treat him with cool detachment.

If Honey Fitz hoped to make a political comeback, he needed to win back Archbishop O'Connell's support. Cognizant of the archbishop's view that all good Catholics should attend Catholic schools, Honey Fitz informed his daughter Rose that she would not be allowed to attend Wellesley College—the secular school she had her heart set on—but would have to enroll in the Convent of the Sacred Heart in Boston.

"For seventeen years [Rose's father] had offered her everything, telling her she could do or be whatever she wanted," Doris Kearns Goodwin writes. "Now he was taking it all back and telling her, in essence, that she was only an appendage to his political needs. . . . It was as if a mask had fallen, allowing her to see her father for the first time, tainting forever the quality of his reactions with a recognition of his self-absorption."

Having betrayed Rose and sacrificed her girlhood dreams on the altar of his ambition, Honey Fitz concluded that it was time to put some distance between himself and the city he had scandalized. And so, in the summer of 1908, he took his wife, Josie, and two of their daughters, Rose and Agnes, to Ireland on a voyage into the past.

The Fitzgeralds left at two o'clock in the afternoon on July 18, 1908, aboard the liner *Cymric*. Among the Boston politicians who came to see them off were P. J. Kennedy and a personal envoy sent by the Mahatma, who no doubt wanted a trusted eyewitness to confirm that his chief nemesis was out of the way.

The high point of the trip for Honey Fitz was a visit to his father's homestead in Bruff. It was in this small village in County Limerick that the former mayor heard from a local historian that his ancestry could be traced back to the noble Italian family of Geraldini, whose members arrived in Ireland with the Norman invaders in 1169.

"The Fitzgeralds were planted in Ireland by the British," Patrick Cronin, a leading authority on the Fitzgeralds, told me during an interview in Limerick in the spring of 2001. "They were insolent, nasty people, bullers [lady's men], kings and nobles who fought a lot of bloody battles over land. They grew too big for their boots, and one Fitzgerald turned on his own. In their coat of arms, you see a chain-mailed arm holding a number of arrows, one of which is broken as a symbol that something is wrong with the Fitzgerald family. And in fact, a lot of what subsequently happened to them was ill-fated."

In the village of Bruff, another local historian, Pat Quilty, said, "Over time, the Fitzgeralds became more Irish than the Irish, and joined the Catholics against the Protestant English. They were tall, husky, burly men, brawlers who fought with fists, boots, stones, shovels, spades, scythes, and sickles. When they went into politics, they took their aggressiveness with them."

The earl of Desmond, who was head of the Munster branch of the *fitz* (meaning "son of") Geralds, erected a splendid castle on a lake at Shanid, and *Shanid Abu!*—which translated from the Gaelic means "Shanid Forever"—became the Desmond Fitzgeralds' war cry.

According to a legend that is recounted in W. B. Yeats' *Fairy and Folk Tales of Ireland*, the castle had a secret room in which the four-teenth earl of Desmond performed magic spells. One day, or so the story goes, he invited his wife into the secret room to observe him on the condition that she remain silent, no matter how frightened she became. But as soon as the earl began assuming a different magical shape, his wife let out a shriek, which broke the taboo of silence. The castle sank to the bottom of the lake, and the earl was said to dwell there, waiting for an auspicious moment to return and restore the grandeur of his reign.

This legend made a powerful impression on Honey Fitz, and in the years to come he repeated it often to his children and grandchil-dren. One who was especially fond of the story was John Fitzgerald Kennedy, who must have been struck by its similarity to the messianic legend of King Arthur, the "sleeping king" who, it was hoped, would return and restore a golden age.

"Irish Americans like Honey Fitz were eager to make up for the glorious defeat of the United Irishmen by the British in 1798," the historian Kevin Whelan told me. "They taught their sons and grand-sons that the patriot dead had a call on the living, that the torch was passed from generation to generation in an apostolic succession, and that someday a hero would emerge, like King Arthur from the Isle of Avalon, to rescue his countrymen in the hour of their direst need."

The identification with the Arthurian legend stemmed from the Kennedys' narcissistic need to see themselves as superior beings who resided above the common herd. As little gods, they felt immune to mortal laws and the consequences of their deeds. And as we shall see, this pathological fantasy put them on a fatal collision course with re-ality.

In the early eighteenth century, the Desmond Fitzgeralds' castle at Shanid was used for secret meetings of the Hell-Fire Club, a notorious group of aristocratic hedonists who indulged in every form of depravity—drunken revels, "blazings" (duels), gambling, whoring, pornography, sadomasochistic orgies (both hetero- and homosexual), cross-dressing, phallic worship, and mock religious ceremonies called "black masses" that were celebrated on the naked bodies of debauched noblewomen.

The Knight of Glin, a member of the Fitzgerald clan, and one of the oldest hereditary titles in the British Empire, was among the Hell-Fire "Bucks" who spent their nights swigging scaltheen, a rancid mixture of Irish whiskey and melted butter. Many of the Bucks had mistresses, mostly prostitutes or local girls looking for excitement. But ladies of society also appeared at the Hell-Fire Club, wearing masks so that they would not be recognized by their husbands.

"Seduction was a sport to be shared, analyzed and duly debated by club members," writes Donald McCormick. "It was generally, though not always, accepted that marriage was a matter of financial arrangements convenient to both parties, and that sexual adventure was to be sought outside the sphere of matrimony. There was a juvenile attitude to this quest for adventure, and club members not only compared notes and exchanged mistresses, but kept lists of approved harlots with detailed memoranda of their qualities and foibles."

Clubs bearing the name Hell-Fire sprang up in other places—Dublin, Edinburgh, London, and Paris—but the Hell-Fire Club situated in the Fitzgerald castle at Shanid was, at least for a time, the most notorious. "Who knows," writes a club historian, "but the curse of the Kennedy family might well be as a result of the blasphemy and irreverence associated with the club. . . . [Perhaps it] was payback time by the good Lord himself."

When he returned home to Boston, Honey Fitz was considered damaged political goods. Thus, it was a huge story when he announced to the newspapers in 1909 that he was going to run again for mayor.

Honey Fitz's second mayoral campaign was memorable for three things: first, he accused his blue-blooded opponent, James Jackson Storrow, of being anti-Catholic ("Religion should not be an issue in this campaign," he said, a phrase that would be sounded over and over by his grandson John F. Kennedy in his 1960 campaign); second, he broke into song at campaign rallies (forever linking his name in the mind of Irish Americans with the words to "Sweet Adeline"); and third, he won a thumping victory.

In his second term as mayor, Honey Fitz ran a remarkably scandal-free government. And he got along so well with the city's usually fractious ward bosses, including Martin Lomasney, that they urged him to run for a third term in 1913. Honey Fitz was only too happy to oblige.

It turned out to be a monumental mistake. Honey Fitz had made many enemies during his long career, notable among them Daniel Coakley, the lawyer who had vowed to make Honey Fitz pay for his shabby treatment of Michael Mitchell.

Coakley wasted no time in plotting Honey Fitz's destruction. He went to see James Michael Curley, who was also running for the mayoral nomination, and spun a lewd tale about one of his legal clients, a beautiful young woman named Elizabeth Ryan, who worked at a suburban roadhouse, where she was employed as an "entertainer" under the name of Toodles. Among Toodles's many admirers, according to Coakley, was Mayor John Francis Fitzgerald.

"Vivacious and cheerful, [Fitzgerald] would always tell [Toodles] how rich in beauty she was and would often invite her to join his party, where he would pull her close to him and flirt with her for hours," writes Doris Kearns Goodwin. "Proud of their friendship, he pursued her shamelessly; when they danced, he would press her tightly against his chest and smother her with kisses."

That Honey Fitz would feel sexually attracted to Toodles, a woman who was clearly his social inferior, is typical narcissistic behavior. "This position [of social inferiority]," writes Alexander Lowen, "alleviates [the narcissist's] fear of women and permits him to feel strongly excited on a genital level. Yet without a feeling of love or affection for his partner and respect for her feelings as a human being, the sexual act is largely a narcissistic expression. It amounts to exploitation."

On December 1, 1913, Curley had a black-bordered letter addressed to Honey Fitz's wife, Josie, delivered to the Fitzgerald home on Wells Avenue in Dorchester. If her husband did not withdraw from the mayoral race, the letter warned, Honey Fitz's relationship with Toodles would be exposed, and the entire Fitzgerald family would be disgraced.

When Honey Fitz came home that night, his wife and daughter Rose (who, at twenty-three, was the same age as Toodles) were waiting for him in the hallway. Brandishing the letter, Josie demanded that her husband save the family from humiliation by withdrawing from the race. But Honey Fitz—who later described the scene with his wife and daughter as the worst moment of his life—said that he preferred to call the blackmailer's bluff.

Three days later, while inspecting a cheap lodging house for building violations, the stressed-out mayor narrowly escaped death. He fell headlong down a long flight of stairs and, according to a report in the *Boston Herald*, "came within an ace of falling over the railing to a narrow hallway 20 feet below."

While the injured Honey Fitz was convalescing at home, Curley ratcheted up his campaign of intimidation. He announced that he would deliver a series of lectures on such themes as "Great Lovers in History: From Cleopatra to Toodles" and "Libertines in History from Henry the Eighth to the Present Day."

"Lying in bed that night," writes Curley's biographer, "John Fitzgerald knew what he must do. He must head off the Toodles lecture. . . . The next day, saying that he was acting on his doctor's orders, he announced his withdrawal from the race."

Five times over the course of the next quarter century—in 1916, 1918, 1922, 1930, and 1942—Honey Fitz attempted to make a political comeback. And five times he failed. Once, he won a seat in the U.S.

House of Representatives, only to be thrown out of that chamber on charges of ballot stuffing. The last time he ran for office—in the Democratic primary for a Senate seat from Massachusetts—he was seventy-nine years old; although he made a respectable showing, he lost again.

Eight years later, in 1950, long after he had retired from public life, his arch political rival, James Michael Curley, suffered a double tragedy: his grown daughter Mary Curley and his son Leo both died on the same day of the same cause—a cerebral hemorrhage. Their bodies were laid out, side by side, in the hallway of James Michael Curley's redbrick Georgian house, and more than fifty thousand mourners lined up to pay their respects, among them John Francis Fitzgerald's grandson and namesake, thirty-three-year-old Congressman John Fitzgerald Kennedy.

After the wake, Jack Kennedy visited his grandfather at his apartment in the Bellevue Hotel. The once-sprightly Fitzgerald was now eighty-seven years old. His hair was snow-white, his face deeply lined, his step no longer as light as a leprechaun's. But he was still in possession of all his faculties, and he listened with keen interest as his grandson described the extraordinary spectacle he had just witnessed at the Curley house.

It was not the raw human emotion displayed by the mourners that impressed Jack Kennedy; feelings never interested him much. He was fascinated by power and control—specifically, by how the old scoundrel James Michael Curley had stood at the head of the receiving line, proud and ramrod-straight, shaking hands and exchanging a personal word with every one of the thousands of people who filed past the biers of his dead children.

"No matter what you say of him," Jack told his grandfather, "you have to admire him for his great courage."

"When he had looked about the room and seen the astonishing variety of faces crowded together to lend support to an old politician who had been variously acclaimed and reviled, he had suddenly appreciated the indestructible rapport that springs up in political life," writes Doris Kearns Goodwin. "And now his grandfather, having achieved an unmistakable presence from the cumulative effect of his days in public life, was passing on the same message.

" 'You are my namesake,' Fitzgerald told his grandson that night, describing for him one last time the long road that had taken him from a tenement on Ferry Street to the happy years he had spent in political life. 'You are the one to carry on our family name. And mark my word, you will walk on a far larger canvas than I.' "

The Honey Fitz story illustrates how an otherwise brilliant and cunning man could be destroyed by his self-inflicted wounds. On the scale of grand tragedy, however, his tale pales by comparison with that of his son-in-law, Joseph P. Kennedy. Joe Kennedy not only destroyed his chances of becoming President of the United States but, in projecting onto his children his own unfulfilled longings and desires, provided the Kennedy Curse with its lethal gale force.

PART TWO

AFFLICTION

CHAPTER THREE

JOSEPH PATRICK KENNEDY

SPEAKING THE LANGUAGE OF HIS AGE

ON A BALMY JUNE EVENING in 1937, a Packard limousine made its way along the leafy bank of the Potomac River and passed through the gates of Marwood, an opulent 125-acre estate set deep in the Maryland countryside. When the automobile came to a stop in front of Marwood's main house, a French-style château, the chauffeur jumped out and opened the rear door for his passenger, James Roosevelt, the eldest son of the President of the United States.

At thirty-one, Jimmy bore a striking resemblance to his famous father. The son was over six feet tall and possessed the high patrician forehead, easy bearing, and good looks of the men of the Roosevelt clan. If there were signs of serious character defects in Jimmy's face, they were camouflaged under a year-round tan, which he acquired as a houseguest of rich and powerful men, who used him to finagle favors from the President.

A law school dropout and serial failure as a businessman, Jimmy had been reduced to selling insurance as a way of making a living. However, the previous January, at the start of Franklin Delano Roosevelt's second term in the White House, Jimmy's father had appointed him as his personal secretary. When Jimmy arrived at 1600 Pennsylvania Avenue to take up his new duties, he brought his insurance business with him. He liked to impress prospective clients by phoning them through the White House switchboard.

Understandably, members of President Roosevelt's staff and cabinet were uncomfortable dealing with Jimmy, for they knew that he had no compunction about profiting from his powerful new position. But the President loved his son and frequently sent him on sensitive political missions, such as the one Jimmy was on that night.

Jimmy greeted the Marwood doorman and swept through the foyer. The huge mansion contained twelve bedrooms, a two-hundred-seat underground movie theater, and a vaulted dining room copied from the original dining hall of King James I of England. A Chicago retailing heir by the name of Samuel Klump Martin III had built the mansion for his *Ziegfeld Follies* bride. But for the past two years, it had been rented to Joseph Patrick Kennedy, the fourth-richest man in America.

Joe was seated at one end of Marwood's enormous dining table when Jimmy Roosevelt entered the room.

At Marwood, fourteen miles from Washington and hundreds of miles from his family, Joe lived like a bachelor-potentate with a pack of his Irish American cronies. Each morning, Joe rose early and went for a horseback ride along the private bridle paths or for a nude swim in the pool. He was usually at his desk by seven-thirty. In the long summer evenings, he sat out on the veranda listening to Beethoven's *Fifth* or other classical pieces. When his aides begged him to put some livelier music on the Victrola, Joe growled, "You dumb bastards don't appreciate culture!"

Since he moved into Marwood, Joe had become one of the most-talked-about personalities in New Deal Washington. Reporters were amused by Joe's shameless self-promotion. The Kennedy beat was considered a plum assignment thanks to the lavish buffets and cocktail parties that Joe threw at Marwood and the fact that he kept many of the journalists on a secret payroll.

Joe's hospitality was not confined to the ink-stained wretches of the Fourth Estate. He was on equally good terms with their bosses—publishing barons such as William Randolph Hearst and Colonel Robert McCormick, the isolationist owner of the *Chicago Tribune*. When Henry Luce ordered *Fortune* magazine to run a feature on Joe, the press magnate allowed his friend to see drafts of the article and make corrections.

Joe had installed an elevator at Marwood for his most important guest—the wheelchair-bound Franklin Roosevelt. The President made occasional sorties to Marwood for a swim in Joe's pool, dinner, and a Hollywood movie in the basement auditorium. Guests at these impromptu presidential suppers sipped Scotch provided by Joe's liquor-importing company and ate lobster flown down from Boston on Joe's private plane.

"The President enjoyed Joe," said James Landis, who served under Joe when he was head of the Securities and Exchange Commission. "Joe would get films before they were released, and the President used to kid him about this."

After dinner, Roosevelt would regale Joe's guests with faintly ribald stories or break into old campaign ditties in his rich tenor-baritone. Joe would settle back in his chair, a smile of contentment on his Irish face. Having the President of the United States as a guest in his home made Joe feel important.

"How about a drink, Jimmy?" Joe asked the President's son.

Jimmy had a keen appetite for liquor, women, and luxuries that were beyond his means—all things that Joe was able to provide in abundance. As Joe once told an aide, "Jimmy is so crazy for women he would screw a snake going uphill."

Joe had sized up Jimmy the moment they met in 1932 on a cross-country whistle-stop tour for FDR aboard the *Roosevelt Special*. At the time, Joe was a Hollywood producer and major Roosevelt campaign contributor, and he impressed Jimmy as "a rather fabulous figure to a very young fellow on his father's first campaign train."

Sensing that Jimmy could be easily suborned, Joe set him up in the insurance business in Massachusetts. He also turned his Palm Beach home into a resort for Jimmy and his wife, Betsey, and supplied the young man with chorus girls through his friend, the singer Morton Downey.

Following the end of Prohibition, Joe promised to cut the President's son in on a lucrative liquor-distribution deal in London. The partnership with Jimmy, which implied that Joe had the imprimatur of the White House, cemented Joe's position as the leading distributor of Scotch whiskey in America, which was one of the major sources of Joe's fabulous wealth.

"You know as far as I'm concerned," Joe had written Jimmy and his wife a few months earlier, "you are young people and struggling to get along, and I am your foster-father."

"I can't tell you how much I appreciate what you did for me," Jimmy once thanked Joe. "And anyway, words mean so little that I hope my actions will sometimes make you realize how grateful I will always be."

Tonight, Joe intended to find out if Jimmy was as good as his word. He waited until Jimmy poured himself another drink, then steered the conversation to the subject foremost on his mind—a proper reward for his generous campaign contributions and political service to the President.

A number of rich businessmen had contributed to the President's election victories in 1932 and 1936 and had legitimate claims to jobs in the New Deal. But Joseph Kennedy, who had a grandiose idea of his own importance, had fully expected to be awarded with the biggest plum in Roosevelt's cabinet, the job of Secretary of the Treasury. From that prominent perch, Joe intended to become the power behind the White House throne.

Joe's grandiosity may have been the engine of his ambition, but it also made him do stupid—and sometimes self-destructive—things.

Contrary to all available evidence, he insisted on believing that Franklin Roosevelt, like his son Jimmy, had a weak character and a limited intellect. And in conversations with friends, Joe did not bother to hide his disdain and contempt for the President.

"I found Kennedy very frank in his expressions of understanding Roosevelt's immaturity, vacillation and general weak-kneed character," said Frank Howard, the scion of the powerful Scripps-Howard newspaper chain. Kennedy, said Howard, believed he would "be able to go a long way toward molding Roosevelt's thought processes and policies along lines agreeable to him."

In the business world, Joe had demonstrated a knack for turning the appetites and weaknesses of other men to his own advantage, as he had with Jimmy Roosevelt. But in the more complex world of politics, where men used power for ends that were often devious and obscure, Joe's imagination failed him.

For instance, it never occurred to Joe that President Roosevelt was using him, rather than the other way around. As the historian Michael Beschloss writes: "There was something about Roosevelt—the quality that moved men to lower their guard and overestimate their importance to him—that would confound Joseph Kennedy again and again."

When the President did not tap him for the Treasury post, Joe was crestfallen. "I told [Roosevelt]," Joe wrote his eldest son, Joe Jr., "that I did not desire a position with the government unless it really meant some prestige for my family."

In the end, however, Joe settled for what he could get from Roosevelt. He became the founding chairman of the Securities and Exchange Commission and, later, head of the federal Maritime Commission. But neither job satisfied his ravenous hunger for rank and station.

Now, as Michael Beschloss describes the scene in his definitive study, *Kennedy and Roosevelt*, Joe turned to Jimmy Roosevelt and said, "I'd like to be ambassador to England."

Jimmy was speechless. He pictured Joe as a "crusty old cuss," not at all the sort who could move gracefully through the elegant corridors of power in class-conscious England.

"Oh, c'mon, Joe," Jimmy said. "You don't want that."

Kennedy looked him straight in the eye.

"Oh, yes, I do," he said. "I've been thinking about it, and I'm intrigued by the thought of being the first Irishman to be ambassador from the United States to the Court of St. James's."

London had been on Joe's mind ever since Robert Worth Bingham, the current ambassador and publisher of the *Louisville Courier-Journal,* had fallen ill with malaria. The post was considered the premier diplomatic assignment in the world and, not coincidentally, the only government position, except for the presidency, that carried the social clout to impress the people Joe envied the most, the members of the WASP establishment.

No fewer than five ambassadors to the Court of St. James's—John Adams, James Monroe, John Quincy Adams, Martin Van Buren, and James Buchanan—had gone on to be elected President of the United States. Joe's most fervent wish was to become the sixth in this illustrious line of succession.

Joseph Kennedy craved power and prestige the way some men crave alcohol and drugs. Luckily for him, he came of age at a moment in American history that rewarded ambitious, talented rule breakers. He established the Kennedy name across the entire continent—from Wall Street to Hollywood and back again to Washington. His impressive achievements should have afforded him a great deal of satisfaction and contentment. Instead, he felt his successes were never enough.

The reason for this is not hard to find. Centuries of virulent prejudice against Irish Catholics—first in Ireland, then in the United States—had left the Kennedys with a severely damaged sense of their identity. One moment Joe felt that the Irish were smarter, tougher, and better than everyone else. The next he felt as though the Irish blood that flowed in his veins made him a despised outcast.

When Joe was growing up, his parents taught him that the WASP world was a hostile place for Irishmen. This translated into a paranoid attitude toward the world at large and became ingrained in Kennedy family mythology. Life outside the home was pictured as a brutal, no-holds-barred struggle, where ethical rules did not apply and the ends always justified the means. Unfortunately for Joe and future generations of Kennedys, he was never taught an even more important lesson—namely, that people who break the rules are ultimately broken by them.

The scorn that Joe's father, P. J. Kennedy, felt for his wild and rebellious fellow Irishmen was conveyed to Joe in many unspoken ways. One was the old saloonkeeper's attitude toward alcohol, the traditional curse of the Irish. Booze was to be sold, rarely drunk. When P.J. was asked to celebrate an occasion with a toast, he filled a shot glass with beer, not whiskey. And when Joe attended Harvard, P.J. told him that he had to stay sober and in control of his emotions if he wanted to beat the WASPs at their own game.

As a father, P.J. was an excessively demanding figure. But it was Joe's mother, Mary Augusta, who was the greatest influence on her son's life. A social climber and shameless poseur, she tried to hide her humble origins and boasted about the prominence of her Hickey ancestors. When Joe was born and P.J. told his wife that he wanted a namesake, Mary Augusta reversed the order of the child's Christian names, admitting to friends that Joseph Patrick sounded "less Irish" to her ear than Patrick Joseph.

Joe's mother ladled out her love according to his achievements. She obsessed over "my Joe," quizzing him on his academic work and encouraging him to make friends with his social betters. Remember, she told her son, people judge you by the company you keep.

To Mary Augusta, politics had the taint of the Irish. Business was another matter. After arranging a job for Joe at a millinery shop, where he delivered hats to the homes of Brahmin ladies, his mother instructed her sandy-haired, blue-eyed son how to obscure his Irish origins. "If you are asked your name," she said, "answer Joseph."

"Unconsciously," Nancy Gager Clinch writes in *The Kennedy Neurosis*, "every neurotic wonders who he really is. 'Am I the proud superhuman being—or am I the subdued, guilty, and rather despicable creature?' . . . Such a man has little or no faith in human nature, for he lacks genuine faith in himself. Instead, the neurotic, who feels life as an overwhelming threat, must throw up a defense strong enough to hold back disaster. This seems to be the psychological basis of the fantastic energies that [Joseph] Kennedy displayed in realizing his ambitions. His ambitions, in essence, had to be equal to his fears. This is the core of self-glorification."

Harvard convinced Joe that no matter how hard he tried, he could never hope to climb the rungs of WASP institutions. He failed to make Harvard's prestigious final clubs (his heart was set on the most exclusive, Porcellian), despite the fact that, following his mother's advice, he had befriended WASP classmates who were sure to be admitted.

"Joe sucked up to 'important' people quite ingloriously and without scruple," one classmate told authors Peter Collier and David Horowitz. "He tried to get some reflected glory by selecting roommates who were All-America football players and the like."

Joe earned a varsity letter in baseball during his senior year at Harvard by playing in the last inning of the annual game against Yale. To make sure that Joe would get into the game, his father bribed the team captain, who wanted P.J.'s help in opening a movie theater. When Joe caught a pop fly to end the game, he flouted tradition by refusing to hand over the game ball to the captain.

"In years to come," writes Richard Whalen, one of Joe's biographers, "Kennedy adopted an attitude toward Harvard that friends and classmates sadly described as hatred."

In order to start at the top in business, Joe had to play on a field of his own choosing. After graduating from Harvard, he got himself elected head of the Columbia Trust Company and put out a press release noting that, at age twenty-five, he was the youngest bank president in the country. He failed to mention that P. J. Kennedy and his friends owned the bank.

Still, over the next fifteen years, employing means both fair and foul, Joe made a fortune trading securities in the bull market and producing films in Hollywood. But his fabulous material success never provided a bulwark against his overwhelming feeling of failure.

In 1929, when *Queen Kelly*—a film that Joe produced starring his mistress, Gloria Swanson—was a box-office flop, Joe's paranoia got the better of him. He imagined that people all over the country were sneering at him.

Swanson remembered Joe charging into her bungalow. "He held his head in his hands," she writes in her memoirs, "and little, high-pitched sounds escaped from his rigid body, like those of a wounded animal whimpering in a trap. He finally found his voice. It was quiet, controlled. 'I've never had a failure in my life,' were his first words. Then he rose, ashen, and went into another searing rage against the people who had let this happen."

By 1937, Joe Kennedy had become a darling of the media. Reporters churned out reams of copy about him, making him a household name. His friends in the press, especially Henry Luce at *Time* and Arthur Krock, the powerful Washington bureau chief of *The New York Times,* promoted Joe as a presidential contender to succeed Franklin Roosevelt in 1940, when the Democratic incumbent presumably would not seek a third term.

These stories did not please Roosevelt, who never made the fatal mistake of viewing his rivals with benign indifference. As a result, Roosevelt was eager to get rid of Joe. If he sent him to London, Joe would have all the trappings of power but as a subordinate to the Secretary of State, none of the substance. And with Roosevelt's debt to him paid, Joe's objections would be heard as faint cries from across the Atlantic.

Thus, in the fall of 1937, Roosevelt called in his son Jimmy and told him he had been thinking about Joe's request to become ambassador. Roosevelt said he was "kind of intrigued with the idea of twisting the lion's tail a little, so to speak," Jimmy recalled. "He wanted to talk to Joe about it."

Several days later, when Joe entered the Oval Office accompanied by Jimmy, the President was seated behind his large desk in his wheelchair. The amusing scene is described in James Roosevelt's *My Parents*.

"Joe," said the President, "would you mind stepping back a bit, by the fireplace perhaps, so I can get a good look at you?"

Somewhat flustered, Joe complied.

"Joe, would you mind taking your pants down?" said the President, full of mischief.

In disbelief, Joe asked if he had heard correctly.

"Yes, indeed," said Roosevelt.

Joe undid his suspenders and dropped his pants, and stood there in his shorts, looking "silly and embarrassed," as Jimmy recalled.

Roosevelt coolly looked him up and down.

"Someone who saw you in a bathing suit once told me something I now know to be true," he said. "Joe, just look at your legs. You are just about the most bowlegged man I have ever seen. Don't you know that the ambassador to the Court of St. James's has to go through an induction ceremony in which he wears knee breeches and silk stockings? Can you imagine how you'll look? When photos of our new ambassador appear all over the world, we'll be a laughing stock. You're just not right for the job, Joe."

Joe was notorious for poking fun at others, but he had no sense of humor when it came to himself. He looked at Roosevelt like an earnest schoolboy.

"Mr. President," he said, "if I can get the permission of His Majesty's government to wear a cutaway coat and striped pants to the ceremony, would you agree to appoint me?"

Roosevelt played along.

"Well, Joe, you know how the British are about tradition. There's no way you are going to get permission, and I must name an ambassador soon."

"Will you give me two weeks?" Joe asked.

Roosevelt responded laconically: "OK."

Two months later, when Ambassador Bingham was moved to a critical-care unit at Johns Hopkins University Hospital in Baltimore, Joe Kennedy told his two eldest sons, Joe Jr. and Jack, to make plans to move to London. But autumn came and went, and there was still no announcement from the White House of Joe's appointment. Instead, rumors began circulating in Washington that a number of the President's men were bitterly opposed to Joe's nomination.

Every time Joe came home to Bronxville to visit his family, Rose met him at the front door with the same question, "What has the President said?"

Like her mother-in-law, Rose stoked the fires of Joe's grandiosity.

"I felt that Joe deserved something better," Rose said, "something really special in the government, and I told him so."

What Rose did not say was that she missed the days when *she* had been the center of attention back in Boston at the side of her flamboyant father, Mayor John "Honey Fitz" Fitzgerald. She had married a man who was like her father in many ways, except the one that mattered most: Joe did not make her a partner in his public life.

Aside from a lavish allowance for shopping trips to the Paris couturiers, Joe had given Rose few opportunities for a life outside the home. She had spent her entire married existence bearing and rearing children: Joe Jr., was born nine months and two weeks after her wedding day, and Teddy, her youngest, was still only five years old. Rose believed that Joe's ambassadorship would give her the opportunity to be indispensable to her husband on the public stage.

With her natural poise, European education, and command of languages, Rose was a natural fit for embassy life, even if her brassy, impatient husband was not. "Joe spoke no foreign languages and had no 'ear' or natural facility in languages," she wrote. "Thus the suitable possibilities were reduced to one post."

The one post left by Rose's self-serving process of elimination happened to be the flagship of the U.S. diplomatic service. As the ambassador's wife in London, Rose would have the highest possible visibility in Anglo-American society. She would, for example, select the American debutantes to be presented to King George VI and Queen Elizabeth. "That power," as Laurence Leamer writes, "[would make] her the most important woman in America to a number of women who only a few weeks ago would have snubbed her."

The need to wash away the stain of being Irish ran even deeper in Rose Fitzgerald Kennedy than it did in Joe. The Kennedys merely hated the English. The Fitzgeralds wanted to be like them.

True, when Rose's father was campaigning for votes in Boston's Irish wards, he put on a thick brogue, danced jigs, and sang "Sweet Adeline." But for all his Gaelic theatricality, Honey Fitz was a snob. His greatest pleasure lay in putting on aristocratic airs. He rode polo ponies, participated in foxhunts, and consorted with European royalty. He did not approve of Joseph Kennedy as a prospective son-in-law because Joe's father plied the stereotypical Irish trade of saloonkeeper.

Only when Joe Kennedy was elected president of Columbia Trust did Honey Fitz finally relent and support Rose's wishes to marry him. The message that Honey Fitz conveyed to Rose was consistent: in order to be accepted by the "right people," she had to make herself over in their image.

Now, as a married woman, Rose had the task of making over Joe, too.

And so Rose came to reinforce Joe's worst tendencies. Few people, for instance, would have expected President Roosevelt to remove his trusted Treasury secretary, Henry Morgenthau, to make room for a campaign contributor and fly-by-night adviser like Joe Kennedy. But when Joe despaired of this, Rose offered an explanation that fit within their narrow sense of entitlement.

"Mrs. Morgenthau and Eleanor were such great friends," Rose recalls in her memoir *Times to Remember*, "and dispensing with Henry could have resulted in friction not only in the Dutchess County neighborhood [where the Roosevelts and Morgenthaus maintained country houses] but in the Roosevelt home."

Rose's attitude meshed well with Joe's view that promotion to high places in government service led to promotions in WASP society. Rose had a fine sense of which ribbons were worn in the social realms to which she and her husband aspired. And in narrowing Joe's field of vision to London, she strengthened his belief that his only safe route out of the political wilderness led across the ocean.

Through the frosted window of a White House car, Jimmy Roosevelt stared at the passing landscape of the wintry Maryland countryside and pondered how best to carry out his father's latest assignment. The President was being pelted by protests from liberal advisers and members of Congress, who were deeply disturbed by reports that Joe Kennedy was about to be appointed ambassador to London. Something had to be done, and Roosevelt had chosen this cold December evening to dispatch his son to Marwood again, this time to talk Joe out of the job.

When the young man arrived, he found Joe dining with the *Times'* Arthur Krock, Joe's closest confidant and Marwood's most frequent visitor. A short, stubby man who stabbed the air with his cigar as he talked, Krock was a more expensive Kennedy retainer than Jimmy Roosevelt had ever been. In addition to accepting lavish gifts (such as all-expenses-paid vacations to Europe), Krock pocketed $25,000 a year in cash to keep the Kennedy name front and center in his influential *Times* column. For the past year, he had been using the pages of the *Times* to float trial balloons in favor of Joe's appointment to London.

Normally Jimmy would have enjoyed spending an evening in the company of Joe Kennedy and Arthur Krock. The three friends had shared women on previous occasions. But Jimmy did not have time for such diversions this night. He needed to speak with Joe alone.

Joe escorted Jimmy out of the dining room, pulling the door shut behind them. Though Krock could not hear their words, the tone of their loud conversation was unmistakable. Each sentence from Jimmy drew an explosion from Kennedy. After half an hour, the pair emerged. Jimmy made his good-byes and departed hurriedly through the mansion's front door. Joe returned to the table. His face was flushed and his slate-blue eyes were flashing.

"You know what Jimmy proposed?" he told Krock. "That instead of going to London, I become Secretary of Commerce! Well, I'm not going to! FDR promised me London, and I told Jimmy to tell his father that's the job, and the only one I'll accept other than Secretary of the Treasury."

Krock took another puff on his cigar as he waited for Joe's pulse to subside. The *Times* man recognized that the time had come for him to swing into action and earn his secret Kennedy payola.

Under the dateline Washington, D.C., December 8, Arthur Krock planted a front-page story in *The New York Times* reporting that the Roosevelt administration had definitely decided to nominate Joseph Kennedy to be America's next ambassador to London. To disguise the fact that Joe himself was the source of the story, the *Times* said, "The appointment to the Court of St. James's, premier post in the Foreign Service, will come as a complete surprise" to Joseph Kennedy.

When the President read the story, he hit the roof. He called a press conference on December 21 and, speaking off the record, said he was "very, very sorry to see the story break" in *The New York Times* "because I didn't think it helped for old Bob [Ambassador Robert Bingham]" to read it.

In an unpublished private *aide memoir* that Krock wrote for his files, he disputed the President's interpretation of events. "But at the press conference of December 21," Krock wrote, "Mr. Roosevelt, who was in the midst of charging the press with responsibility for the business recession, named other journalistic sins as he saw them and added he 'thought the premature publication may have hastened Bingham's death.' (The ambassador had submitted to an operation . . . from which he did not rally.) The President left the impression that the White House had nothing to do with the 'premature publication'!"

Later that day, in a meeting with his White House advisers, the President's mood was dark. According to Treasury secretary Henry Morgenthau, Roosevelt called Joe "a very dangerous man" and made it clear that he intended to send him to England with the clear understanding that the appointment was for only six months. Furthermore, he said, by giving Joe the appointment, any obligation he had to him was paid.

"Well, Mr. President," Morgenthau said, "England is a most important post, and there have been so many people over there talking against the New Deal. Don't you think you are taking considerable risks by sending Kennedy, who has talked so freely and so critically against your Administration?"

Roosevelt replied sharply, "I have made arrangement to have Joe Kennedy watched hourly, and the first time he opens his mouth and criticizes me, I will fire him. Kennedy is too dangerous to have around here."

The press saw Joe's appointment as a delightful novelty. Some gushing accounts went so far as to describe him as an Irish American Rockefeller, who had single-handedly fulfilled the American Dream. The Boston papers pulled out all the stops. In the *Post* and the *American*, a series on Joe's career carried a genealogy headlined KENNEDY FAMILY HAS ROYAL BLOOD ANTEDATING THE KING'S.

Honey Fitz was quoted in *The New York Times* as saying that the ambassadorship was "the most important job the Administration has to give out." Dozens of congratulatory letters poured into the Kennedy family homes in Bronxville and Palm Beach. An old friend of Joe's father wrote: "I thank God I have lived long enough to see Kennedy's name spread all over the world the way I like it."

Knowing that the Irish story line would fade soon enough, Joe got out in front of the inevitable questions about his diplomatic inexperience.

"I wouldn't consider the position unless I felt that there was some chance of doing a really worthy job," he wrote the eminent Boston banker Ralph Lowell. "If I do take this job, and I don't feel that I am doing as much in it as I would like, then I am through with that."

There was only one Cassandra among his correspondents.

"You are a sincere man, Joe," his friend Boake Carter, an isolationist, right-wing columnist, warned him. "You possess that great faith that so many Irishmen have—the faith that no matter what he tackles, he can't be licked. You are an honest man. But the job of Ambassador to London needs not only honesty, sincerity, faith and an abounding courage—it needs skills brought by years of training. And that, Joe, you simply don't possess. . . .

"In view of the fact that the probable welfare of 130 million [American] lives may hang on the results of the conduct of that post, you tempt all the Gods of the world by diving into the Court of St. James's as an expert. Joe, in so complicated a job there is no place for amateurs. . . . For if you don't realize that soon enough, you are going to be hurt as you were never hurt in your life."

The SS *Manhattan* set sail from New York harbor for Southampton, England, on February 23, 1938, four days after Joe's swearing-in ceremony in the Oval Office at the White House. On the rain-soaked promenade deck, Joe made his way through hundreds of tightly packed well-wishers to his cabin, where photographers waited to take his picture.

Eight of Joe's nine children were there to see him off. Rose had stayed behind after having undergone an emergency appendectomy, which the children would learn about only when it was reported in the newspapers.

Out at sea, Joe stood on the deck with Harvey Klemmer, an aide he had brought along from the Maritime Commission. Klemmer worried aloud several times about war coming to Europe. But nothing made a dent in Joe's ebullient mood.

"Oh, Christ, Harvey," he scolded. "Drop that war business. You're just a pessimist."

On the afternoon of May 5, 1938, Ambassador Joseph P. Kennedy and his wife stepped out of an embassy car and made their way toward a magnificent eighteenth-century town house situated in the northeast corner of St. James's Square in London.

Joe looked resplendent under the blue-gray sky. He wore the same crisp morning clothes he favored at official functions, a decision that allowed him to stand out as a distinctly American figure among the diplomats and ministers who donned knee breeches in observance of protocol.

Rose, who had already exhausted her Parisian wardrobe in just six weeks of hectic London social life, wore one of the English dresses fitted for her by Captain Edward Molyneux, the city's leading couturier.

The mansion at 4 St. James's Square belonged to Lady Nancy and Lord Waldorf Astor, London's leading hosts. The Astors' only social rivals, Emerald, Lady Cunard, and Sybil, Lady Colefax, had suffered a grievous blow when their chief patron and prize guest, Edward VIII, had abdicated the British throne two years earlier to marry Wallis Warfield Simpson, an American divorcée. The Astors' social triumph over the Cunards and Colefaxes carried some irony, for like Edward's controversial bride, Lady Astor was also American and divorced.

However, unlike Mrs. Simpson, the Virginia-born Nancy Astor commanded unprecedented influence as the leading political hostess in Britain. Twenty years earlier, Nancy had succeeded her wealthy husband to become the first woman ever to serve in the House of Commons. A diminutive five-foot-two, Nancy possessed aquiline features that set off her piercing blue eyes, and an aggressive, magisterial manner that underscored her reputation. Known for her sharp tongue, the doyenne met a rare match in Winston Churchill, who served alongside her as a backbencher in Parliament. They detested each other.

"How many toes are there in a pig's foot?" Churchill had once asked at a party in an attempt to stump the guests.

Nancy Astor shot back, "Take off your shoes and count."

She had taken Rose Kennedy under her wing shortly after the ambassador's wife arrived in March, and she was fast becoming the dominating presence in Rose's new life. On her say-so, Rose had become the honorary president of the American Women's Club of Great Britain. The Kennedys were already regular guests at Cliveden, the Astors' stately, forty-six-room house in Buckinghamshire, where Nancy presided over a rotating assortment of leading diplomats, Oxford dons, journalists, and society figures.

The mistress of Cliveden, who chewed gum while wearing a $75,000 diamond tiara, amazed one and all with her vitality, public-spiritedness, and incomparable wit. She fascinated the repressed and devoutly religious Rose.

"Nancy Astor has the most amazing energy of anyone I have ever seen," Rose wrote in her memoirs. "She went to the Christian Science church, had huge lunch with twenty-eight to thirty, went off to play 18 holes of golf. . . . She is great fun anyplace, talks about everything, anything, intelligently and with gusto and with an inexhaustible sense of humor. Also she is a clever mimic, and when she puts in a pair of false teeth she changes her whole facial expression and is marvelous."

But associating with the Astors was as risky as it was pleasant for the American ambassador. By the late 1930s, the Cliveden salon had coalesced into a group of Oxford-educated intellectuals with a shared belief in the manifest destiny of Anglo-Saxon culture and a disdain for European entanglements, especially military intervention to subdue Nazi Germany. Among the upper-crust members of the Cliveden coterie there were a number of outright Nazi sympathizers. As a result, the Astors' reputation had begun to curdle.

The left-wing journalist Claud Cockburn had scored a bull's-eye when he characterized "the Cliveden Set" as a "shadow cabinet" that had subtly engineered the British government's appeasement policy toward Hitler. The appellation "Cliveden Set" had stuck, especially in the wake of Hitler's annexation of Austria just days after the Kennedys arrived in England. To those with a deep appreciation for geopolitics— a group that definitely did not include Joe Kennedy—it seemed only a matter of time before the Cliveden Set would be tarred with the brush of treason.

The Kennedys eagerly slipped through the front gate and up the steps, past a crowd of photographers, who were frequently stationed outside the Astors' door. Joe and Rose took their seats in the lesser of two paneled dining rooms among a small luncheon party that included the Irish-born dramatist George Bernard Shaw, recipient of the Nobel Prize in literature; William Bullitt, the genial American ambassador to France; and Charles and Anne Morrow Lindbergh, who had exiled themselves to England after the infamous kidnapping and murder of their thirty-month-old son.

Even in such company, the Kennedys commanded considerable attention, and talk soon turned to Joe's first official act as ambassador. Rose had persuaded Joe to abolish the tradition in which rich young American women were presented at the Court of St. James's. At the spring debut a week hence, only the daughters of diplomatic or other U.S. government personnel would be presented—a move that provoked howls of anger from wealthy Americans but earned Joe plaudits throughout England and back home in egalitarian America.

All this was rich stuff to those who understood that Joe's own daughters would now have unparalleled status at the season's premier social event. "That neat little scheme you cooked up . . . to kick our eager, fair and panting young American debutantes in their tender, silk-covered little fannies, certainly rang the bell," the journalist Frank Kent wrote Joe. "A more subtle and delightful piece of democratic demagoguery was never devised."

Lady Astor, who as usual had placed the table settings uncomfortably close together to encourage more lively, intimate conversation, leaned toward George Bernard Shaw and asked whether he approved of Joe's decision.

"Certainly not," the playwright replied, in a quip that was to ricochet through the London press. "We don't want the Court to have only *selected* riff-raff."

Joe had never met Charles Lindbergh, but in the space of a few minutes they became fast friends. Lindbergh had recently toured Germany at Hitler's personal invitation and concluded that the Luftwaffe was the strongest air force in the world. He then had publicly declared the Führer a "great man" who had "done much for the German people." For these comments, Hitler would award Lindbergh the Service Cross of the German Eagle, the highest decoration the Nazis could bestow on an *Ausländer*.

Joe shared Lindbergh's views about the Führer and Britain's scant chances of defeating Germany in the event of war. Over lunch, he was pleased to discover that Lindbergh had closely followed several isolationist speeches Joe had given in London.

"Kennedy interested me greatly," Lindbergh wrote after the luncheon. "He is not the usual type of politician or diplomat. His views on the European situation seem intelligent and interesting. I hope to see more of him."

Five days after the luncheon, Joe sent Nancy Astor a clipping of "Washington Merry-Go-Round," the muckraking syndicated column written by Drew Pearson and Robert Allen. The relevant item began, "Latest American to be wooed by the Clivedon [sic] group is genial Joe Kennedy, new Ambassador to Britain. Reports are that Joe has been taken in just a bit by the Clivedon charm, not on the Nazi-Fascist theories, but on the idea of cooperating with the Tories of Great Britain."

In response, Joe had frantically cabled Pearson: "I know you and Bob don't want to hurt me unless you have definite reasons. Your story on the Cliveden Set is complete bunk. There is not one single word of truth to it and it has done me great harm."

The note that Joe sent along with the clipping to Lady Astor, however, conveyed an upbeat tone: "Well, you see what a terrible woman you are, and how a poor little fellow like me is being politically seduced. *O weh ist mir!*"

As ambassador to the Court of St. James's, Joe had taken to heart Roosevelt's hints that he would be a short-timer. And although he had confided to Joe Jr. that his new duties exhausted him, he was enjoying a honeymoon in London that seemed as if it would last forever.

Some Britons had scoffed at the coarse American amateur, who had immediately assimilated the British cuss word *bloody* into his already scatological vocabulary, put his feet on his desk at press conferences, called the queen a "cute trick," and flouted convention at his debut at Windsor Castle by directly approaching Her Majesty to dance rather than wait for a footman to invite him.

But others were charmed by a living stereotype of an American abroad. Lord Halifax, the foreign minister, toasted him as "so representative of modern America." And the British press delighted in everything he did. A few days after arriving, Joe had played a round of golf and shot a hole in one, and his preternatural instinct with reporters did not fail him.

"I am much happier being the father of nine children and making a hole in one," he declared, "than I would be as the father of one child and making a hole in nine."

The Kennedy children arrived in London in much-publicized waves, and newspapers chronicled every detail of the bedlam at 14 Prince's Gate, the ambassador's official residence opposite Kensington Gardens. Raucous touch football and baseball games convened spontaneously in the backyard, and little Teddy was said to have commandeered the elevator and ferried the housemaids up and down the floors in a game of "department store."

Joe broke convention by allowing unposed pictures of the children in every situation, including shots of Kathleen hitching up her gown in preparation for her May 11 debut before the queen. The extroverted "Kick," to whom Lady Astor had taken an especial liking, outstripped even Joe with her dizzying social life.

She took British society by storm. "Oh, kid, what's the sto-o-ory," she would say, bounding up to a young earl whose proper dates spoke of little but begonias and lineage. The forbidding duke of Marlborough, charmed by Kick's unself-conscious daring, was pleased with the nickname she gave him: "Dukie Wookie."

President Roosevelt, who followed the British press coverage from Washington, was delighted by the overwhelming success and originality of Joe's debut. "When you feel that British accent coming on you and your trousers riding up to your knees," the President ribbed Joe, "take the first steamer home for a couple weeks' holiday."

But as time went on, Roosevelt began to eye Joe's official activities with increasing concern. He had expected Joe to be content to soak up London's social life and use his position to further his business interests. And in fact, Joe had set about enriching himself by instructing his aide, Harvey Klemmer, to reserve scarce shipping capacity for thousands of cases of whiskey for his Somerset Importers. What Roosevelt had not expected was for Joe to launch a personal crusade against American intervention in a future war with Germany.

Hitler's *Anschluss* (the bloodless 1938 annexation of Austria) did not alter Joe's views in any way. "The march of events in Austria made my first few days here more exciting than they otherwise might have been," he complaisantly wrote Arthur Krock on March 21. "But I am still unable to see that the Central European developments affect our country or my job."

He dismissed his staff's horrified reaction to Germany's thuggish behavior as "semi-hysterical." Diplomats on the American desk at the British Foreign Office, who quickly came to detest and even fear Joe, began compiling a secret dossier known as the "Kennediana" file.

"The minute books of the Foreign Office filled with confidential accounts of the deeds and sayings of the American envoy," Michael Beschloss wrote. "As one diplomat noted, it was gossip—'but gossip which very probably has more than a grain of truth to it.' Occasionally cruel, occasionally exaggerated, the reports scrawled across bound foolscap reflected growing antagonism. . . . 'Kennedy's real ambition is the White House,' observed a British intelligence officer, 'and he has a great chance of achieving it.' "

Joe took it upon himself to be a sort of superambassador for Britain and the Continent, issuing a series of increasingly isolationist declarations that were not in sync with Roosevelt's policies. To Joe's way of thinking, economics lay at the root of all problems. Anything that threatened a solid international economy, particularly war, would render America powerless and imperil Joe's own financial well-being.

Like many nouveaux riches, Joe lived in constant fear that cataclysmic events could obliterate everything he had worked for. But economic considerations were only part of the story. He had less creditable motives as well. His lifelong love affair with power led him to admire men like Hitler, who exemplified the theories of Friedrich Nietzsche, the nineteenth-century German philosopher. A nominal Catholic, Joe personally rejected Christianity's "slave morality" and glorified Nietzsche's *Übermensch,* or superman. Only grandiosity on such a monumental scale—and a narcissist's infatuation with power— could explain how Joe, an otherwise brilliant man with a keen understanding of human nature, was so blind to the perverted ideology of Nazi Germany.

"No one knew then that Hitler was criminally insane and had no intention of living by humane standards except his own demented ones, and that his promises meant nothing to him," Rose would later write in defense of her husband.

But that judgment is demonstrably false. Joe chose to ignore evidence that was reaching London of brutal persecution against Jews and other despised minorities in Germany. When Harvey Klemmer returned from a trip to Germany, he gave Joe a personal briefing on how Nazi storm troopers molested Jews in the streets, destroyed Jewish-owned businesses, and committed mayhem and murder in Jewish neighborhoods.

"Well, they [the Jews] brought it on themselves," Joe said.

He expanded on that belief in a meeting with Herbert von Dirksen, the German ambassador to London, that June. Von Dirksen reported to his superiors in Berlin that Joe had told him the Nazi program to rid Germany of Jews was not so much the problem as "the loud clamor with which we accompanied this purpose. He himself understood our Jewish policy completely: He was from Boston and there, in one golf club, and in other clubs, no Jews had been admitted for years." Von Dirksen added that Joe had gone on to praise Hitler and believed "there was no widespread anti-German feeling in the United States outside the East Coast, where most of America's 3,500,000 Jews were living."

Joe had nothing but contempt for the powerless Jews in Hitler's Germany, who allowed themselves to be pushed around. The haunting fear of his own weakness rendered him incapable of seeing Hitler in moral terms. Frightened by Lindbergh's dark reports of superior Nazi armament and Hitler's own aggressive moves in Europe, Joe had little faith that the American and British democratic systems could mount an effective defense.

"He was worried that fascism might very well sweep the world and that we would have to prepare ourselves," Jimmy Roosevelt recalled.

The prospect of war drew out Joe's innermost fears on an epic scale, and the same paranoia that had gripped him during the Great Depression now drove him to respect and fear the Nazi military buildup. As a result, Joe's tone with Roosevelt had grown increasingly shrill, and he alarmed the President by stating that America, softened by depression and social unrest, "would have to come to some form of fascism."

———

By the time the summer of 1938 arrived, Joe was convinced that the only way to avert a general European war lay in a joint Washington-London effort to strike an economic deal with Germany. And the surest way to accomplish that, Joe concluded, was to get himself elected President in 1940.

And so Joe began to supplement his regular diplomatic dispatches to Roosevelt and Secretary of State Cordell Hull with private letters to an array of important American politicians and members of the press, all containing reckless attacks on Roosevelt's nuanced European policy. A good number of these letters floated his notion of leading a new administration fully committed to isolationism. Some opinion makers who received the letters were persuaded and took the idea public.

"Ambassador Kennedy would make a very strong [presidential] candidate," William Randolph Hearst observed. "He may not want to consider the matter himself, but other people are considering it seriously—and if he could get the country out of this mess, he would have no right to refuse."

Of course, Joe had masterminded the presidential boomlet through trusted emissaries, chief among them Arthur Krock of *The New York Times*. By May 1938, *Liberty* magazine ran a story under a headline asking WILL KENNEDY RUN FOR PRESIDENT? And a number of newspapers quickly followed suit.

Roosevelt, who was contemplating an unprecedented third term—a possibility Joe had now become aware of—finally had had enough. He could not recall Joe from his post and risk giving him a way to create mischief in the United States. But Roosevelt was Kennedy's superior at planting stories in the press, and the President summoned his press secretary, Stephen Early, and told him to telephone Walter Trohan of the *Chicago Tribune*.

"You're a friend of Joe Kennedy?" Early asked Trohan, a conservative with whom Joe had regularly planted criticisms of the liberal Roosevelt brain trust.

"Yes," the reporter offered.

"You know Joe wants to be president."

"Yes. He has as much chance as I do."

"Would you rake him over the coals if it were justified?" Early asked.

"Any time I can get a New Dealer, I'm delighted," Trohan answered.

Early sent Trohan the full batch of Joe's "private" letters, all of which had found their way to the White House. On June 23, the *Tribune* ran a front-page story under the headline KENNEDY'S 1940 AMBITIONS OPEN ROOSEVELT RIFT. The article stated that Joe hoped to use his ambassadorship as a stepping-stone to the White House and had directed a stealth campaign from abroad through "a prominent Washington correspondent." Presidential intimates now considered Kennedy "the soul of selfishness." And one high administration official (a cover for Stephen Early himself) was quoted as saying, "Joe Kennedy never did anything without thinking of Joe Kennedy."

After the story broke, Joe immediately sailed home and demanded to see the President. Looking Joe in the eye, Roosevelt denied that he had had anything to do with the leak to the *Chicago Tribune*.

"In this way," Joe recalled years later, "he assuaged my feelings, and I left again for London. But deep within me I knew that something had happened."

On the evening of October 19, 1938, Joe strode briskly to the podium at a London dinner club and readied his notes for a speech that he believed would be the most important of his life. The large hall was packed with bemedaled admirals and other ranking officers of the Royal Navy, many of whom had fought in World War I. At the invitation of George Ambrose Lloyd, president of the Navy League, Joe was to be the first American ambassador to deliver the official address on Trafalgar Day, the annual commemoration of Admiral Horatio Nelson's historic sea victory against Napoleon in 1805.

The Trafalgar Day speech always commanded public attention,

but recent events in Europe ensured that Joe's turn at the podium would receive unprecedented exposure. All summer long, the Nazis had threatened to invade the Sudetenland, the mountainous Czech border region that contained Czechoslovakia's German population, and Europe was in the grip of war hysteria.

In Germany, Hermann Göring, Hitler's propaganda minister, had issued a steady stream of diatribes against the Czechs: "This miserable pygmy race without culture is oppressing a cultured people, and behind it is Moscow and the eternal mask of the Jew devil." To back up Göring's inflammatory rhetoric, Hitler had assembled ninety-six German divisions and issued a deadline of October 1 for the Czechs to hand over the Sudetenland, or face invasion.

Joe had worried that France, bound by treaty to defend the Czechs, would drag Britain and the United States into war. He had already irked Roosevelt by asking permission to deliver a speech that said, in effect, "for the life of me I cannot see anything involved which could be remotely considered worth shedding blood for."

In Washington, the President had invited Henry Morgenthau into his private study, where the two men read the proposed draft of Joe's speech and excised the craven comment. A year earlier Franklin Roosevelt had delivered a rousing speech in Chicago in which he asserted the United States would "quarantine" dictator nations. Roosevelt had no intention of letting Hitler think that he had nothing to fear from the United States. Joe Kennedy, the President told his treasury secretary, "needs his wrists slapped rather hard."

Roosevelt had finally come to the conclusion that Kennedy was a hopeless dupe of the Cliveden Set.

"Who would have thought the English could take into camp a redheaded Irishman?" he told Morgenthau.

But Joe was euphoric as he stood before the top ranks of the British navy. The past three weeks appeared to vindicate everything he had been saying all along. Just a day before the German deadline, Prime Minister Neville Chamberlain had returned exhausted from a last-minute conference in Munich, with Hitler's word that Germany would curtail all further ambitions if handed the Sudetenland.

War had been averted. "I believe it is peace for our time," Chamberlain announced as church bells pealed and Londoners filled the streets to shout their approval. Joe felt he had played a large part in Chamberlain's success, and he boasted to the gossip columnist Walter Winchell that Chamberlain had "depended on me more than anybody for judgment and support."

As plates were cleared and cigar smoke began to fill the great room, Joe relished this public chance to lord it over President Roosevelt, who had slapped him down. Joe had been polishing his Trafalgar Day address for the past ten days, agonizing over every nuance, and this time he had slipped it through the State Department vetting process just a day in advance, making it unlikely that Roosevelt himself would ever see it.

"As pleased as I am to be here, I must confess that your invitation has involved me in definite difficulties," Joe told the navy brass with affected modesty. Using an old rhetorical trick, he went on to list several things he was *not* supposed to talk about in his muffled diplomatic position. Then he dropped his bomb.

"It has long been a theory of mine," he said, "that it is unproductive for both democratic and dictator countries to widen the division that now exists between them by emphasizing their differences, which are self-apparent. Instead of hammering away at what are regarded as irreconcilables, they can advantageously bend their energies toward solving common problems and attempt to re-establish good relations on a world basis. The democratic and dictator countries differ ideologically, to be sure, but that should not preclude the possibility of good relations between them. After all, we have to live together in the same world, whether we like it or not."

Joe's words of appeasement amounted to a rebuke of his own President. Within hours of his Trafalgar Day address, calls and telegrams flooded the White House and State Department, inquiring whether Joe's comments heralded a major shift in American foreign policy.

Roosevelt took to the radio to disavow his ambassador's words, a move that Joe considered "a stab in the back." But what really stung Joe was the lightning speed with which many of the men he had cultivated in the Fourth Estate now turned on him.

"For him to propose that the United States make a friend of the man who boasts that he is out to destroy democracy, religion and all other principles which free Americans hold dear . . . that passes understanding," the *New York Post* editorialized. Heywood Broun, a columnist who had been at Harvard with Joe, suggested that his classmate be dunked in Boston Harbor "so that his Americanism might be restored by resting awhile among the alien tea."

The most influential broadside came from Walter Lippmann, America's leading public intellectual. Three days after Joe's speech, the columnist derided Joe as one of the "amateur and temporary diplomats [who] take their speeches very seriously. Ambassadors of this type soon tend to become each a little State Department with a little foreign policy of their own."

Joe Jr., then twenty-three and serving as one of his father's secretaries, penned an open rebuttal that branded Lippmann's column "the natural Jewish reaction. . . . I know this is hard for the Jewish community in the U.S. to stomach, but they should see by now that the course which they have followed the last few years has brought them nothing but additional hardship."

Joe himself turned on the same scapegoat, blaming "a number of Jewish publishers and writers" for warping his comments into more than the "pet theory" he said he had intended to offer. "The tactics of this group may someday be analyzed," he wrote. "Some of them in their zeal did not hesitate to resort to slander and falsehood to achieve their aims. I was naturally not the sole butt of their attack but I received my share of it."

———

On the evening of November 9, which became known as Kristallnacht, the Nazis razed 200 German synagogues, destroyed 1,000 Jewish shops and homes, murdered nearly 250 Jewish women and children, and deported more than 20,000 Jews to concentration camps. The barbaric shape of the Holocaust was becoming clear to the whole world.

Smarting from the deluge of criticism of his Trafalgar Day speech, Joe sought to turn Kristallnacht to his own advantage. He began working with Chamberlain on a plan to evacuate German Jews to Africa and South America.

Joe made sure that daily updates on "the Kennedy Plan" were fed to the press. George Rublee, a Washington lawyer who had been working on such an evacuation scheme for months, noted that he had tried to interest Joe in the plan before, but he "never gave me any real support or assistance."

Joe encountered the same obstacles as Rublee had: no government was willing to provide a safe haven or logistical support to make the plan work. The idea languished as the State Department questioned why Joe had never brought the matter up with anyone in the U.S. government. Meanwhile, *Life* magazine, run by Joe's friend Henry Luce, noted that the plan "will add new luster to a reputation which may well carry Joseph Patrick Kennedy into the White House."

In December 1938, when Joe returned to Washington for consultations with the President, observers predicted a tremendous confrontation. James Farley, the postmaster general, who himself had designs on succeeding Roosevelt, noted that the President was "terribly peeved" with his ambassador. "When Joe comes back, that will probably be the beginning of the end."

Instead, Roosevelt purposely glossed over their differences. The President predicted that the Munich agreement would fail and confided to Joe his plans for dealing with Europe: "He would . . . help [England] with arms and money, and later, depending on the state of affairs, get into the fight," Joe recalled. By all rights, Joe should have resigned on the spot. He had no intention of supporting a clandestine effort that might lead the country into war.

But Joe began a campaign to persuade Roosevelt that only extraordinary measures could provide security against Hitler and the Soviet communists, whom he feared even more. The heavy sacrifices required to match the Nazi arms buildup would not be possible in the squabbling American and British democracies.

"To fight totalitarianism," Joe told the President, "we would have to adopt totalitarian methods."

Joe also proposed a more grandiose version of his old plan for an economic deal with Hitler. In a strange memo to Roosevelt, he unveiled a new master plan in which the great powers, including Germany, Russia, Britain, Japan, and China, would divide the world into spheres of influence and "settle down to a long peace and security in which the forces for freedom everywhere would once more have an opportunity to develop."

Roosevelt was familiar with Joe's utter lack of faith in democratic government. He once told his interior secretary, Harold Ickes, "Joe Kennedy, if he were in power, would give us a fascist form of government. He would organize a small but powerful committee under himself as chairman and this committee would run the country without much reference to Congress."

Even when Hitler rolled though Czechoslovakia in March, flouting the Munich agreement, and brought the world to the brink of war by massing his forces on the border with Poland, Joe Kennedy continued to believe that the dictator could be bought off. To an increasingly befuddled Neville Chamberlain, Joe suggested that Roosevelt pay Germany a larger cash sum than Hitler could possibly realize from his next military adventure.

"After all, the United States will be the beneficiary of such a move," Joe said. "To put in a billion or two now will be worth it, for if it works we will get it back and more."

To those who knew Joe well, his amoral response to the greatest moral dilemma of the century was not surprising. Roosevelt's aide Tommy Corcoran, who had supported Joe far more often than other liberal New Dealers, remembered Joe's cynical sermons with mixed emotions.

"He was speaking the real language of his age," Corcoran said. "Joe would say, What end is there? Only power. What delight is there but to be part of great events; the sheer sense of control. There isn't any other end. 'Power is the only end and if you don't like the code of the game, what is it then? Love of country? Let me see it in people who really command.' How did the Tudors, Cecils, Brahmins rise? The source of power is money."

At a London dinner given by the diplomat Harold Nicolson and his wife, Vita Sackville-West, Walter Lippmann informed Winston Churchill of a recent afternoon he had spent with Joe Kennedy. Lippmann conveyed Joe's prediction that Britain would inevitably be "defeated" in a war with Germany.

This information brought a powerful response from Churchill.

"No, the ambassador should not have spoken so, Mr. Lippmann," Churchill thundered, punctuating each phrase with a wave of his whiskey and soda. "He should not have said that dreadful word. Yet supposing—as I do not for one moment suppose—that Mr. Kennedy were correct in his tragic utterance, then I for one would willingly lay down my life in combat, rather than, in fear of defeat, surrender to the menaces of these most sinister men."

Minutes before dawn on September 3, 1939, a Sunday, the telephone rang at the ambassador's residence at 14 Prince's Gate. Joe was wide awake; in fact, he had hardly slept in days. An aide delivered the message: Joe was to report to 10 Downing Street, the residence of the prime minister, within the hour. Neville Chamberlain wished to read the ambassador a draft of an address he planned to deliver a few hours later.

The summons filled Joe with dread. On Friday, German tanks had rolled across the border of Poland, crushing twelve brigades of mounted cavalry that stood against them. German bombs rained down on Polish cities, and Warsaw had called on Britain and France to honor their commitments to defend Poland. The Allies issued an ultimatum to Berlin: remove all German forces from Polish soil by noon on September 3, or face war.

Three hours remained before the deadline, and still no answer had come from Hitler. Joe entered the prime minister's office, and Chamberlain's voice quavered as he began to speak the words that would darken the House of Commons later that morning: "Everything that I have worked for, everything that I had hoped for, everything that I have believed in during my public life has crashed in ruins."

That sentence might just as well have described Joseph Kennedy. Before Chamberlain was done, the ambassador's eyes welled up with tears.

Joe made his way back to the embassy and dispatched a triple-priority cable to Cordell Hull conveying the substance of what he had just heard. Then, although it was four A.M. in Washington, he put in a call to the White House.

Franklin Roosevelt could barely recognize Joe's shaky voice. At a time when the President of the United States shouldered an epic burden, he found himself consoling his hysterical ambassador. Joe unleashed a torrent of dire predictions: A new Dark Age was descending. Economies would crumble. His own sons would be lost in war.

"It's the end of the world," he cried over and over. "The end of everything."

Later that morning—on the way to the packed Strangers' Gallery to hear the prime minister deliver his formal war speech to Parliament—Joe, Rose, Jack, Kathleen, and Joe Jr. were caught in a stampeding crowd as air-raid sirens sounded, a false alarm brought on by the hair-trigger mood in London. People rushed into the embassy, which had no shelter. Joe had the staff herd his family and aides across the street, to the nearest refuge he knew—the sturdy basement of Rose's couturier, Edward Molyneux.

Joe scrambled to book berths for Rose, his nine children, and members of his entourage on the SS *Washington,* the first available liner to New York, which did not leave until September 9. But fifteen thousand anxious American expatriates were clamoring for scarce spaces aboard the few American ships in Britain, and it suddenly struck Joe that news of his family's mass evacuation would go over like a lead balloon in the press.

Instead, he sent his family back in waves, a mirror image of the way they had come, this time without the fanfare. Rose, Kathleen, and Bobby left first; then Joe Jr., who defended his father's reputation to reporters when he docked in New York. Pat, Jean, and Teddy took a third boat, and Jack, serving at the embassy, flew home aboard a Pan Am Clipper before September was out.

Only one child remained. "We decided to let Rosemary stay on awhile because she was doing so well at her special school, which was far in the countryside and almost surely safe from any bomb damage," Rose recalled.

Joe was panicked by the threat of German air raids. He spent long stretches near Rosemary in rural Hertfordshire at Wall Hall, an abbey that J. P. Morgan Jr. had restored for the use of American ambassadors. But no ambassador could remain so far away from London. Without authorization from the State Department, and at his own expense, Joe rented St. Leonard's—a vast, seventy-five-room country mansion beyond Windsor, about twenty-five miles from the city—"as a place outside London in the event of heavy bombing." When the Blitz came, Joe would be widely despised for his lack of solidarity with the British people, while the king and queen won their hearts forever by striding through the London rubble.

Ensconced in these country abodes, Joe sent Roosevelt updates that focused less on the British war effort than on his own notions of what should be done and on the subject closest to his heart—money

President Kennedy's grandfather Patrick Joseph (P.J.) Kennedy, age twenty-two, in 1880. The tragedies that struck the Kennedys and those associated with them can be traced back to the nineteenth century.

(John F. Kennedy Library, Boston)

Patrick Kennedy, Rose Fitzgerald, John F. "Honey Fitz" Fitzgerald (first, second, and third from left) and Joseph P. Kennedy Sr. (second from right) at Old Orchard Beach, Maine. One must go back to the ancient Greeks and the House of Atreus to find a family that has been subjected to such a mind-boggling chain of calamities. *(Corbis)*

FITZGERALD DENIES HE EVER KISSED "TOODLES"

Supt Pierce Also Disavows Charges Made Regarding Miss Ryan.

Names of Prominent Men Used in Trial of Suit Against Mansfield.

"I NEVER KISSED HER."

"I never kissed 'Toodles,' nor do I remember ever seeing any more than a picture of the Ryan woman," said Ex-Mayor John F. Fitzgerald last evening in an address before John J. Williams Council, K. of C., of Roslindale, in Fraternity Hall.

Nearly 200 members and friends of the organization gathered to hear him speak on local current events. Mr Fitzgerald came late and explained that he was detained through having to attend to a denial of the newspaper headlines reflecting upon his actions at the Ferncroft Inn.

"One of the disagreeable features in public life, and one that keeps many a good man out of it, is the ease with which a man can be attacked, and for which there is no redress. In my 20

Continued on the Sixth Page.

WHERE NAMES COME IN

It was full of thrills, the session of the Ryan-Mansfield breach of promise case in the third session of the Superior Court yesterday afternoon, but it required little effort on the part of the court to restrain the thrills.

> Ex-Mayor Fitzgerald—"It's a lie, pure and simple."
> Supt of Police Pierce—"There is not a word of truth in it."

The testimony was more interesting to the crowded courtroom than it has been for the past few days. This fact only made the waiting line outside the more patient, and at the same time more determined to wait for a chance to get in.

Continued on the Sixth Page.

TOP LEFT Elizabeth Ryan, an "entertainer" whose nickname was Toodles. Among Toodles's many male admirers was Boston's Mayor Fitzgerald, who showered her with hugs and kisses. *(Reprinted courtesy of* The Boston Globe*)*

TOP RIGHT The Toodles scandal made headlines, like this one in the January 20, 1915, issue of *The Boston Globe,* and forced Honey Fitz to withdraw from the Boston mayoral race. *(Reprinted courtesy of* The Boston Globe*)*

ABOVE Mayor Fitzgerald struts his stuff in a Boston parade. A born politician, Honey Fitz earned a nickname for his excessive talkativeness: Fitzblarney. *(AP/Wide World Photos)*

ABOVE (from left) Teddy, Jean, Bobby, Pat, Eunice, Kick, Rosemary, Jack, Rose Kennedy, and Joe Kennedy, c. 1933 in Palm Beach. When one of the Kennedy children failed to come in first, he or she was sent to the kitchen to eat alone. Victory—and parental acceptance—had to be won over and over again. *(Photofest)*

RIGHT Ambassador Joseph P. Kennedy in London on the eve of World War II. Joe's love affair with power led him to admire Hitler, who exemplified the superman theories of Nietzsche.
(John F. Kennedy Library, Boston)

ABOVE Ambassador Kennedy and Rose flank King George VI and Queen Elizabeth in 1939. Rose's attitude meshed well with Joe's view that promotion to high places in government service led to promotions in WASP society. (*Photofest*)

LEFT Navy Lieutenant Joseph P. Kennedy Jr. in World War II. "Nobody in my family needs insurance," Joe Jr. boasted just before taking off on a suicidal mission. (*Bettmann/Corbis*)

ABOVE Kathleen (Kick) Kennedy and William Robert John Cavendish, Marquess of Hartington, smile at their London wedding in 1944. Even broad-minded members of the Cavendish family were wary of Kick's Catholicism. (*Bettmann/Corbis*)

LEFT Peter Fitzwilliam dancing at a hunting ball. Kick was attracted to the married, Protestant Fitzwilliam because he was like her father—older, sophisticated, and a rogue male.

(Illustrated London News *Picture Library*)

The Brothers Kennedy—Jack, Bobby, and Teddy—in an undated photograph. "Our father wanted us to be able to smile no matter how tough things were," Teddy remarked. " 'I don't want any sour pusses around here,' he would say." *(Photofest)*

RIGHT Joseph Kennedy with his sons (from left) Edward, John, and Robert. It was the Kennedys themselves, not their detractors, who were the first true believers in the Kennedy Curse. *(John F. Kennedy Library, Boston)*

BELOW President Kennedy kisses his father after Joe's stroke. Jack's compulsive womanizing could be seen as a desperate effort to obtain what was missing from his life—a genuinely intimate parental connection. *(John F. Kennedy Library, Boston)*

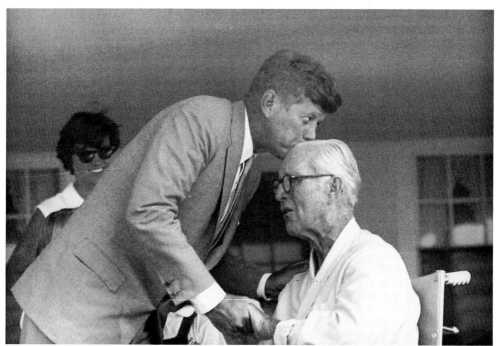

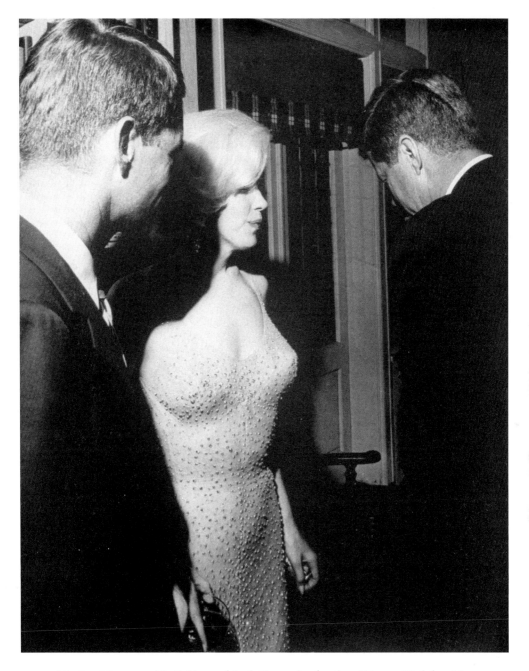

Marilyn Monroe with Bobby and Jack Kennedy after her "Happy Birthday, Mr. President" performance at Madison Square Garden. Suspicions lingered that the Kennedy brothers were somehow implicated in Marilyn's death. *(Cecil Stoughton/TimePix)*

Three generations of Kennedys, in Hyannis Port, September 1962. Four decades later, the Kennedys were like the tail of a comet whose blinding brightness had passed. (*John F. Kennedy Library, Boston*)

TOP President Kennedy strolls in Boston with Dave Powers and his Secret Service detail. Drinking and sex became part of traveling with the President and led some Secret Service agents to fall victim to the Kennedy Curse. *(Bettmann/Corbis)*

BOTTOM Jacqueline Kennedy scrambles onto the trunk of the presidential limousine in Dallas. "We're heading into nut country," Jack informed Jackie prior to his assasination. *(Bettmann/Corbis)*

TOP John Jr. and Caroline with their nanny, Maude Shaw, in Hyannis Port, August 1963. After the President's assassination that year, John's impulsive behavior developed into a serious problem. *(Cecil W. Stoughton/John F. Kennedy Library, Boston)*

BOTTOM Jackie chastises young John Jr. in Hawaii, 1966. "I always told John he's got to be careful never to do anything that could darken the family name," Jackie told the author. "But I'm not sure he's listening." *(Photofest)*

TOP Spectators watch the police inspect Senator Edward Kennedy's car after it was pulled from the water on Chappaquiddick Island. Teddy's life had been fractured by his brothers' assassinations. *(Photofest)*

BOTTOM Teddy after Chappaquiddick. "The serious lawmaker in Ted Kennedy would turn now and then into a drunken, overage frat-house boor, the statesman into a party animal, the romance of the Kennedys into a smelly toxic mess," wrote *Time* magazine.

(John Loengard/TimePix)

TOP An infamous paparazzi shot of Teddy Kennedy atop an unidentified woman on a powerboat on the Cote d'Azure in 1989. The photo prompted another senator to say to Kennedy, "Well, I see you've changed your position on offshore drilling." *(Pierre Aslan/Sipa Press)*

BOTTOM An aeriel view of the Kennedy compound in Palm Beach, Florida. The promise of "a quiet drink at the house" was a surefire technique for luring women back to the family playground for sex. *(Bob Shanley/Palm Beach Post)*

LEFT JFK Jr. in Hyannis Port, 1980. To get attention, John often indulged in exhibitionist stunts, like appearing shirtless in Central Park, or having his picture taken while sailing with Carolyn. *(Paul Adao/New York News Service)*

BELOW JFK Jr. and Carolyn Bessette cruising Cape Cod. The author's conversations with Jackie led him to believe that, had she lived, she would have disapproved of John's choice of Carolyn. *(Paul Adao/New York News Service)*

Caroline Kennedy and her husband, Edwin Schlossberg, leave their Manhattan apartment on their way to an exhibition of her mother's White House clothes, April 2001. After her brother's death, Caroline picked up the torch and assumed a larger public role. *(William Reagan/AP/Wide World Photos)*

and financial security. In one notorious message sent just a week after the war began, Joe suggested that Roosevelt step in where England and France could not, to make his own Munich-style deal with Hitler.

"It appears to me that this situation may resolve itself to a point where the President may play the role of savior of the world," Joe wrote obsequiously.

Roosevelt called it "the silliest message I have ever received."

The President did not lack field intelligence, however. By the time war broke out, he had wholly circumvented Joe, sending numerous emissaries to London and the Continent who reported directly to him. Roosevelt sent Churchill a note inviting him to open a back channel of communication with the White House. Joe was given the thankless task of ferrying the cables, which were encoded and sealed in pouches and underscored the ambassador's growing irrelevance.

By the fall of 1940, Joe wanted out. He was being left in the dark on decisions of importance and was routinely unable to answer basic questions at meetings. He protested to Roosevelt that he was "seriously considering going home. As far as I can see, I am not doing a damn thing here that amounts to anything."

In several heated telephone exchanges, some of which escalated to shouting matches, Roosevelt firmly told him to stay put. Quitting in defiance of the President during wartime would ruin Joe's reputation and end his public aspirations. Joe remained in exile, alone and afraid.

Finally, Joe found a lever, albeit an exceedingly dangerous one: blackmail. On October 16 he sent a cable to Roosevelt asking again to be released. Then he telephoned Sumner Welles, the undersecretary of state, vowing that he was "coming home anyhow." If he did not get a positive response to his request this time, Joe told Welles, he would have his trusted private secretary, Eddie Moore, release a written account to the press of his mistreatment at the hands of Roosevelt.

For months Joe had been amassing a cache of the clandestine cables between Roosevelt and Churchill that revealed the American

President had been secretly cooperating with the British military effort. Joe had persuaded Tyler Kent, an embassy code clerk, to provide him with deciphered copies, then stood by silently as British counterintelligence agents arrested Kent for harboring the material.

Joe sent the cache back to New York with Eddie Moore. Revelations of this material, at a time when many Americans and members of Congress bitterly opposed entering the war, could well cost Roosevelt the 1940 election. Joe was, of course, untroubled by the larger implication—that isolationists might use the scandal to undermine tacit American support of the Allies and tip the outcome of World War II in favor of Nazi Germany.

A few hours later Joe received approval for a Washington visit, and then this cheerful and apologetic cable from Roosevelt:

Dear Joe:

I know what an increasingly severe strain you have been under during the past weeks and I think it is altogether owing to you that you get a chance to get away and get some relief. The State Department has consequently telegraphed to you by my desire to come back during the week of October 21. . . . I need not tell you that a great deal of unnecessary confusion and undesirable complications have been caused in the last few months by statements which have been made to the press by some of our chiefs of mission who have been coming back to this country. . . .

I am, consequently, asking you specifically not to make any statement to the press on your way over nor when you arrive in New York until you and I have had a chance to agree upon what should be said. . . .

Yours very sincerely,
As ever,

F.D.R.

The presidential election of 1940 was only ten days away, and speculation was mounting that Joe would use the occasion of his return to endorse Wendell Willkie, the Republican candidate, and thus break with Roosevelt for good. However, if Joe had any intention of talking to reporters before setting foot in the White House, he saw that it would not be possible. When his plane touched down in Washington, he was met by a large reception committee consisting of Foreign Service officers, policemen, and others, which served as a muscular escort to his destination.

At his first opportunity, Joe telephoned the White House, where the President was lunching with House Speaker Sam Rayburn and Lyndon Johnson, then a special duty officer in naval intelligence.

"Ah, Joe, it is so good to hear your voice," Roosevelt intoned. "Come to the White House tonight for a little family dinner. I'm dying to talk to you."

Johnson, who idolized the President, said he watched in awe as Roosevelt, while pronouncing the word *dying,* looked at his companions and conspiratorially drew his finger across his throat.

Rose knew nothing about the recent machinations, except that Joe had angrily talked of throwing his political support to Roosevelt's Republican opponent, a move that might influence many of the nation's 25 million Catholic voters. Yet she considered Franklin Roosevelt "the most charming man in the world," and on the flight down to Washington, Rose told her husband that "no other President" would have sent a Roman Catholic to England as ambassador. She cautioned him against any disloyal act that might brand him an "ingrate" and jeopardize Joe Jr.'s political future.

At seven P.M. Roosevelt's private secretary, Missy LeHand, greeted the Kennedys in the President's study, where they were soon joined by Roosevelt, Eleanor, and Senator James Byrnes, the powerful South Carolina Democratic, and his wife—"proving," as Joe later fumed, "that the President didn't want to have it out with me alone."

Roosevelt had no illusions about the high stakes involved with his dangerous ambassador, and not a minute of the next two hours went unscripted. As Missy LeHand led the six to an adjacent room for a casual Sunday dinner of scrambled eggs, toast, and sausages, Roosevelt began working on Rose, talking incessantly about her beloved father, Honey Fitz.

Byrnes had the main assignment, and he engaged Joe in harmless chitchat that drew stock compliments about the President from Kennedy. Suddenly, Byrnes beamed: "I've got a great idea, Joe! Why don't you make a radio speech on the lines of what you have said here tonight and urge the President's re-election?"

But Joe did not take the bait. As the supper party returned to the study, Roosevelt still had not taken him aside or discussed anything of substance.

Finally, Joe piped up tensely.

"Since it doesn't seem possible for me to see the President alone," he said, "I guess I'll just have to say what I am going to say in front of everybody. In the first place, I am damn sore at the way I have been treated. I feel that it is entirely unreasonable and I don't think I rated it."

There was a "second place," and a "third place," and so on, as Joe continued to rant about everything from the frequent dispatch of shadow emissaries to end-run him in London to the State Department's keeping him in the dark.

He continued, disingenuously, "Mr. President, as you know, I have never said anything privately in my life that I didn't say to you personally, and I have never said anything in a public interview that ever caused you the slightest embarrassment."

Roosevelt responded by attacking the State Department officials Joe had named with even more ferocity than Joe had. All of this was a total surprise, the President said with the appearance of growing indignation. After the election, he was going to have a "real housecleaning" and throw out all the villains who had wronged his ambassador.

Rose, whom the President had buttered up all evening, "chimed in at this point," Joe recalled, "and said it was difficult to get the right perspective on a situation that was three thousand miles away."

According to Joe's memoirs, he suddenly softened and agreed to give the pro-Roosevelt radio speech, salving his ego by saying, "But I will pay for it myself, show it to nobody in advance, and say what I wish."

But as Joe, Jimmy Roosevelt, and others would reveal later, the President did indeed take him aside. Clasping his arm around the ambassador, Joe was given the impression that he had Roosevelt's blessing for the 1944 Democratic presidential nomination—an "offer" that several other men would receive. Roosevelt also played expertly on Joe's ambition for his sons. As Joe would tell Clare Booth Luce, a former mistress who had urged him to switch to Wendell Willkie, "I simply made a deal. We agreed that if I endorsed [FDR] for President in 1940, then he would support my son Joe for governor of Massachusetts in 1942."

At nine P.M. on Tuesday, October 29, Joe sat before a microphone in a studio at the Columbia Broadcasting System, which had arranged to carry his words over 114 stations.

"Unfortunately," he told his fellow Americans in the seventy-five-minute speech, "during this political campaign there has arisen the charge that the President of the United States is trying to involve this country in the World War. Such a charge is false."

Joe even flaunted his most precious asset for the cause. "After all, I have a great deal at stake in this country. My wife and I have given nine hostages to fortune. Our children and your children are more important than anything else in the world. The kind of America that they will inherit is of grave concern to us all. In light of these considerations, I believe that Franklin D. Roosevelt should be re-elected President of the United States."

The telegram from Roosevelt came seconds after Joe went off the air:

WE HAVE ALL JUST LISTENED TO A GRAND SPEECH MANY
THANKS STOP LOOKING FORWARD TO SEEING YOU ALL TOMOR-
ROW EVENING

FRANKLIN D ROOSEVELT

Press reviews were equally ecstatic. "As a vote-getting speech, it was probably the most effective of the campaign," declared *Life* magazine, which was controlled by Clare Luce's husband, Henry.

The next night all the threads of Roosevelt's scheme came together in a brilliant tapestry. The President chose Boston Garden to deliver the final speech of his campaign, and thousands of Irish eyes were on the man who sat beaming at his elbow.

"Let me welcome back to the shores of America that Boston boy, beloved by all of Boston and a lot of other places, my ambassador to the Court of St. James's, Joe Kennedy," Roosevelt said to thunderous applause.

Then he uttered those famous words so convincingly isolationist that even the antiwar Willkie knew he was done for.

"I have said this before, and I shall say it again and again and again," Roosevelt said. "Your boys are not going to be sent into any foreign wars."

Joe stood for the ovation and clapped as loudly as all the rest.

The Friday after Election Day, Joe sat in his shirtsleeves in a suite at the Ritz-Carlton Hotel, eating apple pie and hunks of cheddar cheese. His stature, after a two-year slide in London, was miraculously restored. Roosevelt had beaten Willkie in an electoral landslide, and conventional wisdom in Washington had it that the President would reward Joe with a high-profile position in his new administration. What's more, the political rise of Joe's eldest son was all but assured.

Three newspapermen sat around the ambassador, busily scribbling down his every word and gesture. Louis Lyons of *The Boston Globe* had arranged an interview for what promised to be a fluff piece in the coming Sunday paper. Two other reporters, Ralph Coghlan and Charles Edmondson of the *St. Louis Post-Dispatch,* had called that week to get background on Joe. To Lyons's annoyance, Joe had decided he would hold an informal bull session with all three at once.

When he wasn't snapping up the telephone receiver to take congratulatory calls, Joe fired off a series of blunt quips that always endeared him to reporters. The ninety-minute interview was not supposed to cover politics or foreign affairs—Joe had received explicit orders from the State Department on that—but he soon drifted into familiar territory, anyway. Once he got going, the reporters couldn't believe their ears, and they took down every word.

"Democracy is finished in England, and it may be here," he said. "Because if it comes to a question of feeding people, it's all an economic question. I told the President in the White House last Sunday, 'Don't send me fifty admirals and generals. Send me a dozen real economists.' It's the loss of our foreign trade that's going to change our form of government. We haven't felt the pinch of it yet. It's ahead of us."

And there was more as he worked himself into a froth and said everything that popped into his head. Would America refuse to trade with Hitler if the Nazis won the war? "That's nonsensical." It was "bunk" that England was fighting for democracy; instead, it was "self-preservation."

Before the interview was over, Joe had said the queen of England should personally negotiate with Hitler ("She's got more brains than the Cabinet") and dismissed Eleanor Roosevelt, with whom he had stood on the campaign platform just days before, as someone who "bothered us more in our jobs in Washington to take care of all the poor little nobodies who hadn't any influence than all the rest of the people down there together. She's always sending me a note to have some little Susie Glotz to tea at the embassy."

Two days later Lyons's front-page dispatch in *The Boston Globe* carried the banner headline:

KENNEDY SAYS DEMOCRACY ALL DONE IN BRITAIN, MAYBE HERE

Joe had the article read to him over the phone and was so pleased that he called the *Globe* reporter with hearty congratulations.

"Well, the fat's in the fire, but I guess that's where I want it!" he boasted.

The rest of the country, increasingly sympathetic to the British cause, didn't see it that way; nor for that matter, was the queen or Eleanor amused. Newspapers from coast to coast picked up the sensational remarks, and thousands of Americans wrote the White House calling for Joe's summary dismissal.

"I hope you put Joe Kennedy in a bag and pull the string tight," one read.

All the good Joe had done himself with the pro-Roosevelt radio address evaporated into thin air. When he realized his mistake, he repudiated the interview, claiming that he had understood the meeting to be off the record, but he did not dispute the substance of his comments. The *Globe* rejected his demands for a retraction and suffered the loss of thousands of dollars in advertising from Joe's Somerset Importers.

Franklin and Eleanor Roosevelt spent the weekend before Thanksgiving at Hyde Park. The vivid reds, oranges, and yellows of autumn in Dutchess County had faded, and a cold wind whipped through the bare elms along the Hudson River. As they sat with the President's mother, Sara Delano Roosevelt, the talk turned to Joe's *Globe* interview and what to do about it.

"We better have him down here," Franklin concluded, "and see what he has to say."

A few days later Eleanor met the morning train at Rhinecliff and took Joe directly to see the President. The two men disappeared into Roosevelt's private study in the front of the mansion. Ten minutes later an aide came to Eleanor and whispered, "The President wants to see you right away."

"This was un-heard of," Eleanor recalled. She rushed into the office and found her husband rooted to his desk, "white as a sheet." Roosevelt had asked Joe to step outside.

"Get him out of here," he told Eleanor with a shaking voice. "I never want to see that man again as long as I live."

"But, dear, you've invited him for the weekend, and we've got guests for lunch and the train doesn't leave until two," Eleanor said.

"Then you drive him around Hyde Park, give him a sandwich, and put him on that train," Roosevelt said.

Eleanor had always disliked Joe, but she understood the extent of her husband's anger only when she took Joe to her private cottage at Val-Kill, where she was forced to listen to his dire forecasts of British defeat and paeans to German military might. By the time she finally dropped Joe off at the train depot, she was emotionally exhausted.

Twenty years later, at a lunch with the writer Gore Vidal, Eleanor laughed when she recalled that afternoon as "the most dreadful four hours of my life." Her husband, long since dead, had never told her exactly what had transpired, but she knew it was "very bad."

About a year after Joe Kennedy's falling-out with Franklin Roosevelt, his favorite daughter, Kathleen, landed a job as secretary to the editor of the *Washington Times-Herald*. Soon, Kathleen began dating the paper's star feature writer, John White, the oddball son of an Episcopal minister.

"One evening soon after they had begun seeing each other," writes Kathleen's biographer, Lynne McTaggart, "she turned to White and made a coquettish reference to North Carolina. *How the hell does she know where I'm from?* he had wondered. Later she dropped bits and pieces of knowledge about his background that he was certain he had not given her. Finally he had to ask, 'Where the Christ are you getting all this information about me?' "

Kathleen's reply, reports McTaggart, left White "speechless."

"Every time one of us goes out with somebody new, we have to call our father," Kathleen said.

"Has he run a check on me?" White asked.

"You bet he has," she replied.

"Then how on earth can he let you go out with me?"

"Oh, he considers you frivolous but harmless," she said.

It was at about this time that Kathleen began making an effort to break away from her father's suffocating control. But she succeeded only in becoming another victim of the Kennedy Curse.

PART THREE

TRIBULATION

CHAPTER FOUR

KATHLEEN KENNEDY

THROWING CAUTION TO THE WIND

KATHLEEN KENNEDY GAZED UP at the soaring glass-roofed vault of St. Pancras Station. The sky over London looked uncommonly clear for March, a welcome reprieve from the freezing rain and fog that had rolled across wartime Britain for the past several weeks late in the winter of 1944. Great shafts of mote-choked light flooded the packed station, which echoed with the accents of American servicemen who were in England preparing for the invasion of Nazi-occupied Europe.

Kathleen cut a stylish figure in her couture suit and plumed Robin Hood hat. At twenty-four years of age, she was in the full flush of young womanhood: a petite, five-foot-three-inch Irish American lass with bright, gray-blue eyes, incandescent skin, and the prominent teeth of the Fitzgerald clan. The vivacious Kick, as everyone called her, had inherited her charismatic personality from her grandfather Honey Fitz. But beneath the charm, she was all Kennedy. Like her father, she subscribed to the view that rules were made for other people.

Being a Kennedy meant that Kick always traveled first-class, even if she did not possess a first-class ticket, which was the case on this particular day. And so she set about plying a conductor with the same charm that she ordinarily used to beguile the sons of dukes, viscounts, and earls. Soon she was comfortably settled, free of charge, in one of the train's most luxurious carriages.

She shared the compartment with five people—an English couple, a British army captain, and two American officers. The Americans passed around some chocolates, filling the cabin with their loud, grating voices, no doubt reminding their fellow passengers of the saying in wartime London: "The trouble with the Yanks is that they're over-paid, oversexed, and over here."

"Your name—it's Kennedy, isn't it?" one of the Englishmen asked her.

"Yes, it is," she replied.

"I remember seeing your face five years ago in the newspapers and then again the other day."

Kick was flattered by the remark. She had inherited her parents' craving for attention and social acceptance. But whereas Joe and Rose Kennedy were weighed down socially by the large chip on their shoulder, Kick was a blithe spirit who always seemed to find ardent devotees among the best people in Britain. When the European war broke out in the fall of 1939, Joe Kennedy forced Kick to return home to the safety of America, thereby depriving her of the spotlight she had enjoyed as one of the bright young things of London society.

Now, four and a half years later, she had finally made it back to England, and she was setting out on a momentous journey. The train cut through the western suburbs and made its way toward the North Country. Kick's stop, the Derbyshire village of Bakewell, was a gateway to the vast estates of the Cavendish family, the wealthiest and most powerful clan in Britain after the royals. Kick knew that her next two days as a guest of the Cavendishes could determine the future course of her life, as well as the fate of her family.

At Bakewell, a chauffeur greeted Kick and took her things to an idling car. They turned onto a narrow, twisting road that ran out of Bakewell toward Churchdale Hall, the fourteenth-century Cavendish residence in the neighboring medieval village of Ashford-in-the-Water.

The formidable Mary, duchess of Devonshire, had invited Kick to her family's countryseat to discuss the young woman's prospective engagement to her eldest son, William Robert John Cavendish, marquess of Hartington. As heir to the Devonshire dukedom, Billy Hartington was considered the most eligible bachelor in England.

Kick's journey that day was the culmination of years of social striving. She had been plotting to marry someone like Billy ever since her spectacular London debut in 1938, which was arranged by her father. Her success, which was widely publicized in the London papers, gave Kick grandiose notions about what she could accomplish in British society. And indeed, she succeeded in captivating one noble heir after another with her wit, fearless nature, and seductive wiles.

"I think she probably had more sex appeal than any girl I've ever met in my life," recalled a friend of Kick's brother Jack.

Kick had a special knack with stiff British aristocrats, who marveled at her American informality but never thought her crude. A temperamental twin of her brother Jack, she never betrayed personal feelings in her merry-go-round flirtations. Few of her escorts suspected that in the back of her mind, she was shrewdly cataloging each of them according to his wealth and potential influence.

On that score, Billy Hartington easily topped the list.

"Kick was after Billy," one member of her circle observed. "He had a nice big fat title and estate coming, and all that. That is not a nice thing to say, but it was so well known and terribly obvious."

A graceful but shy young man, Billy was thrilled by Kick's boundless energy, and the two became an unlikely item. The match was even physically incongruous: at six feet four, he towered more than a foot over her. Considering Billy's future role as a pillar of English society and the Anglican Church—he was often mentioned as a prospective suitor for Princess Elizabeth—few people could believe that his relationship with Kick was anything more than a youthful dalliance.

But Kick never gave up on her glorious dream. None of the American boyfriends she juggled back home compared with Billy Hartington in terms of social prestige and wealth—the things that really mattered to her. When Page Huidekoper, who worked with Kick as a junior reporter at the *Washington Times-Herald,* announced that she planned to wed a well-born American serviceman whose family had no money, Kick scoffed, "But Page, I thought you were *ambitious.*"

During the early years of the war, when Kick was confined to Washington, her London friends started pairing off, and eventually she heard that Billy Hartington had become engaged to Sally Norton, a niece of Lord Mountbatten. Kick immediately started pulling family strings and arranged for a job in Britain as a Red Cross worker. Within a month of her arrival back in London, she had broken up Billy's engagement and placed Billy once again under her spell.

A great deal more than marriage to Billy Hartington was at stake. Billy's mother, Lady Mary, served the queen as mistress of the robes, a hereditary role that made the duchess of Devonshire the second-most-important woman in British society. The position involved ceremonial duties that were closely tied to the governance of the Anglican Church. This fact alone should have ruled out Kick—the Catholic granddaughter of a Boston Irish saloonkeeper—but with typical Kennedy hubris, she saw no reason why she should let hundreds of years of history, ritual, and tradition stand in her way.

And so, like Honey Fitz and Joe Kennedy before her, Kick—a female personification of the Kennedy Curse—put herself on a collision course with reality. Did centuries of bloody religious strife between Catholics and Protestants make marriage between a Catholic Kennedy and an Anglican Cavendish inconceivable? Not in Kick's grandiose scheme of things. Did Billy Hartington refer to their relationship as "a Romeo and Juliet thing"? Kick ignored the ominous implication.

But the facts could not be ignored.

The Cavendishes loathed Catholics. Their antipathy went back four hundred years, to the time when Henry VIII broke with Rome and rewarded his loyal follower, William Cavendish, with a title and vast properties that had been confiscated from the Roman Catholic Church. Billy's grand-uncle William, the first duke of Devonshire, formed a political party with the express purpose of opposing Irish Catholic home rule. In the nineteenth century, the eighth duke of Devonshire, Lord Frederick Charles, was shot and killed by Irish Republicans on his second day as governor of Ireland. And the current duke, Billy's father, Edward William Spencer Cavendish, was a notorious anti-Catholic bigot who half believed that Catholics were out to recapture Anglican bloodlines and property through the subterfuge of intermarriage.

Even broad-minded members of the Cavendish family were wary of Kick's Catholicism. They knew that the Roman Catholic Church would require her to raise her children as Catholics—or face eternal damnation. Kick had hoped, naively, that Billy would follow the example of his cousin David Ormsby-Gore, who had married a devout Catholic and agreed to rear their children in that faith, even though a Protestant barony was at stake.*

But Kick underestimated Billy's determination when it came to matters of religion. Given the great public and religious responsibilities of his peerage, he felt that his parents would be yielding quite enough to allow the marriage at all. Under no circumstances, he told Kick, would he father a Catholic duke of Devonshire.

"It's really too bad because I'm sure I would be a most efficient Duchess of Devonshire in the post-war world," Kick wrote Jack, who was then commanding *PT-109* in the South Pacific. "As I'd have a castle in Ireland, one in Scotland, one in Yorkshire and one in Sussex I could keep my old nautical brothers in their old age."

It was not true love that explained Kick's resolve to charge ahead with her engagement in the face of all these obstacles. In fact, she

---

*In 1961, at President Kennedy's personal request, David Ormsby-Gore was named the British ambassador to Washington.

had admitted to Jack and others that, though fond of Billy, she was not sure she loved him at all.

Something else weighed on the scales. As a woman of her times, Kick's opportunities for self-expression were limited. She could not follow her father and brothers into business or politics. The only arena in which she could compete on an equal basis with the men in her family was in the field of matrimony.

Like so many other Kennedys, she had a seriously impaired sense of self-esteem. She had internalized the negative stereotypes of Irish Americans that were rampant in America's dominant Protestant culture. To counter the feelings of shame associated with being Irish, she had concocted a grandiose self-image, which would be satisfied only by marrying into the highest reaches of the English nobility.

As a Kennedy, there was no substitute for being number one.

As her car rounded a sudden bend in the Derbyshire road, Kick glimpsed the glittering towers of her dreams. Four miles distant, yet impossible to ignore, stood Chatsworth House, the grand Palladian manor from which the Cavendish family commanded a small empire consisting of 180,000 acres—an area more than two hundred times the size of New York City's Central Park.

Chatsworth House was widely considered the most beautiful private home in the entire British Empire. Man-made lakes fed the most elaborate private waterworks in England, and from a distance, the mansion appeared to rise straight out of a shimmering pool. The 1,100-acre gardens, in which wild forest collided with a geometrical grid of buildings and walkways, was the brainchild of the post-Enlightenment landscape genius Lancelot "Capability" Brown.

On closer inspection, however, it became clear that Chatsworth House had seen better days. The entire contents of the main house, including perhaps the greatest private collection of art treasures in the country, had been packed away for safekeeping soon after the outbreak of war. As a result, though Billy's grandfather had died six years before, his father, the current duke, had not yet taken up residence in Chatsworth House. Instead, he and his family continued to occupy Churchdale Hall, a much smaller home on the grounds.

What's more, most of Chatsworth House's 175 windows were shuttered. Many of its rooms were sealed shut. One vast, empty wing had been turned over to three hundred screaming teenage girls—students of Penrhos College, a Welsh school—and their teachers.

The winds of historic change were buffeting the walls of Chatsworth House. The two world wars of the twentieth century had not only robbed Britain of the flower of its manhood, they had also delivered a body blow to aristocratic rule. Drastically reduced wartime revenues had forced the duke of Devonshire to sell off many parcels of land. A corporation now managed the property in his name. Although the duke's wealth probably still surpassed that of most other landed gentry, crippling taxes awaited his inheritors, especially if Clement Atlee's socialist Labour Party assumed power after the war, as many people expected.

After four hundred years of uninterrupted privilege, the Cavendishes faced an uncertain future. They were painfully aware that their declining prospects stood in dramatic contrast to the rising prosperity of nouveaux riche Americans such as the Kennedys, who seemed to grow wealthier with each passing year of war. This explained why Billy's parents remained cordial, even warm, to Kick ever since their son had announced his intention to marry her. From time immemorial, the chief purpose of marriage among British aristocrats had been to secure the continuity and prosperity of their bloodlines. Kick's father, Joseph Kennedy, who was once listed by *Fortune* magazine as the fourth-richest man in America, was in a position to rescue the Cavendishes.

The duchess of Devonshire received Kick in the sitting room of Churchdale Hall, where Billy and his two younger sisters had been born and raised. A horsey woman with bobbed brown hair, Lady Mary hardly looked like the doyenne who would one day preside over the coronation rites of the young Queen Elizabeth.

With the duchess sat a bespectacled old cleric, whom she introduced to Kick as the Reverend Edward Keble Talbot. Father Talbot had been superior of the Community of the Resurrection of Christ, a prestigious Anglican brotherhood, and now served as personal chaplain to the king. After some pleasantries, the duchess excused herself and left her two guests alone to talk in front of the roaring fire.

To Kick's relief, Father Talbot said nothing to discourage her interest in Billy. Instead, he launched into a learned discourse on the fundamental differences between the Anglican and Roman Catholic rites. The Anglican Church, unlike the Catholic Church, depended heavily on the English nobility to bind the congregants to the faith. Billy's heirs would appoint bishops to the Anglican Church and undertake countless ceremonial duties. Plainly, Father Talbot said, they could not do so as Roman Catholics.

One solution—in fact, probably the only solution—was for Kick to convert. While the duke had frequently nudged her on the matter— he once sent Kick a copy of the Book of Common Prayer of the Church of England as a birthday present—Lady Mary had always left such discussions to intermediaries.

"Of course both the Duchess and Father Talbot don't for a minute want me to give up something," Kick wrote her parents defensively. "They just hoped that I might find the same thing in the Anglican version of Catholicism."

When it came time for Kick to leave Churchdale Hall, the duchess showered her with kindness. Billy had returned to his regiment, the Coldstream Guards, to prepare for the Allied invasion of Normandy. Everyone was bracing for heavy casualties.

"It is desperately hard, that you should have all this great unhappiness with the second front always at the back of one's mind," Lady Mary wrote Kick the day after she left. "I know how lonely you must feel and almost forsaken but we must trust in God that things will come out for the best in the end."

The cable from London arrived at the Kennedys' home in Hyannis Port on April 29, 1944. It said that Kick and Billy had found a way out of their religious predicament. They planned to wed in a civil ceremony.

To a devout Catholic like Rose Kennedy, such a marriage was a mortal sin. To Joe, who wore his Catholicism like a loose cloak, Kick's impending marriage was something quite different. Though he could never admit it to his wife, Joe admired the aplomb with which his favorite daughter had pulled off the kind of social coup that had always eluded him.

"You're tops with me," he wrote Kick privately. "I'll bet on your judgment anytime for any amounts."

Joe's only real concern was the potential damage his daughter's civil marriage might inflict on his eldest son's political career. Despite his falling-out with Franklin Roosevelt, Joe believed that the President would still honor his promise to promote Joe Jr. in his bid to become governor of Massachusetts. But the Catholic voters whom Joe was counting on to support his son would not likely forgive Kick for jettisoning her faith and marrying into the despised English establishment.

Joe had to find a way to persuade the Catholic Church to bless the union. He knew that marriage on the Cavendishes' terms would require an extraordinary Vatican dispensation. And so he resorted to his usual methods and sought to put in a fix with the pope.

Before his ascension, Pope Pius XII had been Eugenio Cardinal Pacelli, the Vatican secretary of state. Joe had met him in 1936, when Roosevelt had asked Joe—America's most famous Catholic layman— to escort Pacelli during his first official visit to the United States. Pacelli had bounced young Teddy on his knee in the Kennedys' Bronxville home and had given the boy his First Communion. Later, Joe had taken his family to Rome as Roosevelt's delegate to Pacelli's coronation as Pope Pius XII.

As face-to-face negotiations with a sitting pope were impossible,

Joe enlisted his close friend Francis Cardinal Spellman of New York to mastermind a series of communiqués with the Vatican. Because cables would undoubtedly be read by prying eyes in wartime, Spellman signed his messages "Archie Spell." However, after weeks of back-and-forth, Spellman had to inform Joe that nothing could be done to smooth over Kick's transgression.

As usual when things did not go his way, Joe shut his eyes to reality. Rose, however, was another matter. For weeks she had engaged in psychological warfare with Kick, greeting every mention of Billy's name in Kick's letters by ignoring the subject of marriage. When that tactic failed, Rose retreated into a crushing silence. She had no intention of acknowledging Kick's decision now.

"Naturally I was disturbed, horrified," Rose wrote to a friend after reading Kick's devastating cable. "Talked for a minute on our responsibility in allowing her to drift into this dilemma then decided we should think of practical way to extricate her . . . Heartbroken—think—feel you have been wrongly influenced—Sending Archie Spell's friend to talk to you. Anything done for Our Lord will be rewarded a hundredfold. . . . I thought it would have such mighty repercussions in that if every little young girl would say if K-Kennedy can—why can't I?—why all the fuss, then everyone pointed to our family with pride as well behaved—level-headed and deeply religious. What a blow to the family prestige."

Among the Kennedy children, the two most devout, Eunice and Bobby, sided with their mother and attacked Kick in agitated letters. For his part, Jack, the only sibling to whom Kick had confided her deepest feelings, ridiculed everyone in the family as hypocrites. He wrote his friend Lem Billings, who had professed to have a crush on Kick: "You might as well take it in stride. As sister Eunice from the depths of her righteous Catholic wrath so truly said: 'It's a horrible thing—but it will be nice visiting her after the war, so we might as well face it.'"

The only player in the entire drama who could claim to be free of hypocrisy was Billy Hartington. He admitted that his devotion to

Anglicanism was less a matter of religious conviction than a patriotic stance in favor of king and country.

"I know that I should only be justified in allowing my children to be brought up Roman Catholic . . . if I believed it to be desirable for England to become a Roman Catholic country," he wrote Rose. "Therefore, believing in the National Church of England, as I do very strongly, and having so many advantages, and all the responsibilities they entail, I am convinced I should be setting a very bad example if I gave in, and that nothing would justify my doing so."

Privately, however, Billy provided Kick with a potential way out of her predicament. Like his parents, he was aware that times were changing and that Britain's rigid class structure might not survive the war. If the dukedom was able to maintain its old position of privilege and power, he told Kick, then their children must be raised as Anglicans. But if future social upheavals undermined the institution of aristocracy and severed the historic connection between the dukedom and the Anglican Church, then the children could be raised as Catholics.

Kick jumped at his offer.

News of the engagement broke in the Boston papers on May 4, along with rumors that the wedding ceremony would take place in London two days later.

In Hyannis Port, an increasingly desperate Rose tried to orchestrate a campaign of resistance in the press.

"Members of the Kennedy family here said last night that although Miss Kennedy and Lord Hartington have had 'a very fine friendship' dating back to when her father was ambassador of Great Britain, they did not know of plans for a marriage," the *Boston Herald* reported.

The next day, May 5, the irrepressible Honey Fitz inserted himself into the melodrama. Still playing to the Boston Irish wards, the old pol resorted to his usual muddy logic.

"When non-Catholic young people were week-end guests at the Kennedy home," he told the *Herald,* "Kathleen would take them all to

Mass every Sunday morning. She's all quality, and that boy must have had quality to have won her."

At last, Rose appeared to face the inevitable. Her final cable to Kick—which she could not summon the nerve to send—was an incoherent mass of cross-outs. It read:

ARCHIE SPELL~~MAN~~ HAS MADE INVESTIGATION—ALL CASES THERE & HERE. CAN YOU WRITE OR CABLE WHAT CONCESSIONS YOUR FRIEND ~~CAN~~ WILL CONSIDER—~~MAY BE CONTAINED IN LETTER TO MOTHER.~~ HOPING FOR SOME SOLUTION BUT LOOKS EXTREMELY DIFFICULT.

When reporters inquired whether Rose intended to fly to England for the wedding ceremony, they were informed that she had been hospitalized and was physically unfit to travel. Actually, Rose had checked herself into New England Baptist Hospital in Boston for a routine checkup.

Kick and her eldest brother, Navy Lt. Joseph P. Kennedy Jr., hopped out of a car in central London shortly before noon on Saturday, May 6. They rushed up the town hall steps to the Chelsea Registry Office, dodging a throng of reporters.

Kick had dreamed of being married in Westminster Cathedral. Instead, she found herself in a small, squalid building—a fitting place, as she later wrote, for mixed marriages, drab ceremonies between atheists or agnostics, and worse, the final rites of divorce. The place was decorated with pink Devonshire carnations, misbegotten reminders that Billy would be the first titled Cavendish in four centuries to wed outside the family chapel at Chatsworth House.

The usual bridal materials were scarce in London. Many wartime brides had to settle for gowns that had been worn at several previous weddings. Kick was not among them. Her gown, a very pale pink crepe, street-length dress, had been sewn together the night before by the best fitter in London. Kick had also gotten hold of a turban made of blue and pink ostrich plumes, and she carried a borrowed gold mesh bag with diamonds and sapphires.

Joe Jr. escorted his sister to a drab second-floor office where Billy waited in his crisply pressed Coldstream Guards uniform, flanked by his parents; his grandmother, the dowager duchess; Lady Adele Cavendish, his American aunt and the sister of Fred Astaire; and his younger sisters, Elizabeth and Anne.

Charles Granby, son of the duke of Rutland and Billy's best man, had never seen the inside of a registry before, and he was shocked at the perfunctory, ten-minute ceremony. There was no exchange of vows. Billy slipped a large square-cut diamond heirloom ring onto Kick's finger, Joe and the duke signed as witnesses, and it was all over.

The Cavendishes' lavish London home lay in ruins, the casualty of a German V-1 rocket, and Lord Hambleden, a relative, had offered his Eaton Square town house for the reception.

More than 150 friends turned up, dozens more than were expected under the circumstances. As Kick showed off a diamond bracelet gift from her in-laws, a crowd of Red Cross workers thronged around their famous colleague. A few GIs, drunk on champagne, carried on conversations with society dowagers.

When, several hours later, Kick and Billy prepared to leave on a week's honeymoon at Compton Place, a Cavendish seaside estate, an American sergeant grabbed Billy by the arm.

"Listen, you goddamn limey," he said, stabbing a finger into Billy's chest. "You've got the best goddamn girl America could produce."

While the reception was in full swing in London, Rose Kennedy stepped into a car bound for Boston Airport, where a plane waited to take her to New York. She appeared "wan from two weeks' hospitalization," *The Boston Globe* wrote, exaggerating the length of her stay by eleven days. The paper said she was headed for a "much-needed rest" in Hot Springs, Virginia.

Heavily jeweled, with a silver fox stole on her arm, and wearing a tricorn beret with a black veil pulled low, Rose looked as though she were en route to Kick's funeral.

"I'm sorry, but I don't feel physically well enough to grant an interview," she told reporters on the tarmac. "I'm sorry it has to be this way."

As the plane idled for an hour in bad weather, Rose sat in the waiting room, cradling her head in her hands.

In the weeks that followed, a flood of letters from righteous Catholics on both sides of the Atlantic reminded Kick that she now dwelled in an earthly purgatory of her own making. According to Church dogma, she was living in mortal sin, and was therefore unqualified to receive Holy Communion.

And yet Kick did not seem unduly troubled. She felt certain that her father would eventually come through and arrange a dispensation from the Vatican. As Joe's daughter, Kick was accustomed to getting away with things. Just look at how she had arranged her marriage to Billy Hartington. She had become the marchioness of Hartington while simultaneously remaining a Catholic. She had managed to have it both ways.

"You did everything in your power," she assured her mother. "You did your duty as a Roman Catholic mother. You have not failed. There was nothing lacking in my religious education. . . . [David James Matthew, auxiliary bishop of Westminster,] whom I have consulted so often told me that perhaps at a later date our marriage could be made valid. Until that time I shall go on praying and living like a Roman Catholic and hoping. Please, please do the same."

Kick's only defender in the family, Joe Jr., was a most unlikely ally.

As the firstborn and eldest son, he had been the family drill sergeant, the one who enforced the win-at-any-cost Kennedy code, forever chastising his brothers and sisters for their weaknesses, coolly demonstrating that he could perform any task better than they could.

He was just as stringent in enforcing Rose's Catholic prescriptions, not least with himself. In his English barracks, for instance, he would dutifully kneel down for daily prayers while his squadron mates played poker.

Yet it was Joe Jr. who swept into London the day before Kick's wedding and worked through the union's legal and financial details with Billy's lawyers. It was Joe who took it upon himself to give the bride away and be her official witness. And it was Joe who wrote to his mother: "As far as Kick's soul is concerned, I wish I had half her chance of seeing the pearly gates. As far as what people will say, the hell with them. I think we can all take it. . . . I do know how you feel, Mother, but I do think it will be all right."

Since Joe Jr. had never before challenged his parents, his defiance caught everyone in the family by surprise. Neither his father nor his brother Jack thought it wise to stick his neck out for Kick. Joe Jr. was only half kidding when he told Kick that after Irish Catholics voters opened their newspapers and saw a wedding photo of him standing beside his sister in a non-Catholic setting, he'd be "finished in Boston."

Any explanation of Joe Jr.'s behavior has to take into account a change that had occurred in his standing in the family. Until recently, he had been the anointed son, the one who was expected to carry the Kennedy name into the White House. But the previous summer, Jack—the son from whom little had been expected—emerged as a war hero after a Japanese destroyer sliced his *PT-109* in two in the South Pacific. His elated father transformed this accident into myth, seeing to it that the *Reader's Digest* and *The New Yorker* carried vivid accounts of Jack's successful attempts to save his crew.

Joe Jr.'s upbringing left him utterly unprepared to be replaced in his father's esteem by his younger brother. The previous September, after a judge had raised a glass to Jack's triumph at a birthday cele-bration for Joe Sr. in Hyannis Port, young Joe broke down and sobbed into his pillow for hours into the night. From then on, the family curse seemed to tighten its grip on Joe Jr., who began to engage in increas-ingly reckless behavior in an effort to prove his worth.

———

While on leave in London in October, Joe Jr. joined Kick, William Randolph Hearst, and others for a dinner at the Savoy. Across the table sat Patricia Wilson, a dark beauty with piercing eyes and an infectious laugh. The daughter of a wealthy Australian sheep rancher, Pat had endured a loveless marriage to George Child-Villiers, a wealthy young British earl. She had divorced and remarried, this time to Robin Filmer Wilson, a banker who had been stationed in Libya for two years as a major in the British army.

Captivated by Pat, Joe eagerly accepted an invitation to Crastock Farm, her country home an hour north of London. Until then, Joe Jr. had always followed his father's example and treated women as throwaway objects. But his affair with the married Pat Wilson was different. By all accounts, he wanted to marry her—an act that, like his sister's marriage, would have to take place outside the Catholic Church.

As D-Day and the invasion of Europe approached, Kick and Billy joined Joe and Pat at Crash-Bang, as they christened Pat's house. They spent long hours playing gin rummy and bridge, dancing, and performing pranks. Kick could not get over the change in Joe. The old family enforcer seemed to be rushing headlong into his own state of mortal sin.

On July 26, Joe spent what was to be his last weekend in England with Kick and Pat at Crastock Farm.

He had completed his assigned thirty-five bombing missions and was scheduled to return stateside. He had flown his final sorties with careless abandon, in one case defying orders by diving low over the German-controlled island of Guernsey, a needless flyby that left his fuselage riddled with bullets.

Now he revealed to Kick and his family that rather than go home, he had decided to extend his stay in England. He did not want to leave Pat Wilson; and perhaps to impress her, he had volunteered for a new top-secret mission. He could not discuss the details.

"I am going to do something different for the next three weeks," he wrote his parents. "It is secret and I am not allowed to say what it is, but it isn't dangerous so don't worry."

From America, his father wrote back a beseeching note: "Joe, don't tempt the fates. Just come home."

Kick was granted only five weeks with her new husband before Billy was ordered to ship out with his regiment to join the Allied assault on France following D-Day.

Shortly after Billy left, his cousin David Ormsby-Gore drove Kick and his wife, Sissy, to a Catholic church north of London. Kick envied the Ormsby-Gores. They had adapted to Roman Catholic ways over the objections of David's Anglican family. Inside the small church, Kick watched as David and Sissy rose during Communion, a ritual from which Kick was now excluded.

Before her wedding, Kick had sought comfort from Father Martin D'Arcy, a London Jesuit who had converted her friend, the famous satirical novelist Evelyn Waugh, to the Roman Catholic Church and was renowned for his subtle interpretations of Catholic dogma. Instead of providing a dispensation or even a pat on the head, Father D'Arcy had painted a frightening picture of her spiritual future—an empty life as a nonparticipant, followed by eternal damnation. Her only chance of redemption would be confession in the event of Billy's death, a verdict that she considered perverse.

After church, Kick returned to Compton Place, where she was spending the summer on the beach with the duke, the duchess, and Billy's sisters, Anne and Elizabeth. Kick was using the time to learn her new duties as the marchioness of Hartington. Although her in-laws treated her warmly—Anne and Elizabeth had become staunch allies—Kick felt unsure of her hold on the old duke.

"Even though his present daughter-in-law has acquiesced to his demands," Kick wrote her family, "[the duke] always sees within me some sort of evil influence. I shall just have to prove myself over a period of years, I suppose."

Two weeks later, on a languid Sunday afternoon in London, Kick sat in the flat that the Devonshires had rented for her in Billy's absence. When she answered a rap on the door, she was greeted by two sober-faced officers of the British Royal Air Force.

They had been trying to reach her all day. Joe Jr.'s plane had exploded the day before, twenty-eight minutes after takeoff. Fifty-nine buildings had been damaged as the plane splintered over the English coastal town of Newdelight Wood. There was no sign of a body. Speculation was that a faulty electrical system had sparked the explosion.

A short while later, Mark Soden, Joe's roommate, telephoned Kick to tell her of her brother's last wish. She was to receive his most prized possessions—an Underwood typewriter, a Zenith radio, a Zeiss camera, and the Victrola he and Kick had played for hours on end at Crash-Bang.

Kick collapsed in sobs.

"I'm so sorry I broke down tonight," she wrote Soden a few hours later, telling him where to send the items. "It never makes things easier. I don't know whether I'll ever want to use the much-discussed typewriter but it will make me always think of that hard-talker Joe."

Kick learned from Pat Wilson a few weeks later that Joe had bragged to a friend before his flight that he would have only a fifty-fifty chance of making it back alive.

The odds were probably lower, and he knew it. Joe had volunteered for a top-secret project, code-named Anvil, that was a last-ditch attempt to destroy impregnable German bunkers from which V-1 rockets had been launched over England. His hollowed-out PBY 4 bomber had been packed with ten tons of TNT—enough explosives to make it one of the largest bombs ever created.

If Joe had been successful, it was all but certain that he would have received the Navy Cross, the second-highest naval military honor and one that would put him well ahead of Jack, who had received the lesser Navy and Marine Corps Medal for his role in *PT-109*.

The night before takeoff, Earl Olsen, the mission's electronics offi-cer, had taken Joe aside and told him that he wanted to delay the mission to change the circuitry of the panel that would ignite the bomb. Olsen was worried that the circuitry was faulty and that the plane might explode prematurely. Higher-ups had refused to delay the flight, and Joe, the commander, had no interest in doing so, either.

"Don't you see," Olsen protested, "you're risking your neck for nothing."

Officers on the tarmac, accustomed to Joe's bravado, speculated that his reaction was less a death wish than a monumental belief in his own invulnerability and omnipotence. Before Joe took off, one of them asked him whether his insurance was paid up. Joe flashed them a Kennedy grin. His final words amounted to a defining statement of the Kennedy Curse.

"Nobody in my family needs insurance," he said.

On Labor Day weekend in Hyannis Port, Jack invited a houseful of his *PT-109* buddies for a reunion. Kick joined them out on the bluff. She had stayed on after returning home for Joe Jr.'s memorial service.

As the evening wore on, the laughter turned raucous, and the noise brought Ambassador Kennedy, as he was still called, to his bedroom window. Kick's biographer Lynne McTaggart describes how Joe leaned out and acidly silenced the partygoers with a request to keep quiet out of respect for his dead son.

Half a beat later, Bobby, a scrawny young navy cadet at nineteen, ran out of the house and slavishly delivered the same message.

"Dad's awfully mad," he said.

Kick turned on Bobby.

"You're frightening our houseguests out of their wits!" she said.

But these agitated Kennedy outbursts soon passed. They were re-placed by an attitude of stoic resignation.

"I am a Kennedy," Kick wrote Jack's friend Lem Billings. "I have a very strong feeling that makes a big difference about how to take things. I saw Daddy and Mother about Joe, and I know that we've all got the ability not to be got down."

Two weeks later, on a trip to New York City with her family, Kick picked her way through the second floor of the Bonwit Teller department store, impressed by the mountain of merchandise that was so scarce in London. She was clutching a bundle of presents for her aristocratic English friends when Eunice appeared early for lunch.

"Before we go, I think we should go back and talk to Daddy," Eunice said, her bright tone slipping.

"Something's happened," Kick remarked.

"Why don't you talk to Daddy?" her sister repeated halfheartedly.

They walked a dozen blocks in silence to the family suite at the Waldorf-Astoria Towers. Joe Kennedy was waiting at the door to his bedroom. A telegram sat on the writing desk nearby.

He told Kick that her husband, Billy Hartington, was dead.

Later, Joe called Patsy Field, a friend of Kick's, and asked her to come to the hotel. His children were avoiding the subject of Billy with Kathleen, he said, and Kick needed somebody to talk to.

"What have you been doing since you received the news?" Patsy asked Kick after she arrived.

"Mostly going to Mass," Kick replied glumly. "Mother keeps saying, 'God doesn't send us a cross heavier than we can bear.' Again and again she keeps saying it."

Kick had not been able to sleep, and Patsy gave her a vial of sleeping pills.

When Kick awoke several hours later, she took out her diary.

"So ends the story of Billy and Kick!!!" she wrote, then quickly crossed out the exclamation points.

Kick returned to London for Billy's memorial service.

She took up residence with the Devonshires and her sisters-in-law. She spent time with Billy's blue-blooded friends. Among these friends, a rumor began to circulate that Kick's fanatically religious mother, in a bizarre twist of logic, had managed to cast a positive light on the twin deaths of her son and Billy Hartington.

According to the story making the rounds, Rose told Kick that she believed both Joe Jr. and Billy were cut down in their prime as divine retribution for Kick's unholy marriage. Their deaths cleared the way for her daughter to return to the Catholic fold.

And, as things turned out, the Catholic Church was prepared to welcome Kick back. As Father D'Arcy, the hard-line London Jesuit, put it, all Kick had to do was confess her sin and make an act of contrition.

Kick went through the rituals, even though she felt that she had nothing to atone for. A few days later she wrote a friend bitterly: "I guess God has taken care of the matter in His own way, hasn't He?"

The marchioness of Hartington, née Kathleen Kennedy, stood on the dais in the colossal ballroom of the Dorchester Hotel, greeting guests. It was a June evening in 1946, almost two years since Billy's death, and Kick was back in the social swing as chairwoman of the Commandos' Ball, the most prestigious event of London's first postwar season.

With her hair cut in a fashionable pageboy and wearing a pale pink gown with diamond clips, Kick looked as slim and girlish as the debutante she had been eight years before. The British ruling class felt duty-bound to show its appreciation for the veterans who had saved the country from defeat, and the glittering fund-raiser honored a special military unit that had been created by Winston Churchill in 1940, the bleakest year of the war.

The twenty-seven-year-old American widow shook hands with the dignitaries and paused to curtsy to the young Princess Elizabeth. After a while, her gaze wandered across the room and settled on a tall, ruggedly handsome man who grinned back at her unabashedly. The

Distinguished Service Order, Britain's highest military honor, adorned his broad chest. He had won it for captaining a torpedo boat through a German naval blockade.

Seconds later the war hero, Peter Fitzwilliam, was standing beside Kick. And for the first time in her life, as she later confessed, she found herself blushing uncontrollably.

"I'm so pleased to meet you at last," Fitzwilliam said, grasping her hand and whisking her onto the dance floor.

An aristocrat whose wealth rivaled that of the Cavendishes, the eighth Earl Fitzwilliam was everything the reticent Billy Hartington had never been. He was a notorious gambler, sportsman, and womanizer. He had excelled in daredevil military pursuits. In peacetime, he moved smoothly between the salons of English high society and the after-hours joints of London's demimonde.

Peter Fitzwilliam was a charmer of men and women alike. Even novelist Evelyn Waugh, who had just published *Brideshead Revisited* and had famously called Fitzwilliam "king dandy and scum," found it impossible to resist Fitzwilliam's Anglo-Irish charisma.

"Peter had all the charm in the world, to a rather dangerous extent, really," a wartime comrade, Harry Sporberg, said.

Kick's friend Jane Kenyon-Slaney, who accompanied her to the gala, thought that for Kick, Fitzwilliam's appeal lay in his resemblance to her father.

"He was like Joseph Kennedy himself—older, sophisticated, quite the rogue male," she said. "Perhaps in the last analysis those were the qualities required to make her fall deeply in love."

At thirty-seven, Fitzwilliam was ten years older than Kick. He was not your run-of-the-mill playboy; he had been married for the past thirteen years to the same woman. His wife, the former Olive Plunkett, was an heiress to the Guinness brewery fortune and an accomplished sportswoman. Obby, as she was known, could drink most men under the table and had once become so drunk that she walked through a plate-glass door. Despite the efforts of the best plastic surgeons, her face still bore deep scars from that old accident.

By the time Fitzwilliam ascended to his title in 1943, Obby was a raging alcoholic who managed to match her husband in extramarital affairs. Their marriage was dead in all but name. Still, Obby remained a social figure to be reckoned with; she played a prominent role in that night's gala as the president of the Commandos' Benevolent Fund.

As Fitzwilliam whirled Kick around the dance floor, Obby watched from the sidelines, gulping down drinks, the scars on her face turning bright crimson.

Kick neither drank nor slept around. For all her social spontaneity, she had always been her mother's daughter—a sexually repressed Catholic schoolgirl. But once she became enveloped in the powerful male aura of Peter Fitzwilliam, her inhibitions melted away and she experienced a sexual awakening.

Their affair jeopardized Kick's already-tenuous hold on a place in British society. By then, her in-laws, the Devonshires, had formally announced that the dukedom would pass to their younger son, Andrew. His wife, the former Deborah Mitford, was now the true marchioness of Hartington and in line to become the next duchess. Kick retained an honorary title that carried no official role.

The duke and duchess had encouraged Kick to stay in England, where she would be a living reminder of their beloved son Billy. They bought her a small white Georgian town house on London's Smith Square. She remained a fixture of the city's social scene and attracted several suitors among the British nobility. But after Billy's death had dashed her dreams of becoming the duchess of Devonshire, she became halfhearted in her attempts to marry into any other noble family. For a Kennedy like Kick, that would be like settling for second-best.

During the first few months of her affair with Fitzwilliam, Kick maintained the facade of correctness. When she met Fitzwilliam in public, it was usually for a conventional lunch at the Ritz. They had dinners with friends in her town house. And they took extra precautions in carrying out their furtive, late-night assignations.

Kick found Fitzwilliam's mocking wit—so like her father's—irresistible. They shared off-color jokes that drew disapproving English comments about their Irish "coarseness." Fitzwilliam was like her father in other ways as well. Despite his fortune, he continued to make money through gambling and high-risk business ventures, including what many considered to be the finest horse-racing track in England. Like Joe Kennedy, Fitzwilliam was not concerned about the welfare of his country unless it affected him personally. While other Britons were celebrating V-E Day, Fitzwilliam was attempting to make a quick killing on the Coca-Cola franchise in northern England.

As their affair matured, Kick began to take bigger and bigger risks. She met the married Fitzwilliam in public places without chaperons. She dressed in ostentatious jewelry and clothing. And she mimicked her lover's raffish personal style and habits. One newspaper columnist took to calling her "the gum-chewing marchioness."

Her friends did not know what to make of all this. Kick's behavior seemed to be a deliberate repudiation of everything she had once stood for. She seemed hell-bent on self-destruction.

Fitzwilliam had agreed to marry Kick if he could work out a divorce from Obby that would avoid a major public scandal. But Fitzwilliam proved to be just as adamant as Billy when it came to the question of religion. He had no intention of converting to Catholicism or of allowing his heirs to be raised as Catholics.

However, Kick no longer seemed to care.

"Billy, I think, was a very conscious decision, but not Fitzwilliam," Charlotte McDonnell, a Catholic childhood friend in whom Kick confided, told authors Collier and Horowitz. "It was passion. It was hysterical. It was all 'I gotta do, I gotta go.' If she couldn't marry him, she was ready to run off with him. She just wasn't concerned about consequences."

She was a captive of the curse.

Kick sat with her parents on a large sofa in the ballroom of the Greenbrier Hotel, an antebellum-style resort nestled in the hills of White Sulphur Springs, West Virginia.

Under ceilings covered in pink streamers, waiters carted off tea sets from the tables. More than two hundred dignitaries, celebrities, and international socialites, including the exiled duke and duchess of Windsor, had shown up for the weekend's gala festivities, which marked the reopening of the hotel after the war. Joe Kennedy, who knew the owner, Robert Young, had brought his large family to the celebration to cap off their annual winter gathering in Palm Beach.

In the two months since Kick had arrived for the holidays, society columnists had run a number of tantalizing items hinting about her relationship with Britain's most famous titled scoundrel, Peter Fitzwilliam. Still, Kick had not yet found the courage to raise the subject with her parents.

Suddenly, as though she had been reading her daughter's mind, Rose Kennedy broke the silence.

"He's a divorced man," she said. "This is sacrilege!"

Rose's face grew tight.

If Kick insisted on marrying the earl, she warned, she would disown her daughter. What's more, Rose continued, glancing over at Joe, she would insist that Kick's father cut off her allowance and disown her. For all intents and purposes, Kick would be dead to the family if she insisted on marrying Fitzwilliam.

Kick's eyes welled up with tears. Later she would learn that Rose had told Joe that she would leave him if he did not support her position in the matter of the Fitzwilliam scandal. It was Rose's ultimate threat, one that she had never used despite all of Joe's womanizing, and it was clear from the way she delivered it that she meant exactly what she said.

Kick's marriage to Billy Hartington had driven Rose into a hospital—and impotent silence. This time around, faced with the far messier Peter Fitzwilliam situation, Rose vowed that she would not be a passive bystander.

And so, shortly after she had delivered her ultimatum at the Greenbrier Hotel, Rose found herself sitting in Kick's London drawing room at 4 Smith Square. She and her daughter were surrounded by priceless Cavendish antiques on loan from Chatsworth House and Kick's artful flower arrangements.

For the next four days, Rose lectured her daughter nonstop on the gravity of the sin that she would be committing by marrying Fitzwilliam. And slowly but surely, as Rose continued her harangue, her daughter's willpower seemed to crumble. At last, apparently drained of all resistance, Kick promised that she would obey her mother and not seek a wedding.

But that did not satisfy Rose. She demanded that Kick put her decision in a letter and send it to Fitzwilliam.

When Rose departed, Kick's housekeeper, Ilona Solynossy, entered the room. She had overheard everything.

"You're a twenty-eight-year-old married woman and a British resident," she said. "How could your mother possibly stop you from marrying?"

As things turned out, Kick had no intention of fulfilling the promise she had made to her mother. Instead, she devised a scheme to enlist her father's aid. Her plot was simple: She and Fitzwilliam were planning a romantic, two-day excursion to Cannes, in the south of France, on May 13 and 14. It just so happened that Joe Kennedy would be in Paris on May 15. Kick persuaded Fitzwilliam to stop off in Paris on their return trip so that she could introduce him to the ambassador over lunch at the Ritz.

"I'm going to do all I can to bring the old boy around," Fitzwilliam promised Kick. "If religion is the problem, I'll build him a bloody church if he wants."

On the morning of May 13, Kick stood waiting for Peter Fitzwilliam on the tarmac of Croyden Airport outside London. She was dressed in a navy blue suit and a string of pearls. Her two suitcases were packed with resort wear and a sexy negligee.

After the earl arrived and greeted Kick with a warm embrace, he turned to his hired pilot, Peter Townshend, a former officer with the

Royal Air Force. When Fitzwilliam inquired about the weather, Townshend replied that a squall was developing over the Rhône Valley in
southern France. If they adhered to their flight plan, he told Fitzwilliam, it should not pose a problem. They would easily outrun the bad
weather.

When Townshend touched down at Le Bourget Airport in Paris for a
service stop, Fitzwilliam hopped out of the eight-seat DeHaviland
Dove and telephoned some racing friends in the city. Then, in a typ-
ically impulsive gesture, he commandeered a taxi to take Kick to meet
his friends for lunch at the Café de Paris.

Before they left, Peter Townshend reminded them once again of
their tight schedule and of the need for them to return promptly after
lunch. According to the latest meteorological report, a large thunder-
storm was gathering over southern France and was scheduled to cross
their route at five P.M.

Three hours went by, and Kick and Fitzwilliam still had not returned. Townshend, who flew by the book, grew angrier by the
moment.

"I'm going to be late," he complained to a French official at the
airport. "It's annoying."

At last, he heard the honk of a car horn. Fitzwilliam, Kick, and
their lunch companions poured out of two taxis, their faces flushed
with too much wine.

By then, however, all commercial flights out of Le Bourget had
been canceled and Townshend's manner had turned somber. He
would not take his DeHaviland Dove up in this weather, he told Fitzwilliam. They must wait out the storm.

But Fitzwilliam and Kick were not the kind of people deterred by
reasonable arguments or the forces of nature. To them, a hazardous
storm represented an exciting challenge to be overcome. It was yet
another opportunity to prove their invulnerability.

For the next twenty minutes, they browbeat the cautious pilot. If
they did not leave Le Bourget this afternoon, they said, they would

have to call off their short vacation in Cannes and miss their meeting with the ambassador.

Finally, Townsend relented. And at 3:30 P.M. he lifted his De-Haviland Dove into the darkening sky.

Almost three hours later, Paul Petit sat outside his nine-hundred-year-old red stone farmhouse near the peak of Le Coran, the highest of the Cévennes Mountains in the Rhône Valley. A high-pitched noise caught the farmer's attention, and he looked skyward.

Just then, a small plane burst through a dark cloud to the northeast, made a sharp noise, and then another. One wing seemed to break off from the fuselage, and the hobbled plane plunged straight down and vanished behind the mountain.

Several hours later, as thick rain pounded the topmost ridge of Le Coran, Petit guided a group of gendarmes up the twisting stone path to an eighteen-foot chasm and the wreckage of the DeHaviland Dove. Inside, the bodies of Peter Townshend and his copilot were crushed against the instrument panel. They were dead, as was Peter Fitzwilliam, whose body was huddled under a seat.

Kick's body was the only one the rescue party could reach. She lay outstretched, her seat belt fastened, a lone, deep gash running along her cheek. The gendarmes believed that, at the moment of impact, Kick had been sleeping. She had been jolted awake in the instant before she perished.

Joe Kennedy was the only family member to attend Kick's funeral, which was held at the Farm Street Catholic Church in London.

The patriarch of the Kennedy family appeared stooped under the weight of his grief. He stood during the Mass, surrounded by senior members of the British government and friends of Fitzwilliam and Kick. Almost all the people gathered in the church were upper-class Anglicans—the kind of people who had once snubbed Joe when he was ambassador. Among the flowers and wreaths heaped atop Kick's casket was a handwritten note from the one Briton whom Joe, still the unrepentant isolationist, detested above all others, the wartime prime minister, Winston Churchill.

Despite his heartache, Joe somehow summoned the presence of mind to shape the public perception of his daughter's death with her married lover. It was important that the story not embarrass the Kennedys and harm the political aspirations of Joe's second son, Jack, who had inherited the mantle of the family standard-bearer following the death of Joe Jr.

Though all of London society had been aware of Kick's scandalous affair with Fitzwilliam, Joe Kennedy set about fabricating a story that whitewashed his daughter's reputation and became the established version of her death. An obituary in the *Boston American* was typical of how newspapers on both sides of the Atlantic handled the incident.

CHANCE MEETING LED TO DEATH OF KATHLEEN

While grieving members of the Joseph P. Kennedy family gathered on both sides of the Atlantic today to arrange last rites for Kathleen Lady Hartington, 28, it was learned in London that a chance meeting led to the girl's tragic death in a plane crash on a French hillside.

She died in a twin-engine plane chartered at Croydon Airport, London, by Lord Fitzwilliam, 37, for a visit to racehorse breeders in France.

Kathleen had returned to England only two days earlier from a family reunion in America and was too late to arrange passage on the luxury train, Golden Arrow, for a trip to Paris and a prearranged meeting with her father.

Entering the Ritz Hotel bar, she encountered Lord and Lady Fitzwilliam and during a brief chat was offered a seat on the chartered plane.

In disclosing the chance meeting, Fitzwilliam's secretary added:

"Lady Hartington was an old friend of both Lady and Lord Fitzwilliam. She had been delighted with the offer of a lift."

Rose was certain that Kick had died in a state of sin and that her soul resided in purgatory. But as time went on, she appeared to soften a bit in her public attitude. Whenever she learned that someone was traveling to England, she would suggest that he or she visit Kick's grave at Chatsworth. Then Rose would add, "She was a duchess, you know."

News of Kick's violent death overwhelmed Jack Kennedy, her closest sibling.

"Jack had terrible problems falling asleep at night," his friend Lem Billings recalled. "Just as he started to close his eyes, he would be awakened by the image of Kathleen sitting up with him late at night talking about their parties and dates. He would try to close his eyes again, but he couldn't shake the image. It was better, he said, when he had a girl in bed with him, for then he could fantasize that the girl was Kathleen's friend and that when morning came the three of them would go for breakfast together."

When Jack visited London that summer, he stopped to see Ilona Solynossy, Kick's former housekeeper, and questioned her about every detail of her life with his sister. As he left, he stunned Ilona by remarking in a cool, detached tone of voice, "We will not speak of her again."

The Kennedy clan adopted this line for decades to come. Thirteen years later, when Jack gained the presidency, the official White House literature listed Kathleen Kennedy only as "the sister who died in a plane crash."

CHAPTER FIVE

JOHN FITZGERALD KENNEDY

THE ROAD TO DALLAS

"I DON'T WANT THE BUBBLETOP ON THE CAR," President Kennedy told Kenneth O'Donnell. "I want all those Texas broads to see what a beautiful girl Jackie is."

It was shortly after noon on Wednesday, November 20, 1963, and the President was on his way to the White House pool for his midday swim. Wrapped in a bulky terry-cloth robe and padding along in beach slippers, he hardly resembled the dashing figure who had inspired a generation with the soaring rhetoric of his Inaugural Address. Daily injections of cortisone, used to treat his Addison's disease, had added bulk to his six-foot frame and jowls to his face. The extra weight, plus the burden of a thousand days in office, had aged John Fitzgerald Kennedy and made him look considerably older than his forty-six years.

He had asked his two most trusted aides, Kenny O'Donnell and Dave Powers, to accompany him on the walk to the swimming pool so that they could discuss arrangements for his trip to Texas, which was scheduled to begin the next day. Word had reached Washington that the mood in Dallas, a city known as the "hate capital" of Dixie, had turned murderous. Just a month before, right-wing demonstrators had threatened the life of U.N. ambassador Adlai Stevenson. And in recent days, archconservatives had begun flooding Dallas with hand-bills showing John Kennedy's photo under the headline WANTED FOR TREASON.

In the White House, concern over the President's safety had set nerves on edge. A committee of Dallas's leading citizens had alerted the President's men to the danger of assassination, and some White House advisers were urging Kennedy to cancel the trip. A Southern senator, J. William Fulbright of Arkansas, told him, "Dallas is a very dangerous place. . . . I wouldn't go there. Don't *you* go." And in a draft of a speech that Lyndon Johnson intended to give in Austin after the Dallas leg of the tour—a draft that the President's advisers had presumably seen and approved—the Vice President planned to open with the line "Mr. President, thank God you made it out of Dallas alive!"

Kennedy himself seemed to have intimations of doom. Several weeks earlier, one of his World War II buddies, Paul "Red" Fay Jr., had written a script for a home movie in which the President, Jackie, and some of their friends had roles. In the movie, which was shot by a navy photographer, Kennedy chose to play a character who was assassinated.

Despite these grim omens, Kennedy refused to alter his travel plans. As the leader of the Democratic Party, he felt that it was essential for him to go to Texas, where bitter infighting among Democrats was undermining his chances of carrying that crucial state in the 1964 presidential election, now less than a year away. His approval rating in the Gallup polls had dropped from 76 to 59 percent over the past year, and according to biographer Richard Reeves, Kennedy felt that "the key to winning easily in 1964 was to carry Texas and Florida to make up for any losses in other Southern states."

In light of all the danger signals coming out of Texas, a prudent man would have thought twice about going on such a trip. But as always, Kennedy was more concerned with image than reality. He was worried that a last-minute cancellation might damage the image of rugged masculinity that he so assiduously promoted.

"Jack was determined to go to Dallas because of his stupid hubris," said Jay Tunney, the son of former heavyweight champion Gene Tunney and a close Kennedy family friend. "Jack couldn't wimp out and be cautious. Kennedys weren't put together that way."

As the President and his aides passed the Bouquet Room on their way to the swimming pool, Kenny O'Donnell, who had responsibility for planning the presidential motorcade through downtown Dallas, attempted to sound a note of caution.

"Mr. President," he said, "the Secret Service doesn't want you to ride in an open car."

All presidents resented the protective screen erected by the Secret Service. It obstructed the very lifeblood of politics—intimate contact between politician and voters. Knowing how strongly Kennedy felt, O'Donnell had chosen his words with care. He purposely did not say that *he* thought the President should use the bubbletop. He placed the onus for that advice on the Secret Service.

John Kennedy felt most comfortable with men who, as one biographer put it, "exhibited an almost adolescent macho temperament." Courage—not prudence, compassion, or justice—was the virtue held in highest esteem in the Kennedy White House.

"People are often obsessed by the values which they most doubt in themselves and which have some neurotic meaning for them," Nancy Gager Clinch observes. "Kennedy's fascination with the limits of human courage, both political and physical, suggests that he doubted these qualities in himself."

Those who fell short of this Kennedy ideal felt the wrath of the President, who could be a bully with the members of his inner circle. Press Secretary Pierre Salinger would comment on "his bristling temper, his cold sarcasm."

As a result, the one thing that Kenny O'Donnell feared more than anything else was that he might appear fainthearted in the eyes of the President.

"In the years to come, Kenny could never forgive himself for not doing more to stop the President from going to Dallas," Dave Powers informed me. "He felt he should have tried harder to protect the President."

O'Donnell's daughter Helen agreed. "My father always felt a huge responsibility for what happened in Dallas," she told me. "He always felt that he should have anticipated what happened, that there must have been something that he could have done, and that if he had, he could have changed the course of history."

When the President reached the swimming pool, he turned to O'Donnell.

"Kenny," he said, according to the recollection of Dave Powers, "if the weather is clear and it's not raining, have that bubbletop off. I don't want the Secret Service to ride on the running boards, either. And keep those motorcycle cops back from the sides of the car and out of the line of sight."

After the President sent Kenny O'Donnell to convey his instructions to the Secret Service, he and Dave Powers entered the steamy precincts of the swimming pool. During his daily swim, the pool was off-limits to everyone except four men: Bobby and Teddy Kennedy, Powers, and O'Donnell. Even the White House Secret Service detail was barred from entry.

The walls of the pool were covered with a mural depicting the sunset over St. Croix, in the Virgin Islands. The artwork had been commissioned in 1961 by the President's father from the artist Bernard Lamotte. Music played over the sound system. A pitcher of daiquiris and several glasses were set on a table next to the pool.

Kennedy poured himself a drink, then settled into a lounge chair. Soon the sounds of female voices could be heard coming from the gymnasium. Dave Powers unlocked the door connecting the gym to the pool area, and two women in their early twenties entered.

The Secret Service agents had nicknamed them Fiddle and Faddle. One worked for Evelyn Lincoln, the President's private secretary; the other for Pierre Salinger. Fiddle and Faddle accompanied the President on many of his trips outside Washington and often received calls late at night to report to the President for "duty."

"At one point," writes Thomas C. Reeves, "Peter Lawford [the President's brother-in-law] brought some amyl nitrate to the White House. Knowing that the drug, called 'poppers,' was supposed to increase the sexual experience, Jack wanted to try some. Lawford refused, citing the extreme danger involved and warning the President not to take the risk. So Jack gave the drug to Fiddle and Faddle, and both men watched with interest as the young women fell under the drug's powerful influence, appearing for a time to be hyperventilating."

After the President finished his drink, he slipped off his robe. He wore nothing underneath. He stepped into the water, which was heated to help ease the chronic pain in his back. Fiddle and Faddle followed him in, and the President reached out and pulled them onto his knees. His hands cupped their breasts. Then, in the same authoritative tone of voice he had used to instruct Kenny O'Donnell to leave the bubbletop off his car in Dallas, John Kennedy told Fiddle and Faddle exactly what he wanted them to do.

It was an unspoken rule among the Secret Service agents not to discuss the President's activities behind the locked door of the swimming pool. On this particular day, they suspected that Kennedy was frolicking in the pool with his customary companions, Fiddle and Faddle. But they could not be sure. For in a violation of security procedures, no one had bothered to tell the Secret Service the identity of the women.

If the Secret Service was kept in the dark, the American public knew absolutely nothing about John Kennedy's sexual shenanigans in the White House. Most Americans accepted the picture of the President that was forged by his image-making machine, which portrayed him as the ideal family man—faithful to his wife and devoted to his children.

Marital fidelity was not the only area where myth failed to match reality. Though Americans admired Kennedy for his glowing health, he was, in fact, often laid low by his Addison's disease and was confined to his bed when people thought he was conducting affairs of state. Americans were also impressed by Kennedy's virility; he had gotten Jackie pregnant twice in the past three years—once during the presidential campaign, and then again after he entered the White House. Few people were aware of the fact that Kennedy suffered from chronic venereal disease and that he had infected his wife, possibly causing her to deliver a sickly, premature baby boy the previous August. The boy, who was named Patrick, died after two days.

The presidential image makers were fortunate that their man had arrived on the scene at exactly the right moment—a tipping point in America's cultural history. In the early 1960s, the postwar flood of American affluence was flushing away many of the country's old Puritan restraints, leaving people eager for more personal freedom. Americans had grown tired of fatherly figures like Truman and Eisenhower in the White House. They yearned for a leader who embodied the spirit of the times with its narcissistic emphasis on "nonbinding commitments" and "cool sex."

John Kennedy was nothing if not cool. "His 'coolness,'" writes historian Arthur Schlesinger Jr., "was itself a new frontier. It meant freedom from the stereotyped response of the past. . . . His personality was the most potent instrument he had to awaken a national desire for something new and better."

He was a perfect fit for the popular culture. He had been elected, as historian Theodore H. White has pointed out, "chiefly because he was elegant, gay, witty, young and attractive. It was his image that won him the election; that plus his superlative gamesman's skill at the game of politics; plus the underswell of the times, with old prejudices breaking up and new forms of politics just beginning."

Kennedy's sexual rendezvous were arranged by Dave Powers and other members of the Irish Mafia during Jackie's frequent absences from Washington.

"There was a conspiracy of silence to protect his secrets from Jacqueline and to keep her from finding out," Traphes Bryant, the White House kennel keeper, writes. "The newspapers would tell how First Lady Jacqueline was off on another trip, but what they didn't report was how anxious the President sometimes was to see her go."

Fiddle and Faddle were not the only White House staffers who indulged in sex with the President. His wife's press secretary, Pamela Turnure, a dark-haired beauty who resembled the First Lady, carried on an affair with Kennedy during his years in office. At the height of the Cuban missile crisis, Kennedy's eye was caught by a temporary secretary lent to the White House by the Commerce Department. "Get her name," he ordered Defense Secretary Robert McNamara. "We may avert nuclear war tonight."

According to Peter Lawford, the President liked to include friends in his White House escapades. One time he set up a contest—with a cash prize—to see who would be the first man to have sex with a woman other than his own wife in the Lincoln Bedroom. When Lawford mistakenly picked a lesbian for the competition, she refused to have sex with him. But Lawford pretended that he had been successful anyway, and collected the prize.

When Kennedy grew tired of his in-house dalliances, he had Dave Powers import women from outside. One frequent visitor to the White House was Judith Campbell, the girlfriend of Mafia boss Sam Giancana, who was involved in CIA plots to assassinate Fidel Castro. Another was Mary Pinchot Meyer, a Washington artist and the sister-in-law of journalist Benjamin Bradlee. During their White House lovemaking sessions, Mary Meyer introduced Kennedy to marijuana, cocaine, hashish, and LSD. A third guest was Marilyn Monroe, who donned a brown wig and sunglasses when she traveled with the President on *Air Force One*.

And these were only the most notorious examples. Many other

women, whom the President's men called "happening babes," were brought to the White House—airline stewardesses, Las Vegas show-girls, burlesque queens, campaign workers, Palm Beach socialites, Hollywood starlets, and prostitutes.

"More alarming," writes the historian James Giglio, "Kennedy occasionally had affairs with casual acquaintances and virtual strangers, who surreptitiously entered the southwest service entrance of the White House as the result of solicitations of friends and aides. . . . They came during Jacqueline's frequent absences, joining the President in the pool or in the family quarters."

"[The President's] friends and closest assistants, a few of them appalled by the whole business, pretended it was not happening or treated it as if it were the boss's hobby," writes Richard Reeves. "After all, it took less time than tennis, and partners were often easier to find. It was a rite of passage for some, an excited feeling that they had been accepted into a private Kennedy circle. . . . Sneaking around, cleaning up the mess, covering up was all part of the game. Sharing secrets drew men together. 'We're a bunch of virgins, married virgins,' said one young staff member, Fred Dutton, the secretary of the Cabinet. 'And he's like God, fucking anybody he wants to anytime he feels like it.' "

That John Kennedy felt compelled to have casual sex under his wife's nose says a good deal about how completely his ego was defined by the seduction of women.

"A womanizer like Kennedy was not driven, as people often think, solely by the desire to be a macho person," said Sue Erikson Bloland, the daughter of famed psychoanalyst Erik Erikson and a psychoanalyst herself who specializes in the psychology of well-known people and their children. "Kennedy himself gave us a clue to his pathological behavior when he complained that his mother was cold and distant and never hugged him or showed him any affection. His compulsive womanizing can be seen as the desperate effort of a deeply wounded child to obtain what was missing from his seemingly glamorous life— the experience of a genuinely intimate connection.

"At the same time," Bloland continued, "someone with Kennedy's [Irish] background would consider a dependency on women as a sign of male weakness. And so his promiscuous sexual behavior combined two apparently contradictory needs—to be close to women, and yet to be a freewheeling guy who could love them and leave them."

This picture of John Kennedy as a prisoner of sex was not the one embraced by most Americans during his lifetime. And even to this day, there are people who believe that far too much attention has been paid to John Kennedy's childhood traumas and his adult sex life. These people argue that a President should be judged solely on the substance of his performance while in office, not on the morality or immorality of his personal life.

However, as Americans have had the opportunity to learn from bitter experience with Presidents Johnson, Nixon, and Clinton, a leader's personal character cannot be divorced from his public performance. The President's psyche, as Michael Harrington once observed about Richard Nixon, is a very political question.

"Decision making in the White House clearly involves a President's intelligence, experience, political skill, ideology, and the circumstances of the moment, including advice received and political expediency," Thomas C. Reeves writes in his landmark study, *A Question of Character: A Life of John F. Kennedy.* "Still, character is the vital framework in which these elements are arranged. A knowledge of what the President sees as right and wrong, good and bad, will give us a fuller and more accurate picture of the stature of the man and the nature of his leadership."

By probing John Kennedy's personal life—especially the connection between his relationship with his mother and his later promiscuity—we can better understand the narcissistic disorder at the root of the Kennedy Curse.

It is generally accepted as a fact by historians that Rose was an absentee mother. What is perhaps less well understood is the confusion that Rose sowed in her children's emotional lives. On the one hand, she insisted on outward displays of family solidarity; on the other, she did not permit expression of such anxieties privately, within the confines of their own home. Inevitably, her contradictory behavior left its mark on Jack Kennedy.

"Jack had a total lack of ability to relate, emotionally, to anyone," a longtime female friend said. "Everything was so surface with him in his relationships with people."

Though his father was a tyrant, Jack reserved his bitterest scorn for his cold, remote mother.

"My mother," he told a friend, "is a nothing."

In view of his feelings about his mother, it is hardly surprising that Jack's relations with the women he slept with were shallow and superficial. He frequently did not even bother to learn their names, referring to them the next morning as "sweetie" or "kiddo."

"He was as compulsive as Mussolini," one woman recalled. "Up against the wall, Signora, if you have five minutes, that sort of thing. He was not a cozy, touching sort of man. In fact . . . he was a sort of touch-me-not."

After his romp in the pool, the President put on his robe and slippers and used a private passageway to an elevator that led directly to his second-floor living quarters. Fiddle and Faddle returned the way they had come—via the gymnasium. And Dave Powers opened the door to the sacrosanct pool area and told the Secret Service men waiting outside that the President had gone upstairs to take a postcoital nap.

The agents were furious with Powers; they were supposed to be with the President at all times, and Powers often made their job impossible.

"Dave Powers knew we were trying to protect the President," Larry Newman, who had joined the presidential Secret Service detail in 1961, the year Kennedy entered the White House, told Seymour Hersh for his book, *The Dark Side of Camelot*. "We didn't know if these women were carrying listening devices, if they had syringes that carried some type of poison, or if they had Pentax cameras that would photograph the President for blackmail. Your security is only [as good] as its weakest link, and the weak link was Powers in bringing these girls in."

Of course, Newman understood that Dave Powers was only doing the President's bidding. "You'd have to say it starts at the top and works its way down," he said. "It caused a lot of morale problems with the Secret Service. You were on the most elite assignment in the Secret Service, and you were there watching an elevator or door because the President was inside with two hookers. It just didn't compute."

In the slack moral atmosphere that reigned in the Kennedy White House, women were admitted to the Oval Office without having to record their names in the visitors' log. Few of them were even required to undergo background checks. As a result, the Secret Service constantly fretted that the President was vulnerable to scandal or blackmail—or worse.

"We were told to just not interfere with [the steady stream of women]," Agent Larry Newman told author Hersh. "We didn't know if the President that next morning would be dead or alive."

But the agents found it hard to complain, since many of them participated in the sexual cover-ups. For example, during Kennedy's trips to New York City, where he slept with numerous women, the Secret Service helped him avoid the prying eyes of the press by guiding him through the tunnels beneath the Carlyle Hotel, where Kennedy used the family penthouse.

"It was kind of a weird sight," said Charles Spalding, the President's friend, "Jack and I and two Secret Service men walking in these huge tunnels underneath the city streets alongside those enormous pipes, each of us carrying a flashlight. One of the Secret Service men also had this underground map and every once in a while he would say, 'We turn this way, Mr. President.'"

"His womanizing was so routine and common," former Secret Service agent Anthony Sherman told me, "that we slipped into the nefarious duty of protecting Kennedy from his wife by alerting him if she was returning to the White House unexpectedly."

It is hard to overstate the strain that this reckless behavior put on the men of the Secret Service, who had sworn to protect the President with their lives. They knew that the lackadaisical attitude toward security was wrong, but they were ordered by their supervisors to look the other way.

"You're going to see a lot of shit around here," one supervisor told an agent. "Stuff with the President. Just forget about it. Keep it to yourself. Don't even talk to your wife."

The agents became even more alarmed after they were given an off-the-record briefing late in 1961 by an army colonel, who told them that the CIA had orders to assassinate Cuba's Fidel Castro and that there was a strong possibility that Castro would try to retaliate against Kennedy. The Secret Service agents were also aware of rumors that the CIA had hired the Mafia to carry out the assassination schemes against Castro.

After Kennedy's death, some historians were puzzled by the way the Secret Service had allowed things to get out of hand. In response, the agents tried to justify their behavior on the grounds that they did not have the authority to tighten presidential protection. Only the President himself could do that.

But the real explanation goes far deeper. Many of the agents had grown up in small towns where patriotism was bred in the bone and courage was considered the highest virtue. They idolized John Kennedy as a valorous World War II hero, and their adoration often blinded them to their duty.

"I served with seven Presidents and not all of them were popular, but President Kennedy was very popular with the Secret Service," said Hamilton "Ham" Brown, who was assigned to the White House detail and later became president of the Association of Former Secret Service Agents. "Kennedy truly liked agents. He knew all of us by our first names, and he was personable. He'd see you and talk to you. I thought he hung the moon.

"There's no doubt that Kennedy created a certain aura," Ham

Brown continued. "He was a young, vibrant man. Everybody was in their youth back then. Oh, yeah, there was a whole bunch of testosterone floating around. The agents loved him, which, quite frankly, is a bad thing. You shouldn't get emotionally involved with a protectee."

Under the spell of Jack Kennedy's charm, the agents were made to feel that they were part of the President's inner circle. As Lewis Lapham later wrote of the President's younger brother Edward Kennedy, he could be "defined as a gravitational field, drawing to himself devotees who imagine that their own lives acquire meaning only insofar as they fall within the sphere of a magical object. The same kind of adulation attaches itself to rock stars and celebrated criminals."

The party atmosphere in the Kennedy White House permeated and infected the Secret Service. "Some agents felt that if the President could get away with this kind of stuff, so could they," Agent Anthony Sherman told me. "This happened by osmosis. It took hold of some of the agents and began to affect them. There were a lot of available women around the President, and some of the agents actually became part of the looseness. Drinking, partying, and sex became part of traveling with the President."

It would be no exaggeration to say that many of the Secret Service agents assigned to the President fell victim to the Kennedy Curse. The agents assigned to the White House frequently acted as though they were above the laws of man and God. They experienced a feeling of omnipotence by attaching themselves to the charismatic President. John Kennedy was the drug that became their habit, and this addiction turned out to have the most profound consequences for the President, the Secret Service, and the country.

On Thursday, November 21, at 1:30 P.M. John and Jacqueline Kennedy arrived in San Antonio aboard *Air Force One*. After dedicating a medical center there, they proceeded to Houston for a testimonial dinner and then flew on to Fort Worth, where they spent the night in the Hotel Texas.

While they slept, Friday's edition of the *Dallas Morning News* began rolling off the presses. The paper carried a full-page, black-bordered advertisement placed by a right-wing group accusing the President of the United States of treasonable acts, including "the imprisonment, starvation, and persecution of thousands of Cubans" and of "selling food to Communist soldiers who were killing Americans in Vietnam." The ad was a blatant incitement to violence against John Kennedy.

In the early-morning hours of November 22, while copies of the *Dallas Morning News* were being loaded onto delivery trucks, several off-duty Secret Service agents made their way to the nearby Fort Worth Press Club, where they ordered alcoholic drinks. When the club closed, they moved on to an after-hours beatnik joint called the Cellar Coffee House. Though all the agents had duty assignments beginning no later than eight A.M. that same morning, most stayed at the Cellar Coffee House until three A.M., and one remained there until five A.M.

The agents later claimed that they consumed an average of only one and a half alcoholic drinks apiece during the several hours they were partying. No mention was made of drugs, such as marijuana and hallucinogenic mushrooms, which presumably in the 1960s were readily available in such beatnik hangouts as the Cellar Coffee House. Even if their unequivocal claims of sobriety are true—which seems highly doubtful—Secret Service regulations absolutely forbid drinking or drugging by any agent accompanying the President on a trip. A violation or a slight disregard of these provisions is cause for removal from the service.

And yet after the assassination, the chief of the Secret Service testified before the Warren Commission that he did not take any disciplinary action against the offending agents. To do so, he said, "might have given rise to an inference that the violation of the regulation had contributed to the tragic events of November 22."

The Warren Commission accepted this excuse. In its final report, the commission declared: "It is conceivable that those men who had little sleep, and who had consumed alcoholic beverages, even in limited quantities, might have been more alert in the Dallas motorcade if they had retired promptly in Fort Worth. However, there is no evidence that these men failed to take any action in Dallas within their power that would have averted the tragedy."

The commission's conclusion is an insult to common sense. Alcohol and sleep deprivation dull the senses and make reflexes sluggish, and the agents who had been drinking (and possibly drugging) and got less than five hours' sleep could not have functioned at the top of their form on the day of the President's assassination.

The agents' behavior in Dallas should not come as a surprise to anyone familiar with the debauched and degenerate atmosphere in the Kennedy White House. Over a period of a thousand days, the Secret Service agents had fallen under the spell of the President and lost their professional objectivity. They acted as though they, too, believed they were immune to mortal laws and insulated from the inevitable consequences of their deeds.

And so, in the end, John Kennedy's casual attitude toward danger, which was often mistaken for courage, led the Secret Service to do sloppy advance work for his trip to Dallas. The agents did not even inspect the buildings along the President's motorcade route, despite the fact that Kennedy himself had mentioned the danger from a concealed sniper on the very morning of his assassination.

Staring out the window of the Hotel Texas at a platform set up for his speech, Kennedy said, "Just look at that platform. With all those buildings around it, the Secret Service couldn't stop someone who really wanted to get you."

And when Jackie told him of her fears of an assassin on the trip, JFK agreed, saying, "We're heading into nut country today. . . . You know, last night would have been a hell of a night to assassinate a President. I mean it . . . suppose a man had a pistol in a briefcase." The President pointed his index finger at the wall and jerked his thumb. "Then he could have dropped the gun and briefcase and melted away in the crowd."

Yet despite his concerns, Kennedy continued to insist that the bubbletop be left off his limousine. As the House Select Committee on Assassinations stated in its final report on March 29, 1979, fifteen years after Kennedy's murder:

> Not only did Kennedy enjoy traveling, but he almost *recklessly* resisted the protective measures the Secret Service urged him to adopt. He would not allow blaring sirens, and only once— in Chicago in November 1963—did he permit his limousine to be flanked by motorcycle police officers. Furthermore, he told the special agent in charge of the White House detail that he did not want agents to ride on the rear of his car.

Later some people argued that the plastic bubbletop would not have saved the President's life. After all, they said, the bubbletop was not bulletproof, and therefore its use would have made little difference in the outcome in Dallas. But that ignores an important fact: in the glaring Texas sun of November 22, the spherical bubbletop would have acted like reflecting glass, making it hard for a marksman to draw an accurate bead on the President.

Thus, as the presidential motorcade made its way slowly past the Texas School Book Depository in Dallas and entered Dealey Plaza, there was nothing and no one to obstruct Lee Harvey Oswald's view of the back of the President's head.

Kenny O'Donnell and Dave Powers, riding in the follow-up car, were less than twenty yards away when they heard the shots ring out.

"Kenny," Powers said after the second shot, "I think the President's been shot!"

"I made a quick sign of the cross," O'Donnell recalled. "While we both stared at the President, a third shot took the side of his head off. We saw the pieces of bone and brain tissue and bits of reddish hair flying through the air. The impact lifted him and shook him limply, as if he were a rag doll, and then he dropped out of our sight, sprawled across the backseat of the car.

"I said to Dave, 'He's dead.'"

In their grief over the President's assassination, the members of the Kennedy clan felt more united than ever before. The murder in Dallas fortified their belief in the family's divine mission and stiffened their resolve to replace JFK in the White House with another Kennedy.

"In a strange way," Eunice's eldest son, Bobby Shriver, told Peter Collier and David Horowitz, "[we] felt even more like Kennedys than ever—proud of what Jack had been, determined that our time would come again. But once Uncle Bobby died, there was just this sense of splitting apart."

The impact of Robert Kennedy's assassination, which took place five years after Dallas, was devastating, especially for his eldest sons—Joe, Bobby Jr., and David—who caught the brunt of their mother's scorching anger. When the boys became too much for her to handle, Ethel sent them into exile—Joe to Spain, Bobby Jr. to Africa, David to Austria.

After the boys returned to Hyannis Port, they met on the football field. "[But] the games had turned into desperate Freudian struggles, with Joe looking for opportunities to smash them into the ground while they waited for the inevitable moment when his trick knee went out," write Collier and Horowitz. "When this happened, Joe would writhe on the ground as Bobby stood over him sneering, 'Oh, has our sister hurt his knee?' These were such ugly scenes that Mary Schreiner, one of their sister Kathleen's friends, once yelled at Bobby: 'How can you ever expect to be President if you talk like that to your brother?'"

Christopher Lawford, Patricia Kennedy's first child, told Collier and Horowitz that all the cousins—the Kennedys, Lawfords, Shrivers, and Smiths—felt alone and unprotected. "When Uncle Bobby was alive, [Chris] thought to himself, we knew who we were. But now he's gone. What will happen to us? What comes next?"

PART FOUR

VISITATION

CHAPTER SIX

WILLIAM KENNEDY SMITH

TWILIGHT OF THE GODS

.

IT WAS THE NIGHT OF GOOD FRIDAY, March 29, 1991, and a dozen or so people, including Senator Edward M. Kennedy, were crowded around his family's large dining-room table in Palm Beach. Dinner had been prepared by Jean Kennedy Smith's cook of twenty-seven years, Bridie Sullivan, but no one was paying attention to the food. Instead, the Kennedys were engaged in one of their mealtime free-for-alls— telling bawdy stories, poking fun at one another, and throwing dinner rolls across the table.

The setting for this boisterous meal was a musty old house that had been built back in the twenties for Rodman Wanamaker, the Philadelphia department-store heir. Originally called La Guerida, the oceanfront estate was one of the least-distinguished works by Addison Mizner, a well-known architect who popularized the Spanish style in Palm Beach. In 1933 Joseph P. Kennedy bought and enlarged La Guerida for his family, and over the next several decades, the house gradually fell into disrepair. Nowadays, the slightest tremor, even from a heavy footfall, could send chunks of loose plaster raining down from the ceiling.

Still, the Kennedy compound, as it was now called, ranked as one of the most notable structures in Palm Beach, for it had been used by President John F. Kennedy as the winter White House. Everyone in Palm Beach was familiar with the location of the landmark house on North Ocean Boulevard. But since the cream of Palm Beach society did not mingle with the Kennedys, hardly any of the wealthy winter residents had stepped foot inside the compound's stuccoed walls.

"It's odd, but it's a known fact that the Kennedys have never been accepted in Palm Beach," a well-known hostess who had lived there all her life told Dominick Dunne. "Young Joe and Kathleen were very popular with other young people. But the Kennedys never belonged to any of the clubs, and I think they never felt at home in Palm Beach."

Because few people had seen the Kennedy compound from the inside, the house had acquired a certain mysterious allure, and men in the family often exploited this attraction during their annual Easter hunt for women. The promise of "a quiet drink at the house" was a surefire technique for luring women back to the compound for sex.

Once there, the women might be passed around from Kennedy to Kennedy, then sent on their way. Sex itself was never the primary purpose of these evenings; it was an opportunity for the Kennedys to put on a show of manly swagger in front of one another and to demonstrate that women were discardable objects.

Bringing strange women back to the compound in the middle of the night was a high-risk gamble; there was always the possibility of robbery, assault, blackmail, or a politically embarrassing charge of sexual misconduct. But the Kennedys behaved as though they were invulnerable and had nothing to fear. Palm Beach was their seraglio, a place of licentious pleasure. It was there that they could drink themselves into a state of drunken senselessness and turn sex into a power game of seduction, manipulation, and control.

After dinner Senator Kennedy strolled out to the patio on the seawall overlooking the ocean. The air was scented with jacaranda and hibiscus, and a full moon cast shadows on the beach. The senator sipped his usual Chivas and soda and chatted with his sister Jean and their old friend, a retired FBI agent by the name of William Barry, who had been with Bobby Kennedy the night he was shot and had knocked the gun out of assassin Sirhan Sirhan's hand.

When they ran out of things to say about Bobby, they reminisced for a while about Jean's late husband, Stephen Smith, who until his death the previous summer had managed the family's money and its political campaigns. Considered by many to be as cunning and ruthless as Old Joe Kennedy, Steve had been the master fixer who, as one writer put it, was "the guy who kept the lid on, the ultimate practitioner of media damage control." He saved Ted Kennedy's political career after Chappaquiddick and rescued countless other family members from the consequences of the Kennedy Curse.

This was the first time since Steve's death that the Kennedys had been together as a family. Teddy poured himself another drink and suddenly turned maudlin.

"Steve was like a brother to me," he said. "Something left us all when we buried him. Now Steve's gone, along with Bobby and Jack."

Jean could see that her brother was near tears, and she tried to cheer him up.

"The family is lucky it still has you," she said.

Luck was not a word that people normally associated with Teddy Kennedy, whose life had been fractured by his brothers' assassinations.

"The fracture," *Time* magazine wrote at the time, "set a pattern of sharp contradiction: the 'brief shining moment' would give way to long, sordid aftermaths. Greek tragedy ('the curse of the Kennedys') would degenerate into sleazy checkout-counter revelations. . . . The serious lawmaker in Ted Kennedy would turn now and then into a drunken, overage frat-house boor, the statesman into a party animal, the romance of the Kennedys into a smelly, toxic mess. The family patriarch, the oldest surviving Kennedy male, would revert to a fat, sloppy baby."

Palm Beach was the ideal setting for a Falstaffian figure like Teddy. Its tropical climate and dazzling wealth acted like stimulants to his jaded senses; its congenial police force could be counted on to pardon his transgressions. Even so, Teddy did not confine his escapades to Palm Beach. Tales of his outlandish conduct came from all points of the compass—Hyannis, the Virgin Islands, London, Washington, New York. . . .

"In recent years," Dominick Dunne wrote in *Vanity Fair,* "there [were] confirmed accounts of a drunken tabletop episode with a waitress as well as public fornication with a lobbyist in La Brasserie, a Washington restaurant. There [was] also the by-now-famous photograph of the senator atop a woman on the open deck of a sleek powerboat in the Mediterranean, a picture that prompted another senator to say to Kennedy, 'Well, I see you've changed your position on offshore drilling.' "

As Teddy Kennedy recalled, he retired to his room at about eleven-thirty that night. However, he discovered that despite all the alcohol he had consumed—or perhaps because of it—he could not fall asleep.

He staggered out of his room and past the tennis court, and groped his way in the dark to the bedroom that was being shared by his son Patrick, then a member of the Rhode Island legislature, and his nephew William Kennedy Smith, who was about to graduate with a degree in medicine from Georgetown University.

"They appeared to be asleep when I opened up the door," Teddy said. "I asked them if they wanted to have a couple of beers."

The senator had just turned fifty-nine—an age when most men have long since put away childish things—and took great pride in his role as the father of three and surrogate father to the entire Kennedy clan. And yet he apparently did not see anything wrong or even inappropriate about waking up his twenty-four-year-old son and thirty-one-year-old nephew in the middle of the night and inviting them to join him in a round of drinks that might lead to sexual debauchery.

No one—perhaps least of all Teddy Kennedy—would ever know what went through his mind at the moment he woke up Patrick and Willy. Perhaps he was recalling that just a couple of nights before, the three of them had gone out on the town and brought several women back to the compound for "a quiet drink at the house." And perhaps he was hoping that his young son and nephew could help a drunken, grossly overweight, middle-aged man get lucky again that night.

Shortly after midnight Patrick Kennedy slid behind the wheel of a rented white Chrysler Le Baron convertible in the parking lot of the compound and set out with his father and Willy Smith for Au Bar, the happening place in Palm Beach.

It was the biggest party night of the year, and when the Kennedys arrived at Au Bar, it was crammed with people who had to lean over and shout into each other's ear to make themselves heard over the throbbing music. There were more women than men sitting at the tables in the club's distinctive pink-and-white-striped chairs. Many of these women had traveled a considerable distance from Palm Beach to be there that night. They were looking to get picked up by rich men.

"We walked in," Teddy recalled, "and the bar was crowded two or three deep. . . . Folks were sitting on stools and being around the bar. We passed the main part of the bar to the far end of it, where the waitresses take drinks and serve the tables. It seemed less crowded there, so we stood at the bar at that place."

Teddy ordered a double Chivas and soda and turned to face the room. People standing nearby stared openly at the famous senator and his son, but they hardly noticed Willy Smith, who did not have the familiar Kennedy hair and flashing teeth.

Willy was not much to look at. He had a lumpy body, a messy mop of dark hair, and the crooked smile of someone who was in a state of perpetual befuddlement. He had always been ambivalent about his Kennedy connection; during his sophomore year at Duke University, he was persuaded by his parents to take a semester off to work on Teddy Kennedy's 1980 bid to unseat Jimmy Carter as the Democratic Party's nominee for President. Willy's father, Steve Smith, ran the campaign, and the brooding, introverted Willy worked along-side his wildly extroverted cousins, who referred to him as "the un-Kennedy."

"I never really felt exposed to being a celebrity until the campaign, when it was your role to be a celebrity," Willy told the Duke news-paper.

Like his father, Willy went out of his way to avoid publicity. He once told a pack of photographers who were pestering him that he was just a Kennedy "friend." And on his recent application for a res-idency in internal medicine, he wrote the letter *K* instead of *Kennedy* in the space reserved for his middle name.

Willy resembled his father in yet another way. When Steve Smith drank, he became abusive, especially toward his wife, Jean. Willy ex-perienced a similar personality change when *he* drank. Among his rich friends up and down the East Coast, he was notorious for his uncon-trollable craving for sex; in this respect at least, he was sometimes compared with his late uncle John F. Kennedy, who also suffered from satyriasis. But whereas Jack Kennedy never pressured a woman for sex, Willy was known to become aggressive and rough if a woman rejected his advances.

Half an hour after Willy Smith arrived at Au Bar, he struck up a conversation with a pretty young woman in a dark dress. Her name was Patricia Bowman, and she later remembered thinking that Willy "seemed like a real nice guy."

"He was with his uncle and his uncle's son, and he introduced me to them as Uncle Ted and . . . Patrick," she said in one of several statements she later gave to the Palm Beach police. "He introduced himself as William Smith, and he asked me if I wanted to go dance, and I said yeah."

It took Patty a while to figure out who Uncle Ted was.

"[When] I realized that he was in fact Ted Kennedy," she said, "I laughingly remarked to William, 'You must think I'm pretty slow,' and we laughed about that for a while."

After they finished dancing, Patty led Willy back to her table and introduced him to some of her friends. He said hello to Chuck Desiderio, who worked as the manager of his father's well-known Palm Beach restaurant, Renato's, and had been charged with larceny of auto parts in 1979 in a case that was dismissed. Chuck was currently being investigated by the police on allegations of drug trafficking. Chuck's date was Anne Mercer, a sometime salesgirl at a chic Worth Avenue clothing boutique. And sitting next to Anne was her father, Leonard Mercer, an alleged associate of Philadelphia mobster Nicodemo "Little Nicky" Scarfo. Leonard was out on parole after serving part of a four-year prison sentence on federal tax, perjury, and bank fraud charges.

Patty Bowman had a checkered past of her own. Her father, who had physically and emotionally abused her as a child, had been charged with setting fire to his home and had been ordered to obtain psychiatric treatment. When she was eight, Patty was sexually abused by a gardener; twenty-one years later, she was still seeing a counselor for the lingering trauma. In her teen years, she broke her neck in a car accident and was currently taking prescription drugs for the persistent pain. She also had had three abortions, a child out of wedlock, and trouble with cocaine.

Unlike some of her Au Bar companions, however, Patty did not live on the wrong side of the law—or the tracks. After her parents divorced, her mother married Michael O'Neil, the son of William O'Neil, the founder of General Tire. The immensely rich O'Neil looked after Patty and had bought her a home in an upscale neighborhood in the nearby town of Jupiter.

Thanks to her old reputation as a wild party girl—and the O'Neil connection—Patty was known to friends as Patty O. But since the birth of her daughter, Caroline, two years before, Patty O had put aside her former lifestyle and become a devoted mother. In fact, that night was her first night out in many, many months.

As the crowd in Au Bar began to thin, Patty and Willy found it easier to converse without shouting. She told him that her daughter had been born prematurely and suffered severe medical problems as a result. And she talked about how the abuse she had suffered in childhood still affected her outlook as an adult.

"I never really trusted anybody," Patty said. "A lot of other people have had a lot worse lives than I have, but mine hasn't been that great at times. . . ."

At some point in the evening, Teddy and Patrick Kennedy came over to the table. They had glum expressions on their faces, perhaps because, unlike Willy, neither of them had been able to pick up a woman.

"They just sat down," Patty's friend Anne Mercer recalled, "and it was a very uncomfortable feeling . . . and just to lighten up the atmosphere . . . I looked over at Patrick and I jokingly said to him, 'You look like *you're* having a good time. . . .' Senator Kennedy then says to me, 'Who are you to say anything?' And I said, 'I'm Anne Mercer. Who are you to say anything?' And he goes, 'You don't understand anything about world politics . . . ,' and stood up."

"And then all I remember," said Patrick Kennedy, picking up the story, "was *she* stood up in a sort of imposing way, to my father, and my father, I could sense, was very uncomfortable. . . . I think she could have said, 'You have been drinking too much. . . .' [My father] said, 'You know, Patrick is a Representative,' and that seemed to exacerbate her, because Anne felt she was being slighted in some way."

As Teddy and Patrick got up from the table and prepared to leave the nightclub, a young woman who had declined Patrick's earlier invitations to dance came up to him and grabbed his hand. Her name was Michele Cassone, and she was a waitress at a Palm Beach restaurant called Testa's.

"Are you leaving?" Patrick asked her.

"Yes," Michele Cassone said.

"Would you like to join us for a quiet drink at the house?" Patrick said. "Why don't you follow us back in your own car."

It was about three o'clock in the morning when Willy Smith and Patty Bowman decided to leave Au Bar.

"My uncle's gone," Willy told her. "Can you give me a ride home? I'm living up at the estate."

"Sure," Patty replied. "I know where it is."

They got into her car, a sporty two-seater, and drove the short distance to the Kennedy compound. When they pulled into the driveway, Willy kissed Patty good night, got out of the car, and walked around to the driver's side. He leaned down and asked her if she would like to come in "for a quiet drink."

"And I said yes, because I wanted to see what the Kennedy house looked like," she recalled.

Entering the house through the kitchen, they came upon Teddy and Patrick, both of whom appeared to be quite drunk. As soon as they saw that Willy had a date, they turned and left the kitchen, taking a couple of bottles of wine with them.

"And we stood there talking for a while," Patty said, ". . . and then William asked if I wanted to go swimming, and I said no, but he asked if I wanted to go to the beach, and I said okay.

"When we got [to the beach]," she continued, ". . . it was a beautiful night. . . . I'd met somebody who I thought could become a friend . . . and we kissed a couple of times, nothing big, grand or— who's the guy in *From Here to Eternity*? You know, laying in the surf stuff. None of that. It seemed very innocent to me."

On the seawall patio overlooking the beach, Teddy and Patrick had joined Michele Cassone. Patrick filled their wineglasses from one of the bottles he had brought from the kitchen while Teddy told a sexually explicit joke.

Suddenly Michele pointed at the beach twenty feet below.

"Ted," she said, "there goes a naked woman, walking on the beach into your ocean."

Teddy looked out to the spot where the beach met the water, but even in the light from the full moon, it was difficult to tell whether the distant figure was a woman or a man. In any case, the person's identity did not seem to interest him. He wanted to get back to his joke.

The drunker he got, the dirtier the punch lines became. When at last Patrick announced that he was going back to the house, Michele made it clear that she did not want to be left alone with Teddy.

"Don't leave me here," she told Patrick.

"Michele stood up and my father stood up," Patrick said, ". . . and at that point my father departed. I'm not sure exactly what direction he went. But I know that Michele and I went to my room."

On the beach, Willy Smith had stripped off his shirt and pants and was preparing to skinny-dip in the ocean.

"I got a little embarrassed," Patty Bowman told the police. "I didn't feel that was appropriate, and I turned around, and I heard him go in the water, and I said that I was leaving, and I turned to go up the steps.

"I got to the top of the steps," she continued, "and I think I had one foot on the grass, and then my ankle was grabbed, and I fell, and it was such a weird thought. You know, here's this man who has seemed so nice, but now all of a sudden, somebody has grabbed me. I wondered who's grabbing me, and then I realized that the only person who could be grabbing me was him, and I got real scared and got away and started to run. . . . I thought, if this is playing, that's way too rough for me. I don't play that way. I broke my neck years ago, and I'm concerned about whether I'm fragile or not, and I don't want to be played with that way. . . .

"When I was running, he caught me again and tackled me, and I fell to the ground out by the pool, which is on the south side of the house. . . . All I know is . . . he tackled me and then he had my dress up and his hands in my pants . . . and he raped me. . . . I was yelling *no,* and to *stop,* and he wouldn't. . . . He might have been yelling at me something, but I don't know what it was. . . . All I know is, I was screaming *no,* and to *stop* . . . and I couldn't figure out why, why he wasn't stopping, and why nobody was helping me."

While she was wrestling with Willy on the grass and screaming, Patty suddenly understood why no one was responding to her cries for help. During a taped interview, Detective Christine Rigolo of the Palm Beach Police asked Patty about a startling statement she had made to her friend Anne Mercer.

"There was a comment that you made that 'he was watching . . . he was watching,'" Detective Rigolo reminded Patty. "Do you know what that means?"

Patty's response was vague.

"I had seen Ted and Patrick [Kennedy] on the beach before they . . . took off," she said, "and I thought in my mind . . . this is four or five in the morning. They're not going to go out and have breakfast. They must have been in that house. And I can remember getting upset thinking that they didn't do anything to stop [the rape]. . . ."

In another interview with Patty, Detective Rigolo said, "One of the things that was mentioned is that Ted Kennedy was present."

"I got upset about that because I know I saw [Ted] when I got there," said Patty, who subsequently passed two polygraph tests and a voice-stress analysis. "And, you know, when [Willy and I] went to the beach, [Ted] was there, and I was screaming, *No!* and *Stop,* and I remember thinking, 'Ted Kennedy is here. Why doesn't he come down and stop this man?'"

In the house, Michele and Patrick were lying next to each other on one of the beds in his room.

"It was just a small, messy room with two twin beds," she told investigators. "The beds were unmade, and Patrick and I were . . . making out, kissing, I guess, and laughing and talking.

"About ten minutes at the most later," she continued, "the senator emerged through the door from inside the house . . . and at this time he only has on a button-down oxford shirt. He has taken his slacks off. I didn't see if he had any Jockeys or boxers on [because the shirt] came halfway down the thighs. He was standing there, wobbling, and had no pants on. . . . And I was just really freaked out."

Teddy would later claim that he was wearing a one-piece nightshirt that he used for sleeping. But that made little difference. Michele was sickened by the sight of the drunken, half-naked senator standing in the room and watching his own son in bed with a woman.

"What's going on! What's going on!" Michele screamed.

She bolted from the bed.

"I'm going home right now," she said. "I'm out of here."

After a long struggle, Patty Bowman testified that she finally managed to free herself from Willy Smith's grasp.

She got up and sprinted across the lawn. Behind her, she could hear Willy calling her name. Inside the house, she looked for a place to hide and found a little space behind a water cooler in the kitchen. As she cowered there, she heard Willy's calls growing louder and louder.

She spotted a cordless phone on a nearby counter, grabbed it, and telephoned her friends Anne Mercer and Chuck Desiderio. She told them that she had been raped, and begged them to come to the Kennedy compound to get her.

Later she explained that she did not call the police because the authorities in Palm Beach treated the Kennedys like little gods.

"You hear all about the Kennedys and their political power," she said. "We all know about their previous mishaps with the law, which weren't [prosecuted]. And I was worried whether anybody would believe that a Kennedy had raped me, and what the Kennedys could do to me. . . . I was thinking that this is the Kennedys, these are political people and all that, and . . . maybe they owned the police, and I didn't know what would happen to me. I knew the only people I could trust to come were Chuck and Anne."

The next thing Patty remembered in describing the events to the police, she was standing in the doorway of a book-lined den, facing her assailant, Willy Smith. He was sitting with his legs crossed, a crooked little smile on his face.

"Do you want to talk?" he asked.

"You raped me!" she said.

"No, I didn't rape you," Willy said.

"Yes, you did," she insisted.

"Well, either way," he said, "no one will believe you."

A few minutes later Anne Mercer and Chuck Desiderio pulled up in front of the house in Anne's Jeep.

"Patty was sitting on the steps crying," Chuck recalled, "and I walked up to her and started talking to her and trying to calm her down. . . . She was hysterical . . . crying and screaming . . . and I couldn't make out too much of what she was saying. . . . She wasn't making very much sense."

Chuck followed Patty inside the darkened house. She told him that she wanted to take something so that she could produce proof later that she had in fact been raped at the Kennedy compound, and not someplace else. She picked up a photo of two young men in a plastic frame and a pad with some telephone numbers jotted on it. Chuck grabbed a valuable eighteenth-century vase. And then they ran outside and disappeared into the night.

At breakfast, Willy Smith and Patrick Kennedy bantered about their sexual exploits of the night before. No one was present at the table to overhear their conversation, but Patrick later gave a sworn deposition in which he described what they talked about.

According to Patrick, Willy portrayed Patty Bowman as a dangerously disturbed, "whacked out" woman. She reminded him, he said, of the Glenn Close character in the movie *Fatal Attraction*. She refused to leave the house and threatened to call the police. Her friends Anne Mercer and Chuck Desiderio finally came and picked her up, and before they left, Anne apologized to Willy, saying, "I think we have caused you enough trouble tonight already."

In defense of his cousin, Patrick went on to say that Willy had acted like a perfect gentleman even during sex.

"Did you wear protection?" Patrick asked Willy.

"No, but thank God I pulled out before I came," Willy answered.

That statement, like so many others that emerged from the Kennedy compound over the next several weeks, proved to be untrue. Willy's sperm was found in Patty's vagina.

In fact, much of Patrick's story did not hold water. For instance, when Patrick was asked by Moira Lasch, the tough assistant state prosecutor who was monitoring the police investigation, if he had told his father or Jean Smith or "any of the other older people" at the compound about Patty Bowman's threat to call the police, he answered no.

"Why didn't you tell them?" demanded Moira Lasch, whose nickname was Maximum Moira because of her reputation for seeking the most severe charges possible under the law.

"Because it all seemed sort of surreal," Patrick answered, ". . . and didn't fit into the context of a new day that was bright, and that we had had a tennis game scheduled and, you know, I just never gave it a second thought."

Other witnesses at the Kennedy compound proved to be even less helpful. Jean Kennedy Smith professed total ignorance about the behavior of the men in her family on the night in question—or, for that matter, on *any* night.

"They never discuss—none of them ever discuss what they do in the evening with me," she said. "Except they had fun or if, you know, something like that. Nothing."

For his part, Teddy appeared to get himself tangled in a web of lies and contradictions. He claimed that he never bothered to ask Willy how he got home from Au Bar on the night of Good Friday–Holy Saturday, or whether he brought a woman with him—a statement that was contradicted by Patty Bowman's testimony that she had come face-to-face with Teddy and Patrick in the kitchen that night.

What's more, Teddy stonewalled the police and, at times, interferred with their investigation. When the police showed up at the compound shortly after one P.M. on Easter Sunday—the day after Patty Bowman filed formal charges of "sexual battery" against Willy Smith—they were met at the door by William Barry, the ex–FBI agent, who stated that he handled security for the Kennedy family. Bill Barry told Detective Christine Rigolo, the chief investigator, that the senator was not there and that Willy Smith might have already left town.

"In fact," *Time* magazine reported, "both men were at the house, and a servant later told investigators that Barry and the Senator conferred in the kitchen right after the police left. Police say that when they phoned an hour later, a housekeeper told them Barry had taken the Senator and Smith to the airport. Yet Kennedy did not depart until the next day."

In his deposition, Teddy claimed that he did not grasp "the full dimensions" of the allegations against his nephew until he returned to his Senate office in Washington on Monday, April 1. However, as early as Saturday afternoon Teddy was placing urgent phone calls to Marvin Rosen, a Miami attorney who had helped handle some of the family's legal problems in Palm Beach in the past. Rosen's partner, Mark Schnapp, would end up as part of Willy Smith's defense team.

Another large hole was poked in Teddy's story by a witness who claimed that he overheard the senator discuss the case with Willy Smith at a popular Palm Beach restaurant on Easter Sunday.

"While I was standing behind the senator, I overheard him say, '. . . and she'll say it's rape,' " the witness said.

After Willy flew home to Washington, he called his uncle to talk about the case.

"Do you want the whole story?" Willy asked.

Teddy did not want to be bothered.

"You better tell the whole story to . . . Marvin Rosen," he said.

Before long, it became apparent that the story was turning into a media circus—with unprecedented live coverage on Court TV—and that someone far more cunning and ruthless than Marvin Rosen would be needed to manage the situation.

In the past, that someone had always been Stephen Smith, Willy's father. Steve's most notable accomplishment in damage control was his handling of the 1969 drowning of Mary Jo Kopechne at Chappaquiddick, where Teddy Kennedy failed to report the accident to the police for ten hours. Steve got Teddy off with a suspended sentence for the misdemeanor of leaving the scene of an accident.

Far less famous but equally effective was Steve's crisis management of the 1984 drug overdose death of David Kennedy, a son of Robert and Ethel Kennedy, at the Brazilian Court Hotel in Palm Beach. In an effort to absolve David and the Kennedy family of any connection to drugs, Steve tried to prevent the release of all investigative reports related to David's affairs—the medical examiner's findings, witness statements, police summaries, and photographs.

Steve also made an effort to suppress the testimony of Caroline Kennedy, who was then twenty-seven years old and had been in Palm Beach visiting her grandmother Rose Kennedy at the time of David's death. The police charged that someone had tampered with the evidence in David's hotel room before they arrived, and an unnamed source fingered Caroline as the person who had flushed her cousin's stash of drugs down the toilet.

The unnamed source turned out to be a liar, but that did not alter Steve Smith's intention of keeping Caroline's name out of the papers. In this, he was supported by the state attorney, David Bludworth, who fought to suppress Caroline's statement and preclude lawyers for the defendants from interviewing her.

"What concerned me was the gallant effort to prevent me from seeing [Caroline]," said Michael Salnick, the attorney for one of the hotel bellhops accused of selling drugs to David Kennedy. "I always wondered who was calling the shots."

No one was running the show for Willy.

What's more, Steve Smith had never had to contend with someone as tough-minded and determined as Maximum Moira Lasch, who had watched her boss, David Bludworth, the lead prosecutor in the David

Kennedy drug case, get reprimanded by a judge for being "governed by what the Kennedys want you to do."

"It seems that Lasch learned a lesson," wrote Mary Jordan in *The Washington Post*. "Instead of showing deference to the [Kennedy] family, she has shown defiance."

Clearly, Moira Lasch was preparing to put Senator Kennedy and his entire family on trial. And this time the Kennedys were highly vulnerable. In the seven years since the David Kennedy case, Teddy Kennedy's loutish behavior and sexual escapades had made him a laughingstock. In addition, dozens of newly published books and magazine articles containing sensational charges against the Kennedys had further chipped away at their once-inviolable reputation.

In a biography of Peter Lawford, the former husband of Patricia Kennedy, author James Spada places Bobby Kennedy in Marilyn Monroe's home on the day of her death. Novelist Joyce Carol Oates wrote a chilling fictionalized article in *Lear's* magazine re-creating the Chappaquiddick incident from the point of view of Mary Jo Kopechne. And Thomas Reeves presents a devastating portrait of a sexually out-of-control John F. Kennedy in *A Question of Character*.

Because of this record of malfeasance and depravity, people had come to expect the worst from the Kennedys. Indeed, there was a growing perception in America that the country's royal family lived under a curse from which there was no escape.

And so, the question of Willy Smith's guilt or innocence ceased being the key issue in the upcoming trial. Now it was a question of the survival of the Kennedy political dynasty itself.

With that in mind, Teddy Kennedy turned to an old family friend and Washington power broker, attorney Herbert J. "Jack" Miller Jr., to direct the defense effort as lead counsel. Miller had served under Bobby Kennedy in the criminal division of the Justice Department. He had advised Steve Smith during the Chappaquiddick and David Kennedy crises, and he was Ethel Kennedy's personal attorney.

Jack Miller wasted no time in assembling a damage-control team.

Barbara Gamarekian, a former *New York Times* Washington reporter, was hired to run interference with the press. Cathy "Cat" Bennett, a nationally known jury-selection expert, was put on retainer. More than a dozen expensive expert witnesses, including forensics expert Dr. Henry Lee, were lined up to cast doubt on Patty Bowman's story. And five crack private investigators were brought on board to dig up dirt about Patty, as well as on Anne Mercer and her boyfriend, Chuck Desiderio.

Within a month, Jack Miller's efforts began to pay off. Despite Florida's strict rape shield law, which among other things was aimed at protecting victims from the press, NBC News broadcast a story that identified Patty Bowman by name. *The New York Times* quickly followed suit. The *Times'* unflattering story, which appeared to be based on information leaked by the Kennedy camp, described Patty Bowman as having a "wild streak" and cited as evidence her speeding tickets and out-of-wedlock daughter. The story all but accused her of asking for trouble.

"For days," wrote *Newsweek*'s Jonathan Alter, "the paper was lambasted by critics who compared it to a child. And it responded like one. In classic *Times* form, executive editor Max Frankel, who made the decision, was unavailable for interviews, while the reporter on the story, Fox Butterfield, was prevented by management from defending his own work."

In early May, Jack Miller's defense team let it be known that its investigators had found several witnesses who were prepared to testify that Patty Bowman was a promiscuous, mentally unstable abuser of cocaine. What's more, Miller's private investigators approached Chuck Desiderio and tried to intimidate him into changing his story.

"Two investigators from the Kennedys came to your restaurant?" Moria Lasch asked Chuck Desiderio during a deposition.

"Yes, they did," he replied.

"They told you that if you continued to tell what you had told the police, that allegations were going to be raised against you concerning cocaine?"

"Yes," he said.

"Did you understand that if you testified at trial, that they were going to bring up cocaine during the trial and try to smear you?"

"I felt that is what the insinuation was."

"You have been intimidated in coming forward since the incident?"

"To an extent, yes."

That summer, Jack Miller announced that he was withdrawing from the case in favor of a more experienced litigator. His handpicked successor was noted Miami criminal attorney Roy Black. Nicknamed "the Professor" for his learned manner, Black made a charming, folksy contrast to Moira Lasch's ice queen.

Beneath his gentlemanly demeanor, Black was a battle-hardened warrior who gave no quarter when it came to fighting for his client. In an attempt to pierce Florida's rape shield law and to justify cross-examining Patty Bowman about her sexual history, Black submitted a document to the judge, Mary Lupo, detailing Patty's "bizarre" emotional problems dating back to her teen years. He argued that Patty had made up the rape story because of her history of sexual, physical, and emotional abuse.

To lend credence to the charge, Black hired David Rothenberg, a Miami psychologist and veteran trial witness, and asked him to evaluate both Patty Bowman and Willy Smith. Not surprisingly, Rothenberg supported Black's theory that Patty made up the rape story.

"I'm sure [Patty] thinks she's telling the truth," Rothenberg said. "My question is, whose truth?"

Her sexual encounter with Willy Smith, he said, probably revived Patty's childhood memories of being assaulted.

"Then with Willy, she has this pleasurable experience and realized she's not supposed to be enjoying sex," Rothenberg said. "The echoes say sex is evil, sex is abusive, sex is corrupt. So the way she disavows this feeling of pleasure is by projecting Willy's image on the image of the man who abused her. Willy then becomes the man who assaulted her."

Though damaging to Patty, Rothenberg's report was not all one-sided. After examining Willy's background, the psychologist concluded that Willy was the product of an emotionally deprived and depressed childhood. Willy's emotional insecurities may have intruded on his ability to perform sexually, said Rothenberg, leaving him "sexually dysfunctional."

That phrase fit Moira Lasch's theory about Willy Smith to a tee. In fact, it was exactly what she believed from day one of the case—that Willy was the kind of man who became sexually aroused when he assaulted women.

In July, Moira Lasch went public with her bombshell accusation. She filed documents saying that three other women, who had given sworn depositions, were willing to testify that Willy Smith had attacked them. One of the women claimed that she had been raped in Willy's Washington apartment. A second talked of being assaulted by Willy after a pool party at the Smith family home, though he did not complete the rape. And a third, who was dating Willy's cousin, Max Kennedy, said that Willy had thrown her on a bed and touched her in a sexual manner.

On the eve of the trial in November, Judge Lupo ruled that the women's testimony was inadmissible, since an accused's past actions could not legally be held against him. But by then the damage had been done in the court of public opinion: the three women had told their stories to the media, and similar tales about Willy began cropping up everywhere.

In England, Taki Theodoracopulos, the international social figure, wrote in his weekly column in *The Spectator* that he knew a girl who claimed she had been beaten up by Willy Smith.

"Now we have the case of William Smith, yet another Kennedy nephew," Taki wrote. "He is described by the bunch of Kennedy apologists that the family has been parading in front of the cameras as a quiet, dignified person. He is nothing of the kind. Six years ago, the very same Willy Smith beat up an English girl I know well. When I asked her to testify against him, she told me she was too scared."

The woman Taki wrote about was later revealed to be Alexandra Marr, the daughter of Donald Marr, a stockbroker, and Lady Weir. Before she married, she dated an American businessman named John Bryan.

"Taki and I were in New York," Bryan told Dominick Dunne. "I was going out with Alexandra a lot then, a lot, virtually every night. Then one night she went out with Willy Smith. We saw her the next day. She was beaten to shit by this guy. Taki was going to do an article on it at the time. She said, 'I swear to God, if you do, they will kill me. They told me.' She had a beaten-up face. I remember the absolute terror in her eyes. She was afraid for her life."

Another woman, a former Duke classmate, told Dominick Dunne about Willy's reputation in college.

"He's a creepy guy," she said. "I never heard that he raped anyone, but he did corner girls. I thought he was more pathetic than violent. I heard him referred to as the Presser, because he'd push girls into the corner and then press up against them. He would, to be crude about it, dry-hump people. . . . Everybody did drugs, so he's not alone in that, but he used drugs as a way to get girls. 'Come and do a few lines,' he'd say. I'll tell you one thing he said to me. 'Do you want to do some lines?' I said yes. 'Then you can do them off my cock.' "

Shortly after the trial began in early December, the regulars in Court-room 411 decided that the Professor was going to win the case. And as supporting evidence, they pointed to a number of factors in the Professor's favor.

To begin with, Patty Bowman's story was riddled with contradic-tions. Was she raped once, twice, or not at all? She told Anne Mercer she was attacked twice; later she amended her story to once. And what about her panty hose? She said she could not remember when or where she took them off on the night of the rape. Did she take off her panty hose to walk on the beach? Or did she take them off to have sex with Willy Smith?

Then, the regulars said, there was the matter of Maximum Moira's lackluster performance. Where did she get those dreary clothes? She looked frumpier than a Brooks Brothers catalog. And she gave off the wrong vibes (distant and cold). She never bothered to play to the jury, and she had one tone of voice: shrill. And what was she doing with her left foot? When she sat down at the prosecution table, that foot was in constant motion. She made everybody nervous.

The regulars said that it was a plus for the Professor that the media were happy. And no wonder: the Kennedys were out in full force. Somebody counted nineteen of them: Ethel, Jean, Pat, Eunice, Sargent Shriver—they were all there. They worked in shifts, inside and outside the courtroom, providing great visuals and sound bites for the TV cameras. Even JFK Jr., whose mother begged him to stay away from the lurid trial, was persuaded by his uncle Ted—"for the sake of your own political future, if you want the support of the family"—to put in an appearance. John caused a sensation.

After ten days of testimony, things turned out just as the regulars in Courtroom 411 had predicted. It took the jury seventy-seven minutes to reach a decision to acquit William Kennedy Smith. The curious thing was, when it was all over, the Kennedys, though relieved for Willy, did not seem all that happy.

"After the trial was over, there were requests for TV interviews from all kinds of magazine shows," said Barbara Gamarekian. "I was torn between wanting people to know him better and, on the other hand, allowing him to return to his normal life.

"From the moment he was arrested and indicted, no one really knew him," she continued. "He never gave an interview, never did a press thing. All you saw was that horrible photograph of him—his mug shot—which made him look piggy.

"His mother, Jean Smith, was anxious to get word out, but we decided it wouldn't have helped to do a big PR campaign. Acquittal or no acquittal, people had made up their minds about him. Frankly,

I think that when people think about Willy Smith, they're apt to think about *that rapist.*"

For more than three decades, ever since the assassination of JFK, the Kennedy myth had been nourished by an impossible dream: someday, the family and its supporters fervently hoped, a Kennedy would sit again in the Oval Office.

Even after Chappaquiddick, some Kennedy apologists continued to believe that Senator Edward M. Kennedy could somehow be politically resuscitated. But following the lurid revelations in the William Kennedy Smith rape trial, Teddy was toast.

What's more, other members of the next generation of Kennedys quickly followed their uncle into public dishonor and disrepute. That left John F. Kennedy Jr. as the only member of the family who seemed to have the star power and moral authority to bring about a Kennedy Restoration.

As far as the world was concerned, John was the golden boy with the famous name, matinee-idol looks, private fortune, and the love of a glamorous wife. From all outward appearances, he had survived his family's traumas and avoided the fate of so many Kennedys, who had tangled calamitously with drugs and alcohol and the law. John seemed to have inherited all the Kennedy glory without the Kennedy Curse.

But had he?

CHAPTER SEVEN

JOHN FITZGERALD KENNEDY JR.

CUT FROM THE SAME CLOTH

TO MEMBERS OF THE EDITORIAL STAFF of *George* magazine, their famous boss often appeared listless and withdrawn. This might have been the effects of John F. Kennedy Jr.'s Graves' disease, a thyroid disorder that drained him of energy and made him grouchy. Or it could have been the "family problem" he occasionally referred to when talking with his colleagues.

Something was disturbing him.

But John did not divulge personal matters to the people he worked with. He reserved his confidences for one or two close friends. And to them, he disclosed his worst fear: that his wife, Carolyn, was cheating on him.

Though he did not know it at the time, John's suspicions were not far-fetched. Carolyn had rekindled a relationship with her old boyfriend Michael Bergin, a former underwear model she had met—and fallen in love with—when they were both working for Calvin Klein.

"Michael lived in a second-floor walk-up in Greenwich Village, and I was in his apartment one day, and we were in the middle of something when he was buzzed on the intercom from the apartment building front door," one of Bergin's friends told me. "Michael asked me to leave immediately, and when I went out, I found Carolyn Bessette Kennedy hiding under the staircase.

"I said, 'Hi, Carolyn, what are you doing?' " the friend continued. "And she said, 'Oh, hi, I'm just going upstairs to Michael's.'

"When I got home, Michael called me and said in a kind of panic, 'You saw Carolyn! Why did you talk to her?' He really loved Carolyn, and wanted to protect her.

"Michael decided to stop seeing her. There is something strangely decent about Michael, and he was respectful of marriage vows. He didn't feel comfortable continuing a relationship with a married woman. But Carolyn was obsessed with him. And one day she went up the fire escape to his apartment and broke the window to get in."

Not long after this episode, Michael Bergin left New York to become an actor in Hollywood. Exceedingly handsome and well-built, he joined the cast of the television series *Baywatch* and appeared in a two-hour telefilm for Fox, *Baywatch Hawaiian Wedding*.

When I caught up with Bergin, I asked him about the time Carolyn Bessette Kennedy broke into his Greenwich Village apartment. At first he professed to have no recollection of such an incident. But as we talked, memories of his days with Carolyn began flowing back.

"Carolyn climbing fire escapes doesn't surprise me," Bergin told me. "If Carolyn wanted to get into someone's apartment, she would. If she had to be a spider woman to get into someone's apartment, she would. If she had to throw things, she would.

"There was one time when Carolyn saw me at a bar lighting a cigarette for an ex-girlfriend," he continued. "Carolyn came over, pushed the girl out of the way, got in my face, and screamed and yelled at me, and even drew a little blood from my face.

"I went home, and two minutes later Carolyn was at my door. I had to let her in or she would have knocked the whole building down. I had these tall, heavy religious candles, and she threw one through the window, smashing the windowpane, and another at the mirror above the fireplace mantel, which shattered. Then she knocked my television set and VCR onto the floor and jumped on my VCR and squashed it.

"I ran out of the apartment. I'm very athletic and fast, but she caught up with me, and started yelling at me, and taunting me, calling me a baby. And my adrenaline was flowing, and I turned around and pushed her away from me, and she went flying in the air and landed on the stoop of a building. That put an end to that, and we went back to my apartment.

"Carolyn and I had a very intense love for each other. We were inseparable for a couple of years. And I know deep in my heart that she still loved me even after she married John Kennedy. Some things just don't end."

For a time, Carolyn managed to keep her relationship with Bergin a secret from her husband. But then, during one of their screaming matches, she blurted out the truth.

As John later told a friend, he was thunderstruck. In his narcissistic self-absorption, he found it inconceivable that a woman would choose another man over him.

It took time for him to recover from this devastating blow, but eventually he convinced himself that his wife's behavior was more a reflection on *her* than on *him*. He persuaded Carolyn to see a psychiatrist. He made sure that she took her daily dose of antidepressant medication. To amuse her, he flew her to exotic hideaways for romantic vacations. And in March 1999 he began to join her in marriage counseling.

Nothing worked.

Four months later, on July 12, 1999, Carolyn stormed out of the marriage counselor's office when the therapist raised the subject of her drug habit. Then, in a supreme act of rejection, Carolyn began to sleep in a spare room that John had used to store his exercise equipment.

Humiliated and at his wit's end, John moved out of the North Moore Street loft and checked into a $2,000-a-night suite at the Stanhope. His room overlooked the museum and Central Park, where he had played with his sister as a little boy.

Page proofs and cover mock-ups for the upcoming issue of *George* were strewn over the blue pastel carpet in John's hotel suite. Several different facial expressions of Harrison Ford, *George*'s next cover subject, stared back at John from the floor. As the editor in chief, John assigned all the stories and chose the photographs, and he was particularly proud of an article on Congresswoman Mary Bono, the widow of Sonny Bono, which was illustrated by a photo of the scantily clad U.S. representative.

There was a lot about his role at *George* that John did not like. He was not particularly fond of the circulation battles for prime display space on magazine racks, or the trench warfare for advertising dollars. But he delighted in the side of the job that called upon him to make a good impression—the one-on-one interviews with notorious characters such as Fidel Castro and Larry Flynt, and the television appearances to promote new issues.

It turned out that John was not only attracted to adrenaline-pumping physical activities, like Rollerblading, hang gliding, kayaking, rappelling, skiing, and flying, he loved the thrust-and-parry in the public arena that came with being an editor of a national magazine.

Before the launch of *George,* John had consulted with his mother, who expressed her deep reservations about his magazine venture. Jackie shared these concerns with some of her friends in the media, including me.

"John has never shown the slightest interest in the magazine business before," she told me. "And he has no experience in journalism. Why would he want to start the kind of magazine that pries into people's private lives? He knows I don't approve of that."

The clash between Jackie and John over *George* was, in many ways, emblematic of their relationship. For as much as Jackie loved John, he also caused her a great deal of anguish and grief.

The trouble started early in John's life. After the assassination of his father, John's impulsive behavior developed into a serious problem. He was restless, had a low threshold for boredom, and could not sit still for any length of time. He was disruptive in school and did poorly academically. Jackie constantly had to chastise him.

When John finally got to be too much for Jackie to handle, she took him to see Dr. Ted Becker, a well-known child psychiatrist in New York City. Then, through a referral by a friend—the wife of the chairman of a Fortune 500 company—Jackie found a woman psycho-pharmacologist in Moline, Illinois, and brought her to New York on the chairman's company jet.

The doctor diagnosed John as suffering from ADD, attention deficit disorder, and dyslexia, an impaired ability to read. She prescribed Ritalin, a medication similar in its chemical makeup to the body's natural dopamine, which stimulates neurotransmitters in the brain and helps it work better.

John remained on Ritalin for the rest of his life, but the results were mixed. He flunked eleventh grade at Phillips Academy, a prestigious prep school in Andover, Massachusetts, and had to repeat the grade. After he graduated from Brown University, Jackie refused to let him apply to the Yale Drama School, although acting was clearly his strongest suit.*

The friction caused by John's desire to pursue a career in show business resulted in frequent shouting matches between mother and son. On one occasion, which was witnessed by a friend of Jackie's, John stormed out of a room, slamming the door in his mother's face.

It was at Jackie's urging that John went to law school at New York University, then joined the office of the Manhattan district attorney, which was run by Bobby Kennedy's old friend and colleague Robert Morgenthau (who was the son of FDR's Treasury secretary, Henry Morgenthau).

---

*In the summer of 1985, John appeared in a tiny off-Broadway theater as the male lead in Brian Friel's play *Winners*. The director, Nye Heron, called John "the best young actor I've seen in twelve years."

"John was a very hard worker, very conscientious," Morgenthau told me. "He was under the spotlight all the time and handled it very well. He liked being an assistant D.A., but not so much that he wanted to make a career out of it. I didn't see him much when he was here in my office. I didn't want him to feel he was being treated differently because of who he was. He desperately wanted to be treated like any other assistant D.A. The one time I deviated from that policy I took him to a church in Harlem for Martin Luther King's birthday. They asked me to bring John along. And they loved him."

But John and his mother were humiliated when he flunked the New York State Bar exam twice. Over his strenuous objections, she insisted that he hire a tutor and request a private room in which to take the bar exam—a privilege reserved for those with serious health problems. The third time, he passed the test.

In my conversations with Jackie, she tended to connect John's difficulties to the trauma of his father's assassination. She was pained that John had been robbed of a father figure at such an early age, and although she never came right out and said so, she spoke in an indirect way of her concerns that John might turn out to have sexual-identity problems, or even be homosexual. She sought to compensate for John's lack of a male role model by inviting former members of the Kennedy administration's New Frontier to her apartment to talk to John about his father's legacy.*

But as Jackie probed deeper into her past with her own psychoanalyst, she began to wonder about *her* contribution to John's troubles. Over the years Jackie had given a lot of thought to the subject of mothering. She had always harbored ambivalent feelings about her own mother, Janet Auchincloss, a compulsive perfectionist who was apt to confuse discipline with affection. Jackie loved her mother but was determined not to be like her. Nor did Jackie admire the kind of

---

*For a fuller description of these private tutorials, see the author's *All Too Human: The Love Story of Jack and Jackie Kennedy* and *Just Jackie: Her Private Years.*

mothering practiced by her mother-in-law, Rose Kennedy (a cold, domineering woman), or by her sisters-in-law—Ethel, Eunice, Pat, and Jean—who, Jackie believed, made their children feel as though they were total failures if they did not live up to their uncle, the President, and become powerful and famous in their own right.

As a result of her newly acquired introspection, Jackie began to reassess her relationship with John. Her son's first three years of life coincided with Jackie's own formative years in the White House, when she was changing from a shy, insecure woman in her early thirties into a self-confident First Lady who asserted herself more and more force-fully. During those years, Jackie was completely wrapped up in her role as the President's wife. She took extended trips to India, the Far East, and Europe and frequently weekended in the horse country of Virginia. She spent so much time away from the White House—and her infant son—that someone suggested to a network news anchor that he sign off his evening broadcast with the words, "Good night, Mrs. Kennedy, wherever you are."

"It's funny how we love to think that famous people are devoted parents," said psychoanalyst Sue Erikson Bloland. "But very often what appears like devotion in a mother is really her need to have the child support her own image.

"Down through the years," Bloland continued, "the Kennedys have put on a show of being this extraordinary close family. But it's all a compensation for what they don't have. Their longing for closeness is so powerful that it gives rise to this enormously compelling image that we see in the media. And this evokes a longing in us. 'Oh,' we can't help but say to ourselves, 'they must really have family closeness. I wish I had what they have.'"

John's mother-substitutes during the first few years of his life were his British nanny, Maud Shaw, and his Italian-born governess, Marta Sgubin. When Jackie was around, she took an interest in John's diet, his schooling, what clothes he wore, and how well he behaved in public. Like her own mother, of whom Jackie had once been so critical, she cared passionately about how John and Caroline made her look. Perhaps because she had been thrust by her husband's political career into the public eye, Jackie saw her children as extensions of herself.

The same was true of John's father, the President, with whom the little boy spent only fleeting moments, many of which were staged as photo opportunities (*John running to greet his father as he steps off the presidential helicopter . . . John cavorting under the presidential desk in the Oval Office*). John lived in a state of constant longing, waiting for those rare times when he would be invited into his father's presence.

Guarded by uniformed marines and Secret Service agents, John's father must have struck the little boy as an awesome figure. In the big Oval Office where his father "lived" most of the time, there was a mahogany desk, and on this desk there were buttons that his father used to summon people. His father could summon anyone he wished—not only the dark-suited men who always deferred to him and called him by his other name, "Mr. President," but also John's mother. With a mere push of a button, his father could call John's mother away from whatever she was doing and beckon her to his side. He had that kind of power.

John called his father Pooh-Pooh Head.

"John Kennedy," his father would say, "how dare you call the President of the United States a Pooh-Pooh Head? You rascal, you wait till I get hold of you."

But John insisted: "Pooh-Pooh Head."

Then one day, just before John's third birthday, Pooh-Pooh Head vanished from his life, and suddenly his mother was constantly by John's side, showering him with all the love and affection he had always yearned for. And while everyone around John mourned the death of the President, it was hard to tell from the little boy's behavior exactly how *he* felt. It would have been entirely natural if he rejoiced in the fact that he finally had his mother all to himself.

———

In view of Jackie's frequent and extended absences from the White House, it is ironic that her most famous saying had to do with child rearing.

"If you bungle raising your children," she said, "I don't think whatever else you do well matters very much."

In the 1960s, as historian Thomas C. Reeves writes, America was a nation "preoccupied with raising children and upward mobility." Americans celebrated Jackie as an ideal mother who managed to raise two astonishingly "normal" children under the most difficult circumstances.

Following her husband's assassination, Jackie moved to New York City, where she was able to devote more time to her fatherless children. Even after she married Greek shipping tycoon Aristotle Onassis, she insisted on spending most of her time in New York so that she could supervise her children's education and daily activities. She was praised for this, too. But Jackie told me that she did not think that anyone, herself included, deserved a medal for being a mother.

"Motherhood is a tricky business," Jackie once remarked over lunch.

In the last years of her life, Jackie said that her experience as a mother reminded her of a line from J. M. Barrie, the author of *Peter Pan, or The Boy Who Wouldn't Grow Up*. "The god to whom little boys say their prayers," writes Barrie, "has a face very much like their mother's."

Shortly before Jackie's death, she had a serious discussion with John about his future. She urged him to carry on his father's legacy by entering politics.

In interviews with reporters, John was understandably cagey about his interest in politics, which he referred to as "the family business." His apparent reluctance had nothing to do with his political beliefs, since like the Adams and Bush political dynasties, the Kennedy dynasty was more about sentiment and emotion than ideology.

John was both the beneficiary and the victim of the Camelot mystique. With their short memory, Americans recalled the Kennedys as having presided over a golden age, a time before the country was stained by assassination, Vietnam, racial strife, sexual permissiveness, Watergate, and national disillusionment. People seemed to project onto John all the good things and virtually none of the bad associated with the Kennedys.

Though they had no idea what John stood for politically, large numbers of Americans believed he should run for President. With the possible exception of Robert Lincoln, the Great Emancipator's son, there has never been a figure in American history quite like JFK Jr.

The pressure on John was enormous. And yet he managed to retain his sense of humor. On a visit to Chicago to drum up advertising support for *George,* John told a group of businessmen, "I've come to the city of my family's two biggest purchases—the Merchandise Mart and the 1960 presidential election."

John had been offered—and turned down—a post as an undersecretary in President Clinton's cabinet. And he was the first choice (before Hillary Rodham Clinton) among many Democrats in New York State to run for the seat being vacated by the state's senior senator, Daniel Patrick Moynihan.

However, John's new wife was clearly not ready for prime-time politics. Nor, for that matter, was John. He explored his feelings with Cokie Roberts, the ABC correspondent whose own father, Hale Boggs, had served in Congress with Jack Kennedy.

"Do you think [our fathers] would think that they would have more influence in the media today than in politics?" John asked Cokie.

"It was clearly something that he had spent a great deal of time working over in his own brain and made the decision, at least for the time being, that the place he wanted to be was in the media and that he did that quite intentionally," Cokie said. "He didn't just sort of fall into [*George*]."

Nevertheless, those close to the Kennedy family, such as former Defense secretary Robert McNamara, were certain that the next chapter in JFK Jr.'s life would be politics. And a number of astute observers of the presidency agreed.

Presidential historian Michael Beschloss, for example, believed that JFK Jr. had a "sort of post-modern political sensibility—a grasp of the fact that politics . . . is heavily larded with celebrities, that we're living at a time where especially young people are skeptical about politicians. He was trying to fashion an approach to politics that allowed him to sort of get across the old Kennedy ethic of public service and idealism, but to do it in the new vernacular of Generation X. And had he run for president in the twenty-first century, I think that, to some extent, would have been the basis."

John's uncle, Senator Edward Kennedy, argued that John's destiny was politics. And being the grandiose narcissist that he was, Teddy encouraged his nephew to set his sights on the biggest prize of all— the White House.

By the summer of 1999, Teddy believed the time had come for John to think seriously about a Kennedy Restoration. In Teddy's view, Albany, the capital of New York, would be the strongest possible launching pad for an eventual run for the presidency. He urged John to begin raising money and political backing for the New York governor's race in 2002.

There was only one hitch. John informed his uncle that his marriage to Carolyn was on the rocks and that he was thinking of divorce, even though he knew that such a step would ignite a firestorm of media coverage, put a serious dent in his iconic image, and cloud his political prospects. In an effort to keep his nephew's marriage intact, Teddy took a page out of old Joe Kennedy's playbook on how to handle touchy marital problems. He turned to a prominent Catholic prelate— New York's Cardinal John O'Connor—for help.

"Cardinal O'Connor loved being in the limelight and dealing with important people," said an associate. "At the Kennedy family's request, he got involved and tried to save John's marriage. The Cardinal was acting as a marital mediator at the time of John and Carolyn's death."

After John moved into the Stanhope on July 14, 1999, he spent a great deal of time on the phone, seeking solace from friends. During a long, rambling conversation with one of his closest friends, John said, "It's all falling apart. Everything is falling apart!"

Things were falling apart because John's mother was no longer around to hold them together. During her life, Jackie had been John's anchor in the stormy sea of his emotions. She encouraged him to be bold and courageous—but only up to a point. She drew the line at high-risk Kennedy behavior, which she deemed self-destructive.

For example, when John was a student at Brown University and wanted to take flying lessons, Jackie extracted a promise from him that he would never pilot his own plane. After all, Jackie reminded John, his Kennedy relatives had been dying in plane crashes at the rate of one every seven years for the past fifty years.

"Please don't do it," Jackie told John. "There have been too many deaths in the family already."

In the spring of 1994, when Jackie realized she was dying, she asked her longtime companion, the diamond dealer Maurice Tempelsman, to look after her children, especially John. But John had never felt particularly close to Tempelsman, who occupied a separate bedroom in his mother's apartment. After John's mother died—and before his loft in TriBeCa was ready for occupancy—he let Tempelsman know that he would like to have his mother's apartment to himself. He also suggested that the older man find his own place to live, which Tempelsman did by moving to the Sherry Netherlands Hotel.

John also ignored Tempelsman's advice about flying and began taking lessons at the Flight Safety Academy in Vero Beach, Florida.

"I worry about John flying," Tempelsman told a friend. "He's so distractable."

When John graduated, he presented a photo of himself to his flight instructors with the following inscription:

To Flight Safety Academy,
The bravest people in aviation
because people will only care where
I got my training if I crash.
Best, John Kennedy

Jackie had also cautioned John about the dangers of launching a new magazine. But a year after her death, he went ahead with plans for *George* anyway. At the time of *George*'s launch in September 1995, readers and advertisers flocked to the magazine because they wanted to be part of John's world. As a result, *George* became one of the most successful magazine launches in history, which made John feel like his own man for the first time.

However, Jackie's concerns about *George* eventually came true. The magazine began to hemorrhage money and was expected to lose nearly $10 million in 1999. To John's frustration, *George* never earned the respect of the journalistic community, which considered it an amateur venture.

For John, the failure of *George* was unthinkable. Beyond the private humiliation, the collapse of the magazine could derail his ambitious political plans. And so in recent weeks John had been seeking alternative sources of financing for his ailing magazine. The previous weekend, he and a certified flight instructor flew John's private plane, a single-engine Piper Saratoga, to Toronto to meet a prospective backer. John had also turned for help to his friend Steve Florio, the powerful president of Condé Nast, which publishes such glamorous titles as *Vogue* and *Vanity Fair*.

"I had contracted an infection in my carotid artery in a dentist's office, and had to have open-heart surgery," Florio recalled in an interview for this book. "Shortly before John's fatal crash, he called me and said, 'My cousin Arnold's here.' He put Arnold Schwarzenegger on the phone. Schwarzenegger said he had the same damn thing as I did.

"When I got out of the hospital, John invited me to lunch," Florio continued. " 'Why don't we go to San Domenico, and you can have a piece of grilled fish, and we can talk,' John said. What I thought was going to be just a friendly chat turned out to be a more substantive talk. Hachette had lost interest in *George,* and John wanted to know if we at Condé Nast would be interested in picking it up. And I said, 'Yes, *George* is a good magazine. Let's keep chatting over the next couple of months.' But John died before we could make a decision to save *George.*"

On the day after he checked into the Stanhope, Thursday, July 15, John visited his orthopedic surgeon at Lenox Hill Hospital to have a soft cast removed from his left ankle. Six weeks before, he had fractured his ankle in a hang gliding accident and had been using crutches to get around.

The ankle was still too tender to bear the full weight of his muscular six-foot-one, 190-pound frame. And his surgeon strongly advised him not to fly solo for at least another ten days.

The surgeon was not the only one who counseled caution. A few weeks before, just after John crashed his hang glider, his friend John Perry Barlow expressed concern that John had become overconfident about his flying. Barlow urged John to view his broken ankle as a warning sign.

John's Piper Saratoga II HP, for which he had paid $300,000, was a high-performance plane that seriously taxed his experience, which totaled only thirty-seven hours in the air with a certified flight instructor. No one—not even Carolyn—knew that John's meager hours "in command" did not meet insurance company requirements for high limits of flight coverage. His personal liability insurance did not include aircraft. As a result, John was flying without insurance on his life and those of his passengers.

On his last night alive, John planned to have cocktails at the Stanhope, then go to Yankee Stadium to watch Roger Clemens pitch against the Atlanta Braves. He and his friend Gary Ginsberg, a former editor at

George who was now working for Rupert Murdoch's News Corporation, were to be the guests of the Yankees' principal owner, George Steinbrenner, in his field-side box.

As always, the image-conscious John dressed with care. Then, with the help of his crutches, he made his way to the hotel elevator and descended to the lobby. When the doors opened, John swung himself onto the black-and-white marble floor and negotiated the several yards to the bar. The noisy room fell silent the moment he entered. Heads swiveled as he made his way to a corner table, where two young women were waiting. One of them was his wife, Carolyn. The other was Carolyn's sister Lauren Bessette, an attractive, dark-haired investment banker with Morgan Stanley.

Lauren told a friend that it had been her idea for the three of them to meet for drinks. She was gravely alarmed over Carolyn and John's decision to live apart, and she said that she thought it would be a good idea for them to discuss their problems in front of her. Maybe she could help break their emotional logjam.

But the relationship between John and Carolyn had become so tense and ugly that neither of them was in the mood to talk. They sat in stony silence. As Lauren told the story, she asked John and Carolyn to join her in holding hands. At first they refused. But when Lauren insisted, they reluctantly clasped her hands.

Lauren was aware that Carolyn had vowed never to fly with John in his plane. But as she squeezed her sister's hand, she urged her to make an exception and accompany her husband in his Piper Saratoga the next day to Hyannis Port, where family members and friends were assembling for the wedding of his cousin Rory Kennedy.

With the exception of John himself, Rory had suffered more from the Kennedy Curse than any other member of the family. Rory had never known her father, Robert Kennedy, because she had been born six months after his assassination in 1968. She was a teenager when her brother David died in 1984 of a heroin overdose. And in 1997 a second brother, Michael, died in a freak skiing accident in Aspen,

Colorado, while Rory gave him mouth-to-mouth resuscitation and cried, "Michael, now is the time to fight. Don't leave us!"

Lauren knew that John had promised to attend Rory's wedding. However, it apparently did not cross her mind that John's bad leg would make it difficult for him to work the foot controls of the plane. Nor did she give much thought to John's anguish and state of confusion over his troubled marriage, his failing magazine, and the recent news that his best friend and cousin, Tony Radziwill, was near death with testicular cancer.

No one, least of all Lauren, imagined that John would take up his plane if he thought he would be risking his life and the lives of others. After all, everyone assumed that John was not like his Kennedy relatives—reckless and irresponsible. He was cut from a different cloth.

But that was a fundamental misreading of John's character. In fact, in some respects he was more of a daredevil than the other Kennedys. And the reasons for that should have been obvious to everyone, including Lauren.

It is, of course, every boy's assignment in life to come to terms with his father and, in some ways, to try to outdo him. But John F. Kennedy Jr. bore a unique burden. He was heir to a man of such legendary dimensions that no amount of gossip about sexual romps in the White House swimming pool or dangerous liaisons with mob molls could dim his memory.

In the minds of most Americans, John's father was the most popular President of the twentieth century—the one against whom all Presidents were compared. If it was difficult for an elected President to match the brilliance of JFK, one could imagine the torments his son must have gone through to compete with a father who was more myth than man.

How could John outshine a father who was associated with so much power—political, military, and sexual? How could he eclipse the memory of a martyred President? How could he surpass a man who had been accorded the greatest public funeral in America in the twentieth century?

To measure up to his father, John had to be bolder and more courageous than any Kennedy. He had to ignore the ever-present threat of kidnapping and assassination and become an inveterate risk taker.

And so he traveled without a bodyguard. He attempted every form of extreme sport. He dove for buried treasure. He rappelled down the sides of mountains. He tested himself, pushed himself beyond the limit, flew his plane when he shouldn't have—all in an effort to establish his own identity.

But none of this apparently occurred to Lauren Bessette. She wanted to convince her sister to fly with John to Martha's Vineyard the next day. What would make Carolyn change her mind?

Then, as Lauren remembered the moment, she came up with an idea.

To encourage Carolyn, Lauren offered to fly along with the couple as far as Martha's Vineyard, where she planned to spend the weekend with friends. The three of them would make the flight together.

"Come on," she said, "it'll be fun."

First John, then Carolyn agreed to Lauren's proposal.

"Great," Lauren said. "Then I'll see you guys tomorrow at the airport."

EPILOGUE

THE FALL OF THE HOUSE OF KENNEDY

BY MIDDAY SATURDAY, JULY 17—nearly twenty hours since the plane carrying John, Carolyn, and Lauren had disappeared in the roiling fog over Martha's Vineyard—the major television networks started broadcasting periodic bulletins about the massive search-and-rescue operation.

The news spread like wildfire. Soon Carolyn's friends—some of New York's best-known young clothing designers, hair and makeup stylists, male models, and publicists—were heading downtown to her loft in TriBeCa. They let themselves in with the keys Carolyn had given them and gathered around her TV set in a grim, silent vigil.

With each passing hour, the chances of rescue grew dimmer and dimmer. At a certain point, one of the group—a woman's fashion designer—slipped away and went into the kitchen. There, he opened the door to the freezer compartment of the refrigerator and removed Carolyn's stash of cocaine.

"I didn't want some nosy cop finding Carolyn's drugs and leaking the story to the papers," he explained.

———

It took three days and the combined efforts of the Massachusetts State Police Underwater Recovery Team, the Coast Guard, the U.S. Navy, and the National Oceanic and Atmospheric Administration (NOAA) to find the wreckage of John's plane.

On Monday, July 19—thirty years to the day since Teddy Kennedy drove his car off a bridge into a pond on Chappaquiddick Island—the fragments of John's plane were spotted by the NOAA vessel *Rude* using side-scan sonar.

Thunderstorms and eight-foot waves swept through the area, reducing visibility and hampering efforts by the U.S. Navy recovery ship *Grasp*. When on Tuesday, July 20, navy divers were allowed to descend into the murky, fifty-two-degree water, they found part of the shattered plane strewn over a broad area of seabed 120 feet below the surface of the Atlantic Ocean.

The throttle and propeller controls were in the full-forward position, indicating that the plane had smashed into the water at great velocity. In his last moments alive, John had apparently experienced spatial disorientation, and his plane had gone into a fatal graveyard dive. The force of the cataclysmic crash snapped an engine off its mount truss and tore a large section of the cabin roof from the fuselage. The aluminum seats were buckled.

"The divers went in and recovered the human remains," Captain Burt Marsh, the U.S. Navy's supervisor of diving and salvage, told me. "It took a couple of hours. You can never play down the impact of recovering remains under circumstances like this. No diver likes that idea. It's not their favorite thing."

Flesh and bone had fared even worse than metal.

"At the moment of impact," a rescue expert told me, "John did not go through the windshield. The windshield went through him."

Caroline and her husband, Edwin Schlossberg, a tall, teddy-bearish man who designs museums and theme parks, brought their children— Rose, then fourteen, Tatiana, twelve, and Jack, nine—to the Church of St. Thomas More on Manhattan's Upper East Side for John and Carolyn Kennedy's memorial service.

The three Schlossberg children were rarely seen in public. Rose and Tatiana attended Brearley, an exclusive private girls' school. Jack was enrolled at Collegiate, the alma mater of his uncle, JFK Jr. The children's privacy was zealously guarded by their parents, and as a result, the public knew less about Rose, Tatiana, and Jack than about any Kennedy since the original Patrick arrived in Boston 150 years before.

As the Schlossbergs approached the church, which was ringed by TV cameras, Rose gave a graphic demonstration of just what she and her family thought of the media. She stuck out her tongue.

As the last surviving member of Camelot's First Family, Caroline faced a difficult decision: Should she follow her natural instincts and withdraw into seclusion, or should she pick up the torch dropped by her brother and assume a larger public role?

The answer to that question was not long in coming. A few months after the tragedy, Caroline made an appearance at a gala fund-raiser. She was wearing the spectacular diamond earrings that Aristotle Onassis had given her mother, and she seemed to have blossomed overnight into a stunning woman.

And that was only the first step in her new public diplomacy. With her brother gone, Caroline became the lone presenter of the annual Profile in Courage Award at the Kennedy Library. She had always been a poor public speaker; now she wowed the audience with her confident delivery.

Caroline then published a book of her mother's favorite poetry and edited an updated version of her father's Pulitzer Prize–winning *Profiles in Courage*. To promote these books, she appeared on TV talk shows, where she fielded viewers' questions with aplomb.

To almost everyone's surprise, Caroline accepted an appointment by New York's schools chancellor Joel Klein to become the chief private fund-raiser for the city's hard-pressed public schools.

Caroline was the moving force behind the Metropolitan Museum of Art's hugely popular exhibit of her mother's White House wardrobe. The exhibit moved to Washington, then overseas to Paris. At the black-tie opening at Paris's Musée des Arts Décoratifs, Caroline appeared in a vintage Chanel gown and with a flipped-up hairdo that was reminiscent of Jackie's style.

"She looked dignified but relaxed," said a woman who attended the event. "She read her speech in French, and when she sat down, she looked over at her husband, Ed Schlossberg, and gave him the thumbs-up sign. The crowd was delirious with excitement. Like her mother forty years before when she visited President Charles de Gaulle at the Elysée Palace, Caroline was the toast of Paris."

And what of the other Kennedys?

The current generation of Kennedys was once described to me as the tail of a comet whose blinding brightness has passed. And, indeed, an astonishing number of young Kennedys have begun to disappear from the public scene.

Joseph Kennedy II withdrew from politics after his reputation was sullied by a messy divorce. Max Kennedy, Joe's younger brother, quit his campaign for a seat in Congress after he stumbled in the polls. William Kennedy Smith toyed with the idea of running for office in Chicago, then thought better of it. Andrew Cuomo, who is married to Joe Kennedy's sister Kerry, abandoned his campaign for the Democratic gubernatorial nomination in New York. Mark Kennedy Shriver lost the Democratic primary in Maryland's Eighth Congressional District. And Kathleen Kennedy Townsend, Bobby's eldest daughter, who was once considered a possible vice presidential candidate, lost her bid to become governor of Maryland—the family's first general election defeat since Honey Fitz was beaten in a race for governor of Massachusetts in 1922. (The one exception, Patrick Kennedy, won reelection to the House of Representatives from tiny Rhode Island.)

Whether we are witnessing a political flameout remains to be seen. But one thing is certain: the Kennedys continue to be lashed by savage afflictions. Nine lives have been wrecked by the family curse in the last decade alone.

As the crown prince of the House of Kennedy, John F. Kennedy Jr. must surely have wondered about his place in this dark tale. Now that John is gone, we are left to wonder about the next victim of the Kennedy Curse.

ACKNOWLEDGMENTS

My stepson, Robertson Barrett, a graduate of the John F. Kennedy School of Government at Harvard University, assisted me in researching and editing portions of this book. A whiz in both the Old and New Media, Rob is a gifted writer—and thinker—and was a joy to work with as a collaborator.

My agent, Robert Gottlieb, conceived the idea and the title of this book. His partner at Trident Media, Daniel Strone, was a source of wisdom and encouragement throughout the three years it took me to complete the project. My friend Ronald Kessler played an invaluable role in bringing the manuscript to the attention of St. Martin's Press.

At St. Martin's Press, Sally Richardson, Matthew Shear, and Jennifer Weis provided a rare commodity nowadays—sharp, thorough editing. Their deft no. 2 pencils improved the structure, language, and substance of the text. Their publishing expertise, plus John Murphy's marketing skills and Steve Snider's art direction helped shape the "look" and "feel" of this volume.

Maureen O'Brien got this project off the ground and introduced me to several experts in things Irish American who deserve to be singled out for their generous assistance: Peter Quinn, Michael Coffey, Terry Golway, Malachy McCourt, Terry Moran, and Jay Tunney.

In Ireland, I owe a special debt of gratitude to Kevin Whelan, Fintan O'Toole, Daithi O'Hogan, Pat Quilty, Patrick Cronin, Micky Furlong, Patrick Grenan, Cormac O'Grada, and Anthony and Robbyn Summers.

For insights into the minds of five generations of Kennedys, I am indebted to Drs. Peter Neubauer and Werner Muensterberger, as well as to Sue Erikson Bloland and Dr. Mitchell Rosenthal.

For their valuable help in the voluminous research, I want to extend my thanks to Candace Trunzo, Christopher Carberry, and Robin Rizzuto.

Melissa Goldstein brought an artist's eye and a detective's instincts to bear on the acquisition, organizing, selection, and layout of the photographs.

My children—Karen and Alec Klein—and stepdaughter, Melissa Barrett Rhodes, were unstinting in their encouragement. And, of course, none of this would have been possible without the loving kindness of my wife, Dolores Barrett, who sustained me throughout the long months of creation.

SOURCES

AUTHOR'S INTERVIEWS

Floyd Abrams, Lou Adler, Rachel Altein, Jack Anderson, Joe Armstrong, Dr. Bob Arnot, Hélène Arpels, Jules Asher, Dr. Jiei Atacama, Dr. Michael Baden, Evan Balaban, Peter Beard, Dr. Jonathan Benjamin, Arthur Bennett, Michael Beschloss, Sue Erikson Bloland, Dr. Susan Blumenthal, Captain Greg Brown, Hamilton Brown, Edward Burns Sr., Sean Carberry, David Chalmers, Dr. Robert Cloninger, Michael Coffey, Doug Cohn, Tim Pat Coogan, David Crawford, Susan Crimp, Donald Crocker, Patrick Cronin, Rabbi Schlomo Cunin, Captain Sam DeBow, Linda Degh, Lisa DePaulo, Persi Diaconis, Sante D'Orazio, Dr. Larry Dossey, Keith Estabrook, Dr. Richard Evans, Michael Ferrara, Burt Fisher, Steve Florio, Dr. Bruce Forester, Peter Foskin, Sergeant William Freeman, Tony Frost, Micky Furlong, Nicholas Gage, Edward Galvin, Barbara Gamarekian, Barbara Gibson, Jean-Louis Ginibre, Terry Golway, Doris Kearns Goodwin, Andrew Greeley, Vartan Gregorian, Patrick Grenan, William F. Halsey III, Nigel Hamilton, Patricia Hardy, Professor Michael Harper, Captain Mark Helmkamp, Robert Haydon Jones, Kelly Kapicka, Sheila Rauch Kennedy, Joseph Kopechne, Alexandra Kotur, Barry Krischer, Dr. Richard Kurin, Dr. Eugene Mahon, Mick Maloney, Captain Burt Marsh, Kerry McCarthy, Malachy McCourt, Pat McKenna, Terry Moran, Robert Morgenthau, Dr. Robert Moyzis, Dr. Werner Muensterberger, Dr. Peter Neubauer, Willie Newsome, Cathy Nolan, Cormac O'Grada, Daithi O'Hogan, Fintan O'Toole, Ion Milai Pacepa, David Pecker, Lady Patricia Pelham, Richard Andrew Pierce, Pat Quilty, Peter Quinn, Dr. Chit Ranawat, Neville Raymond, Sean Reidy, John Richardson, Terry Rioux, Ellen Roberts, Robert Scally, John Scanlon, Mark Scheiner, Hank Searls, Kevin Selvig, Lyndal L. Shaneyfelt, Dr. David Skinner, Liz Smith, Thom Smith, the Reverend Lawrence Solan, Christine Stapleton, Jocelyn Stern, Lynn Tesoro, Brett Tjaden, Michael Tomarra, Candace Trunzo, Peter Tufo, Jay Tunney, Roy Wachtel, Leon Wagner, Lieutenant Commander David Waterman, John Weber, Professor Kevin Whelan, Darrell Whiteman, Paul Wilmot, Garrett Yount, Helena Zimny.

DOCUMENTS

Deposition of Patrick H. Barry. Fifteenth Judicial Circuit, Criminal Division, Palm Beach County, Florida. Fink & Carney Computerized Reporting Services, New York, April 30, 1991.

Deposition of Stephen P. Barry. Fifteenth Judicial Circuit, Criminal Division, Palm Beach County, Florida. Fink & Carney Computerized Reporting Services, New York, April 30, 1991.

Bludworth, David H. State Attorney. *Petition for Writ of Prohibition*. Fifteenth Judicial Circuit, District Court of Appeals of the State of Florida, Fourth District, September 10, 1991.

Statements of Patricia Bowman. Palm Beach Police Department, March 30–April 25, 1991.

Statement of Michele Cassone. Palm Beach Police Department, April 5, 1991.

Corcoran Gallery of Art. *Jacqueline Kennedy: The White House Years*. Washington, D.C., March 13, 2002.

Deposition of Chuck Desiderio. Fifteenth Judicial Circuit, Criminal Division, Palm Beach County, Florida. Fink & Carney Computerized Reporting Services, New York, April 30, 1991.

Statement of Chuck Desiderio. Palm Beach Police Department, April 30, 1991.

Glynn, Joseph Martin, Jr., ed. *Manual for Irish Genealogy*. Newton, Mass.: Irish Family Historical Society, 1979.

Deposition of Dr. Lynn Gulledge. Fifteenth Judicial Circuit of Florida. Tyler, Eaton, Morgan & Nichols, Court Reporters, October 26, 1991.

Statement of Dr. Lynn Gulledge. Office of the State Attorney, Palm Beach, Florida, July 21, 1991.

Hamilton, Nigel. Interview with James A. Rousmaniere and Martha Reed. Nigel Hamilton Collection, Massachusetts Historical Society, April 6, 1989.

———. Interview with Frank Waldrop. Nigel Hamilton Collection, Massachusetts Historical Society, May 15, 1989.

———. Interview with John Hersey. Nigel Hamilton Collection, Massachusetts Historical Society, May 26, 1991.

———. Interview with Fred Good. Nigel Hamilton Collection, Massachusetts Historical Society, December 1991.

The Historical Research Center, Inc. *Family Name History: Fitzgerald*. The Historical Research Center, Inc., 2001.

Holmes, Warren D. Letter to Sergeant Keith A. Robinson. Palm Beach Police Department, April 26, 1991.

Irish Department of Foreign Affairs. *Folklore in Ireland*. Dublin, April 1995.

Irish Genealogical Society International. *Families in Ireland from the 11th to the End of the 16th Century*. Philip MacDermott, M.D., ed.

James, Ann. *The Kennedy Family Scandals and Tragedies*. Lincolnwood, Ill.: Publications International, Ltd., 1991.

John Fitzgerald Kennedy Trust. *Dunbrody: Rebirth of an Emigrant Ship, 1845–2001.* New Ross, Co. Wexford, Ireland, February 11, 2001.

Deposition of Edward M. Kennedy. Fifteenth Judicial Circuit, Criminal Division, Palm Beach County, Florida. Fink & Carney Computerized Reporting Services, New York, May 1, 1991.

Kennedy, Kathleen. Letter to John F. Kennedy. JFK Personal Papers, John F. Kennedy Library, December 22, 1944.

———. Letters to family. JFK Personal Papers, John F. Kennedy Library, February 11, 17, and 22, 1944.

Deposition of Patrick J. Kennedy. Fifteenth Judicial Circuit, Criminal Division, Palm Beach County, Florida. Fink & Carney Computerized Reporting Services, New York, May 3, 1991.

Landmark Preservation Commission (Palm Beach, Florida). *1095 North Ocean Boulevard: Designation Report.* April 20, 1990.

Deposition of Lisa J. Lattes. Fifteenth Judicial Circuit, Criminal Division, Palm Beach County, Florida. Fink & Carney Computerized Reporting Services, New York, October 5, 1991.

Statement of Lisa Lattes. Office of the State Attorney, Palm Beach, Florida, July 20, 1991.

Statement of Anne Mercer. Palm Beach Police Department, April 29, 1991.

Deposition of Leonard Mercer. Fifteenth Judicial Circuit, Criminal Division, Palm Beach County, Florida. Mudrick, Witt, Levy & Consor Reporting Agency, Inc., West Palm Beach, Florida, October 17, 1991.

Miller, Herbert J., Jr. Letter to State Attorney David H. Bludworth. May 2, 1991.

New Mexico Board of Examiners. *Application for Approval to Practice as a Resident Physician: William K. Smith.* June 24, 1991.

O'Dowd, Niall. *John F. Kennedy Junior's Irish Legacy.* Irish American Social Club of Sacramento, California, July 25, 1999.

Office of the State Attorney, Florida Fifteenth Judicial Circuit. "Senator Edward Kennedy Chronology," March 31, 1991.

Statement of Lieutenant Thomas M. Perry. Palm Beach Police Department, August 1, 1991.

Statement of Detective Christine E. Rigolo. Palm Beach Police Department, May 8, 1991.

Deposition of Detective Christine Ellen Rigolo. Fifteenth Judicial Circuit, Criminal Division, Palm Beach County, Florida. Fink & Carney Computerized Reporting Services, New York, July 23, 1991.

Rousmaniere, James A. *John F. Kennedy Project*. Oral History Research Office, Columbia University, 1977.

Statement of Stephen Michael Scott. Office of the State Attorney, Palm Beach, Florida, July 2, 1991.

Deposition of Amanda Smith. Fifteenth Judicial Circuit, Criminal Division, Palm Beach County, Florida. Fink & Carney Computerized Reporting Services, New York, April 30, 1991.

Deposition of Jean K. Smith. Fifteenth Judicial Circuit, Criminal Division, Palm Beach County, Florida. Fink & Carney Computerized Reporting Services, New York, April 30, 1991.

ARTICLES

"London Reports Kathleen Kennedy Will Be Married Next Saturday," *The Boston Globe*, May 1, 1944.

"Kathleen Kennedy Soon to Marry Eldest Son of Duke of Devonshire," *The Boston Globe*, May 4, 1944.

"Kathleen Kennedy, 24, to Wed British Lord," *Boston Herald*, May 4, 1944.

"Mrs. Kennedy in Hospital Here; Condition Good," *The Boston Globe*, May 5, 1944.

"Fitz Backs Granddaughter's Choice but Bogs Down on Wedding Details," *Boston Herald*, May 5, 1944.

"Kennedy Daughter Weds in London," *The Boston Globe*, May 6, 1944.

"Mrs. J. P. Kennedy Quits Hospital Today," *The Boston Globe*, May 6, 1944.

"Mrs. Kennedy Leaves Hospital as Daughter Weds in England," *Boston Herald*, May 6, 1944.

"Mrs. Kennedy Leaves Boston by Plane," *The Boston Globe*, May 6, 1944.

"Miss Kennedy Becomes Bride of Titled Briton," *The Boston Globe*, May 7, 1944.

"War Bars Cable to Kennedys as Daughter Is Wed in London," *Boston Herald*, May 7, 1944.

"Earl Killed in Plane Crash," *Boston American*, May 14, 1948.

"Rep. Kennedy Grief-Stricken in Washington," *The Independent* (Boston), May 14, 1948.

"Kennedy Girl, Peer Die in Plane Crash," *Traveler* (Boston), May 14, 1948.

"Chance Meeting Led to Death of Kathleen," *Boston American*, May 15, 1948.

"Kennedys at Hyannis," *Boston Herald*, May 15, 1948.

"Body of Kennedy's Daughter Is Taken to Town from Crash Scene," *The Independent* (Augusta, Me.), May 15, 1948.

"Kennedy Home in Sorrow," *Sunday Post* (Boston), May 15, 1948.

"Kennedy Asks to Be Executor of Sister's Estate," *The Boston Globe,* June 29, 1949.

Lotham, Arnold. "Can't Rest Beside Him," *Photoplay,* December 1970.

Radcliffe, Donnie. "Keeper of the Clan: The Tough Warmth of Ethel Kennedy," *The Washington Post,* June 4, 1981.

Prial, Frank J. "Of Sex, a Senator and a Press Circus," *The New York Times,* April 6, 1991.

Butterfield, Fox. "Views of the Kennedy House: Poignant Past, Busy Present," *The New York Times,* April 8, 1991.

McConagha, Alan. "Kennedy Media Control Slipping," *Washington Times,* April 11, 1991.

"Who's Who in the Palm Beach Rape Case," *The Palm Beach Post,* April 14, 1991.

"The Soul of the Kennedys," *Washington Times,* April 18, 1991.

"Hints of Favoritism Still Swirl Around '84 Kennedy Probe," *Palm Beach Post,* April 21, 1991.

Pallesen, Tim. "Pro-Kennedy Charges Again Haunt State Attorney," *Palm Beach Post,* April 21, 1991.

" 'New York Times' Regrets Action in Kennedy Rape Case," Associated Press, April 26, 1991.

Mailander, Jodi. "Gumshoes Seek Tale of Sleaze to Discredit Kennedy Accuser," *Palm Beach Post,* April 28, 1991.

"Naming the Victim," *Newsweek,* April 29, 1991.

Morrow, Lance. "The Trouble with Teddy," *Time,* April 29, 1991.

Donnelly, John, and Dave von Drehle. "Kennedy Kin Faces Rape Count," *The Miami Herald,* May 10, 1991.

Jordan, Mary. "Willy Smith, the 'Independent' Kennedy, Anonymous No More," *The Washington Post,* May 10, 1991.

Goldberg, Karen, and Joe Dimaola. "Lawyers: Acquittal Probable," *Fort Lauderdale Sun-Sentinel,* May 16, 1991.

"Spotlight on the Senator: What Did Teddy Know?" *Newsweek,* May 27, 1991.

Carlson, Margaret. "When in Doubt, Obfuscate," *Time,* May 27, 1991.

Kacoha, Margie. "Miller a Longtime Lawyer for Kennedys," *Palm Beach Daily News,* June 9, 1991.

Zeman, David. "Smith Switches Attorneys in Rape Defense," *The Miami Herald,* June 25, 1991.

"Maid Disputes Kennedy Friend's Story," *The Miami Herald,* June 26, 1991.

Zeman, David. "Witness Disputes Kennedy," *The Miami Herald,* July 17, 1991.

Clifford, Timothy. "Smith Rape Defense to Focus on Woman's Sexual History," *Newsday,* July 19, 1991.

Stapleton, Christine. "Evidence of Similar Crimes Can Devastate a Defense," *Palm Beach Post,* July 24, 1991.

———. "Smith Assault Statements Similar," *Palm Beach Post,* July 24, 1991.

Ellicott, Val, and Christine Stapleton. "Kennedy Lawyer Tried to Contact '88 Accuser," *Palm Beach Post,* August 10, 1991.

Stapleton, Christine. "Smith Attorney: Woman Is Mentally Ill," *Palm Beach Post,* August 10, 1991.

Zeman, David. "Smith Defense: Alleged Victim Resents Men," *The Miami Herald,* August 10, 1991.

Treen, Joe. "Maximum Moira," *People,* August 12, 1991.

Stapleton, Christine. "Doctor Backs Story Claiming '88 Rape Try by Smith," *Palm Beach Post,* August 22, 1991.

Dionne, E. J. "Changes for Kennedy: Friends See Toll from Palm Beach Incident," *The Washington Post,* August 28, 1991.

"Psychologist Says Smith, Accuser Have Serious Emotional Problems," Associated Press in *Palm Beach Post,* October 6, 1991.

Jordan, Mary. "The Prosecutor Never Rests: Moira Lasch, Building the Case Against William Kennedy Smith," *The Washington Post,* October 30, 1991.

White, Diane. "Willie's Lawyers Dress Down Accuser," *New York Daily News,* November 10, 1991.

Ellicott, Val. " 'Will' Smith Strikes a Pose at Photographers' Request," *Palm Beach Post,* November 11, 1991.

Brock, Pope. "Hot on the Trial," *People,* December 16, 1991.

Hiltbrand, David. "Picks & Pans," *People,* December 23, 1991.

Treen, Joe. "The Most Famous Woman Never Seen," *People,* December 23, 1991.

Dunne, Dominick. "The Verdict," *Vanity Fair,* March 1992.

Cerabino, Frank. "Twists, Tangles in Kennedy Case," *Palm Beach Post,* April 14, 1992.

Perry, Tony. "San Diego at Large: He Leaves No Trash Can Unturned in Digging Up Dirt on Rich, Famous," *Los Angeles Times,* December 6, 1992.

Brozan, Nadine, "Chronicle," *The New York Times,* April 27, 1993.

Gleick, Elizabeth. "Fighting Words," *People,* November 8, 1993.

"In Loving Memory: Jacqueline Bouvier Kennedy Onassis: 1929–1994," *Town & Country,* July 1994.

"Remembering Jackie," *Life: Special Commemorative Edition,* July 15, 1994.

"Love and the Law," *People,* March 6, 1995.

Marvel, Mark. "Life & Liberty," *Interview,* December 1995.

Klein, Edward. "The Man He Might Have Become," *Parade,* August 25, 1996.

Bumiller, Elisabeth. "The Newest Kennedy, Poised for the Part," *The New York Times,* September 29, 1996.

Conroy, Sarah Booth. "JFK Jr., Hitched to Tradition," *The Washington Post,* September 30, 1996.

Collins, James. "By George, He Got Married!" *Time,* October 7, 1996.

Mead, Rebecca. "Caroline, Meet Carolyn." *New York,* October 7, 1996.

"JFK's Wedding: Special Collector's Edition," *National Enquirer,* October 8, 1996.

"Sexy Past of JFK Bride," *Globe,* October 8, 1996.

Gerhart, Ann. "Myth America," *The Washington Post,* October 9, 1996.

"The 25 Most Intriguing People of the Year!" *People,* December 30, 1996.

"Breaking Ranks," *People,* June 25, 1997.

"The Kennedys: The Third Generation," *Life* special issue, July 7, 1997.

Adams, Cindy. *New York Post,* October 19, 1998.

"Jackie's Gift," *People,* October 26, 1998.

O'Brien, Tim. "Forestry to Fund Ship's U.S. Voyage," *Irish Times,* November 9, 1998.

McCarthy, Michael J. "America Saw Itself in DiMaggio, and It Liked What It Saw," *The Wall Street Journal,* March 9, 1999.

"Quote of the Week," *People,* March 29, 1999.

Belkin, Douglas. "A Kennedy Curse?" *The Palm Beach Post,* July 23, 1999.

Kennedy, Edward. Eulogy for John F. Kennedy Jr. in *New York Post,* July 24, 1999.

James, Caryn. "Generating Significance to Apply to Celebrity," *The New York Times,* July 24, 1999.

"Special Report: John F. Kennedy Jr., 1960–1999," *Time,* July 26, 1999.

"Prince of the City," *New York,* August 2, 1999.

"Lost in the Night," *People,* August 2, 1999.

"Remembering John F. Kennedy Jr.," *People,* August 2, 1999.

"Special Report: Ask Not . . ." *Time,* August 2, 1999.

"Hour of Loss," *People,* August 9, 1999.

Peretz, Evgenia. "The Private Princess," *Vanity Fair,* September 1999.

Nickell, Joe. "Curses: Foiled Again," *Skeptical Inquirer,* November 1, 1999.

"JFK's Secret Lover," *National Enquirer,* January 18, 2000.

Weinraub, Bernard. "Just One of the Gals," *McCall's,* May 2000.

"JFK: Heartbreaking Autopsy Secret," *National Enquirer,* July 18, 2000.

"To Have and to Hold," *People,* July 24, 2000.

"Crash Photos: JFK Wreckage Reveals His Final Act of Heroism," *National Enquirer,* July 25, 2000.

Marin, Rick. "Men Are Crazy for Women Who Are, Too," *The New York Times,* February 12, 2001.

"JFK Jr.'s Jeep Sold on eBay," Associated Press, March 23, 2001.

"Farewell Issue," *George,* May 2001.

"JFK Jr.'s Troubled Last Days," *Globe,* January 22, 2002.

Fee, Gayle, and Laura Raposa. "Inside Track," *Boston Herald,* August 14, 2002.

Orin, Deborah. "Clan Baked: Another Kennedy Pol Falters," *New York Post,* August 19, 2002.

Duin, Julia. "Oh Lordy: 40; Baby Boomers Find Life Goes on in Middle Age," *Washington Times,* August 22, 2002.

Brouwer, Julian. "We Need Caroline: Plea to JFK's Girl Over Family Crisis," *Sunday Mirror,* August 25, 2002.

"The Fading Lure of Camelot," *The Economist,* August 31, 2002.

"Magical History Tour: A Busload of Kennedys Pay Homage to the Past—Their Own—on a Summer Road Trip," *People,* September 2, 2002.

Dart, Bob. "Kennedy Mystique Enlivens Maryland Races," *Palm Beach Post,* September 8, 2002.

Espo, Dave. "Campaign Notebook: Republicans Concerned About Gekas Re-election in Pennsylvania," Associated Press, September 9, 2002.

"Inside Track," *Boston Herald,* September 11, 2002.

Barker, Jeff. "For Shriver, Kennedy Ties Not Enough in 8th District; Voters Saw Van Hollen as Stronger vs. Morella," *Baltimore Sun,* September 12, 2002.

"Page Six: Kennedy's Loss Tolls Darkly," *New York Post,* September 13, 2002.

Boyer, Dave. "Shriver's Loss Suggests Kennedy Dynasty Fades; Still, Liberal Followers Say the Younger Generation Can Look to Having a Role in Politics," *Washington Times,* September 15, 2002.

Schlesinger, Arthur. "JFK Revisited," *Cigar Aficionado*, date unknown.

Clines, Francis X. "In Maryland, a Blowout Becomes a Nail-Biter," *The New York Times,* September 15, 2002.

Quinn, Peter. "Looking for Jimmy," *The World of Hibernia*, date unknown.

BOOKS

Aalen, F. H. A., Kevin Whelan and Matthew Stout, eds. *Atlas of the Irish Rural Landscape*. Cork, Ireland: Cork University Press, 1997.

Anderson, Christopher. *The Day John Died*. New York: William Morrow, 2000.

Ash, Jennifer. *Private Palm Beach: Tropical Style*. New York: Abbeville Press, 1992.

Beatty, Jack. *The Rascal King: The Life and Times of John Michael Curley, 1874–1958*. Cambridge, Mass.: Da Capo Press, 1993.

Berlitz, Charles. *The Bermuda Triangle: An Incredible Saga of Unexplained Disappearances*. Garden City, N.Y.: Doubleday, 1974.

Beschloss, Michael R. *Kennedy and Roosevelt: The Uneasy Alliance*. New York: W. W. Norton, 1980.

Bourke, Angela. *The Burning of Bridget Cleary*. New York: Viking, 1999.

Bowen, Croswell. *The Curse of the Misbegotten: A Tale of the House of O'Neill*. New York: McGraw-Hill, 1959.

Bryant, Traphes, with Frances Spatz Leighton. *Dog Days at the White House: The Outrageous Memoirs of the Presidential Kennel Keeper*. New York: Macmillan, 1975.

Cahill, Thomas. *How the Irish Saved Civilization*. New York: Doubleday, 1995.

Campbell, Lily B. *Shakespeare's Tragic Heroes: Slaves of Passion*. Gloucester, Mass.: Peter Smith, 1973.

Carter, Howard, and A. C. Mace. *The Discovery of the Tomb of Tutankhamen*. New York: Dover Publications, 1977.

Chowdhury, Bernie. *The Last Dive: A Father and Son's Fatal Descent into the Ocean's Depths*. New York: HarperCollins, 2000.

Clinch, Nancy Gager. *The Kennedy Neurosis: A Psychological Portrait of an American Dynasty*. New York: Grosset Dunlap, 1973.

Clymer, Adam. *Edward M. Kennedy: A Biography*. New York: William Morrow, 1999.

Coffey, Michael, and Terry Golway, eds. *The Irish in America*. New York: Hyperion, 1997.

Collier, Peter, and David Horowitz. *The Kennedys: An American Drama*. New York: Summit Books, 1984.

Colman, Terry. *Going to America*. Baltimore: Genealogical Publishing Co., 1998.

Cowman, Des, ed. *The Famine in Waterford, 1845–1850*. Dublin: Geography Publications, 1995.

Cronin, Mike. *A History of Ireland*. New York: Palgrave, 2001.

Cronin, Patrick J. *Aubrey de Vere: The Bard of Curragh Chase*. County Limerick, Ireland: Askeaton Civic Trust, 1997.

———. *Eas Cead Tine: "The Waterfall of the Hundred Fires."* County Limerick, Ireland: Askeaton Civic Trust, 1999.

Davies, Robertson. *What's Bred in the Bone*. New York: Viking Penguin, 1985.

Davis, John H. *The Kennedy Clan: Dynasty and Disaster 1848–1984*. London: Sidgewick & Jackson, 1985.

Demaria, Robert. *"That Kennedy Girl": A Biographical Novel*. Port Jefferson, N.Y.: Vineyard Press, 1999.

Dinneen, Joseph F. *The Kennedy Family*. Boston: Little, Brown, 1959.

Dobrynin, Anatoly. *In Confidence: Ambassador to America's Six Cold War Presidents*. Seattle: University of Washington Press, 1995.

Dossey, Larry, M.D. *Be Careful What You Pray For . . . You Just Might Get It*. San Francisco: HarperCollins, 1997.

———. *Reinventing Medicine*. San Francisco: HarperCollins, 1998.

Duncliffe, William J. *The Life and Times of Joseph P. Kennedy*. New York: McFadden-Bartell, 1965.

Eldredge, John. *Wild at Heart: Discovering the Secret of a Man's Soul*. Nashville: Thomas Nelson Publishers, 2001.

Ellis, Peter Berresford. *A History of the Working Class*. New York: George Braziller, 1973.

———. *Dictionary of Celtic Mythology*. Oxford: Oxford University Press, 1992.

Erikson, Erik H. *Young Man Luther: A Study in Psychoanalysis and History*. New York: W. W. Norton, 1958.

Evans, E. Estyn. *The Personality of Ireland: Habitat, Heritage and History*. Dublin: Lilliput Press, 1992.

———. *Ireland and the Atlantic Heritage: Selected Writings*. Dublin: Lilliput Press, 1996.

Finneran, Richard J., ed. *The Collected Poems of W. B. Yeats*. New York: Scriber, 1996.

Fowler, Marian. *Hope: Adventures of a Diamond*. New York: Ballantine Books, 2002.

Gage, Nicholas. *Greek Fire: The Story of Maria Callas and Aristotle Onassis*. New York: Alfred A. Knopf, 2000.

Gatti, Arthur. *The Kennedy Curse*. Chicago: Henry Regnery Company, 1976.

Gibson, Barbara. *Life with Rose Kennedy: An Intimate Account*. New York: Warner Books, 1986.

Gibson, Barbara, and Ted Schwarz. *The Kennedys: The Third Generation*. New York: Kensington, 1999.

―――. *Rose Kennedy and Her Family: The Best and Worst of Their Lives and Times*. New York: Carol Publishing Group, 1995.

Giglio, James. *The Presidency of John F. Kennedy*. Lawrence, Kan.: The University Press of Kansas, 1992.

Gilligan, Carol. *The Birth of Pleasure*. New York: Alfred A. Knopf, 2002.

Golway, Terry. *The Irish in America*, edited by Michael Coffey. New York: Hyperion, 1997.

Goodwin, Doris Kearns. *The Fitzgeralds and the Kennedys: An American Saga*. New York: Simon & Schuster, 1987.

―――. *No Ordinary Time: Franklin and Eleanor Roosevelt: The Home Front in World War II*. New York: Simon & Schuster, 1994.

Graham, Katherine. *Personal History*. New York: Vintage, 1998.

Gregory, Lady. *Irish Myths and Legends*. Philadelphia: Courage Books, 1998.

Halberstam, David. *The Fifties*. New York: Villard Books, 1993.

Hamer, Dean, and Peter Copeland. *Living with Our Genes: Why They Matter More Than You Think*. New York: Doubleday, 1998.

Hamilton, Edith. *Mythology*. New York: Little, Brown and Company, 1942.

―――. *The Greek Way*. New York: Time, Inc., 1963.

Hamilton, Nigel. *JFK: Reckless Youth*. New York: Random House, 1992.

Handlin, Oscar. *Boston's Immigrants 1790–1880*. Cambridge: Harvard University Press, 1991.

Hersh, Seymour M. *The Dark Side of Camelot*. Boston: Little, Brown, 1997.

Higham, Charles. *Rose: The Life and Times of Rose Fitzgerald Kennedy*. New York: Pocket Books, 1995.

Hollett, David. *Passage to the New World: Packet Ships and Irish Famine Emigrants 1845–1851*. Gwent, Great Britain: P. H. Heaton Publishing, 1995.

Jones, January. *Oh, No . . . Jackie-O!: The Unspeakable Is $poken! A Theory*. P. J. Publishing, 1998.

Jung, C. G. *Synchronicity: An Acausal Connecting Principle*. Princeton, N.J.: Princeton University Press, 1973.

Kappel, Kenneth. *Chappaquiddick Revealed: What Really Happened*. New York: Lamplight Publications, 1989.

Kenneally, Thomas. *The Great Shame*. New York: Doubleday, 1998.

Kennedy, Brian Patrick. *The Irish Kennedys: The Story of the "Rebellious O'Kennedys."* Brisbane, Australia: Gaeltachta Publishers, 1998.

Kennedy, Joseph. *I'm for Roosevelt*. New York: Reynal and Hitchcock, 1936.

Kennedy, Rose. *Times to Remember*. Garden City, N.Y.: Doubleday, 1974.

Kennedy, Sheila Rauch. *Shattered Faith: A Woman's Struggle to Stop the Catholic Church from Annulling Her Marriage*. New York: Henry Holt, 1997.

Kennedy, William. *Legs*. New York: Penguin Books, 1975.

Keough, Daire, and Nicholas Furlong, eds. *The Mighty Wave: The 1798 Rebellion in Wexford*. Dublin: Four Courts Press, 1996.

Kernberg, Otto, M.D. *Borderline Conditions and Pathological Narcissism*. New York: Jason Aronson, Inc., 1980.

Kessler, Ronald. *The Sins of the Father*. New York: Warner Books, 1996.

Kibberd, Declan. *Inventing Ireland*. Cambridge: Harvard University Press, 1995.

Koskoff, David E. *Joseph P. Kennedy: A Life and Times*. Englewood Cliffs, N.J.: Prentice-Hall, 1974.

Krock, Arthur. *Memoirs: Sixty Years on the Firing Line*. New York: Funk and Wagnalls, 1968.

Kusche, Larry. *The Bermuda Triangle Mystery Solved*. Amherst, N.Y.: Prometheus Books, 1986.

Lasch, Christopher. *The Culture of Narcissism: American Life in An Age of Diminishing Expectations*. New York: W. W. Norton, 1991.

Laxton, Edward: *The Famine Ships: The Irish Exodus to America*. New York: Henry Holt, 1996.

Leamer, Laurence. *The Kennedy Men: 1901–1963*. New York: HarperCollins, 2001.

———. *The Kennedy Women: The Saga of an American Family*. New York: Villard Books, 1994.

Leigh, Wendy. *Prince Charming: The John F. Kennedy Jr. Story*. New York: Penguin Books, 1994.

Lichte, Shannon McMahon. *Irish Wedding Traditions*. New York: Hyperion, 2001.

Lieberson, Goddard, ed. *John Fitzgerald Kennedy . . . As We Remember Him*. New York: Atheneum, 1965.

Lowe, Jacques. *JFK Remembered: An Intimate Portrait by His Personal Photographer*. New York: Gramercy Books, 1993.

Lowen, Alexander, M.D. *Narcissism: Denial of the True Self*. New York: Collier Books, 1985.

Macken, Walter. *The Silent People*. Dublin: Pan Books, 1978.

Madsen, Axel. *Gloria and Joe: The Star-Crossed Love Affair of Gloria Swanson and Joe Kennedy*. New York: William Morrow, 1988.

Malinowski, Bronislaw. *Magic, Science and Religion, and Other Essays*. Westport, Conn.: Greenwood Press, 1984.

Marvin, Richard. *The Kennedy Curse*. New York: Belmont Books, 1969.

McCormick, Donald. *The Hell-Fire Club*. London: Jarrolds Publishers, 1958.

McCourt, Malachy. *A Monk Swimming: A Memoir*. New York: Hyperion, 1998.

McTaggart, Lynne. *Kathleen Kennedy: Her Life and Times*. New York: Holt, Rinehart, and Winston, 1983.

Morash, Christopher. *Writing the Irish Famine*. Oxford: Oxford University Press, 1995.

O'Brien, Edna. *Mother Ireland: A Memoir*. New York: Penguin Putnam, 1999.

O'Connor, Peter. *Beyond the Mist: What Irish Mythology Can Teach Us About Ourselves*. London: Victor Gollancz, 2000.

O'Connor, Thomas H. *The Boston Irish: A Political History*. Boston: Back Bay Books, 1995.

O'Flaherty, Liam. "Going into Exile," in Roland Hindmarsh, ed., *Waiting and Other Modern Stories*. Cambridge: Cambridge University Press, 1979.

O'Hanlon, Thomas J. *The Irish: Portrait of a People*. London: Andre Deutsch, 1976.

O'Muirithe, Diarmaid, and Deirdre Nuttall, eds. *Folklore of County Wexford*. Dublin: Four Courts Press, 1999.

Olsen, Jack. *Aphrodite: Desperate Mission*. New York: G. P. Putnam's Sons, 1970.

Onassis, Jacqueline, and Lee Radziwill. *One Special Summer*. New York: Delacorte Press, 1974.

Osbourne, Claire, ed. *Jackie: A Legend Defined*. New York: Avon Books, 1997.

Patch, Susanne Steinem. *The Story of the Hope Diamond*. New York: Harry N. Abrams, 1999.

Pierce, John W. *The Kennedys Who Left and the Kennedys Who Stayed*. Dunganstown, Ireland: The Kennedy Homestead, 2000.

Pottker, Jan. *Janet & Jackie*. New York: St. Martin's Press, 2001.

Rachlin, Harvey. *The Kennedys: A Chronological History 1823–Present*. New York: World Almanac, 1986.

Radin, Dean, Ph.D. *The Conscious Universe: The Scientific Truth of Psychic Phenomena*. San Francisco: HarperCollins, 1997.

Reedy, George. *From the Ward to the White House: The Irish in American Politics*. New York: Charles Scribner's Sons, 1991.

Rees, Jim. *Surplus People: The Fitzwilliam Clearances 1847–1856*. Cork, Ireland: Collins Press, 2000.

Reeves, Richard. *President Kennedy: Profile of Power*. New York: Simon & Schuster, 1993.

———. *President Nixon: Alone in the White House*. New York: Simon & Schuster, 2001.

Reeves, Thomas C. *A Question of Character: A Life of John F. Kennedy*. New York: Macmillan, 1991.

Roosevelt, James. *My Parents: A Differing View*. Chicago: Playboy Press, 1976.

Rose, Norman. *The Cliveden Set: Portrait of an Exclusive Fraternity*. London: Pimlico, 2001.

Ryan, Dennis P. *A Journey Through Boston Irish History*. Charleston, S.C.: Arcadia Publishing, 1999.

Scally, Robert James. *The End of Hidden Ireland: Rebellion, Famine and Emigration*. New York: Oxford University Press, 1995.

Schrier, Arnold. *Ireland and the American Emigration, 1850–1900*. Chester Springs, Penn.: Dufour Editions, Inc. 1997.

Searls, Hank. *The Lost Prince: Young Joe, the Forgotten Kennedy*. New York: Harcourt, Brace, 1969.

Shriver, Maria. *What's Heaven?* New York: St. Martin's Press, 1999.

Smith, Amanda, ed. *Hostage to Fortune: The Letters of Joseph P. Kennedy*. New York: Viking Penguin, 2001.

Specter, Arlen, with Charles Robbins. *Passion for Truth*. New York: HarperCollins, 2001.

Sullivan, Gerald, and Michael Kenney. *The Race for the Eighth*. New York: Harper and Row, 1987.

Swanson, Gloria. *Swanson on Swanson*. New York: Random House, 1980.

Taraborelli, J. Randy. *Jackie Ethel Joan: Women of Camelot*. New York: Warner Books, 2000.

Targ, Russell, and Jane Katra, Ph.D. *Miracles of Mind*. Novato, Calif.: New World Mind, 1998.

Taylor, Lawrence J. *Occasions of Faith: An Anthropology of Irish Catholics*. Dublin: Lilliput Press, 1995.

Thomas, Evan. *Robert Kennedy: His Life*. New York: Simon & Schuster, 2000.

Truman, Margaret. *First Ladies*. New York: Random House, 1995.

Whalen, Richard J. *The Founding Father: The Story of Joseph P. Kennedy*. Toronto: New American Library, 1964.

Whelan, Kevin. *Fellowship of Freedom: The United Irishmen and 1798*. Cork, Ireland: Cork University Press, 1998.

Whelan, Ronald E., ed. *Historical Materials in the John F. Kennedy Library*. Boston: John F. Kennedy Library, 2000.

Wills, Garry. *The Kennedy Imprisonment: A Meditation on Power*. New York: Pocket Books, 1981.

Yeats, W. B., ed. *Fairy and Folk Tales of Ireland*. New York: Galahad Books, 1996.

NOTES

INTRODUCTION: AN ILL-FATED HOUSE

The quotes attributed to John F. Kennedy Jr. come from one of John's oldest friends, who was a primary source for the Introduction. This friend had a lengthy telephone conversation with John on July 14, 1999, two days before John's fatal plane crash. The author interviewed the friend, on condition of anonymity, shortly after the accident, while the conversation was still fresh in his mind.

Other friends of John's provided corroborating material regarding the state of his disintegrating marriage to Carolyn Bessette Kennedy and the problems caused by Carolyn's use of cocaine. More than one of these friends had firsthand knowledge of Carolyn's drug taking. It should also be noted that Carolyn's use of drugs was an open secret in New York City fashion circles.

The material on Carolyn's constant meddling in the editorial operations of *George*, which helped wreck John's relationship with Michael Berman, is drawn from interviews with her friends, former members of the magazine's editorial staff, as well as with Jean-Louis Ginibre, the former editorial director of Hachette.

Details of Carolyn's falling-out with Caroline Kennedy Schlossberg were provided by people who attended John's Cumberland Island wedding and knew Carolyn well.

All the quotes attributed to Jacqueline Kennedy Onassis, as well as the author's interpretation of her attitude toward her children and their friends, were drawn from the author's personal conversations with Jackie over more than a dozen years. The author made notes of these conversations at the time in his reporter's diaries.

Books that were used in the Introduction include Anderson's *The Day John Died*; Berlitz's *The Bermuda Triangle: An Incredible Saga of Unexplained Disappearances*; Bowen's *The Curse of the Misbegotten: A Tale of the House of O'Neill*; Carter and Mace's *The Discovery of the Tomb of Tutankhamen*; Chowdhury's *The Last Dive: A Father and Son's Fatal Descent into the Ocean's Depths*; Clinch's *The Kennedy Neurosis: A Psychological Portrait of an American Dynasty*; Clymer's *Edward M. Kennedy: A Biography*; Collier and Horowitz's *The Kennedys: An American Drama*; Davis's *The Kennedy Clan: Dynasty and Disaster, 1848–1984*; Dossey's *Be Careful What You Pray For . . . You Just Might Get It*; Gage's *Greek Fire: The Story of Maria Callas and Aristotle Onassis*; Gatti's *The Kennedy Curse*; Hamer and Copeland's *Living with Our Genes: Why They Matter More Than You Think*; Edith Hamilton's *Mythology* and *The Greek Way*; Handlin's *Boston's Immigrants 1790–1880*; Kernberg's *Borderline Conditions and Pathological Narcissism*; Kessler's *The Sins of the Father*; Kusche's *The Bermuda Triangle Mystery Solved*; Lasch's *The Culture of Narcissism: American Life in an Age of Diminishing Expectations*; Leigh's *Prince Charming: The John F. Kennedy Jr.*

Story; Lowen's *Narcissism: Denial of the True Self;* Malinowski's *Magic, Science and Religion, and Other Essays;* Marvin's *The Kennedy Curse;* Patch's *The Story of the Hope Diamond;* Radin's *The Conscious Universe: The Scientific Truth of Psychic Phenomena;* Thomas's *Robert Kennedy: His Life;* and Wills's *The Kennedy Imprisonment: A Meditation on Power.*

The author conducted on-the-record interviews with Lou Adler, Rachel Altein, Joe Armstrong, Dr. Bob Arnot, Dr. Jiei Atacama, Dr. Michael Baden, Peter Beard, Dr. Jonathan Benjamin, Michael Beschloss, Sue Erikson Bloland, Captain Greg Brown, Dr. Robert Cloninger, Rabbi Schlomo Cunin, Captain Sam DeBow, Lisa DePaulo, Dr. Larry Dossey, Steve Florio, Dr. Bruce Forester, Sergeant William Freeman, Nicholas Gage, Barbara Gibson, Jean-Louis Ginibre, Andrew Greeley, Captain Mark Helmkamp, Captain Burt Marsh, Robert Morgenthau, Dr. Robert Moyzis, Dr. Werner Muensterberger, Dr. Peter Neubauer, Dr. Chit Ranawat, John Scanlon, Lyndal L. Shaneyfelt, Dr. David Skinner, Jocelyn Stern, Brett Tjaden, Candace Trunzo, Lieutenant Commander David Waterman, Paul Wilmot, and Garrett Yount.

1. PATRICK KENNEDY: THE UNINTENTIONAL CURSE

The narrative of Patrick Kennedy's last days in Ireland during the Famine, the account of his Irish roots, his trip to Liverpool and stay there, his crossing to America, and his years in Boston are drawn from numerous published sources. Among them are the following books and pamphlets:

R. A. Pierce's "Patrick Kennedy of Dunganstown, Co. Wexford, Great-Grandfather of the President"; J. A. Pierce's "The Kennedys Who Left and the Kennedys Who Stayed"; Herman Melville's *Redburn: His First Voyage;* O'Grada's *The Great Irish Famine;* Quinn's "The Tragedy of Bridget Such-a-One"; Cronin's *A History of Ireland;* Coffey and Golway's *The Irish in America;* Hollet's *Passage to the New World: Packet Ships and Irish Famine Emigrants, 1845–1851;* Trevelyan's *The Irish Crisis;* Morash's *Writing the Irish Famine;* Mitchel's *The Last Conquest of Ireland (Perhaps)* and "To the 'Surplus Population' of Ireland"; O'Brien's *Mother Ireland: A Memoir;* Davies's *What's Bred in the Bone;* Landry Preteseille's "The Irish Emigrant Trade to North America—1845–1855"; Miller and Wagner's *Out of Ireland: The Story of Irish Emigration to America;* Scally's *The End of Hidden Ireland: Rebellion, Famine and Emigration; Triumph and Tragedy: The Story of the Kennedys,* by the writers, photographers, and editors of the Associated Press; Kraehenbuehl's "The American Wake as a 'Rite of Passage' "; O'Flaherty's "Going Into Exile," in *Waiting and Other Modern Stories;* O'Muirithe and Nuttall's *Folklore of County Wexford;* Schrier's *Ireland and the American Emigration, 1850–1900;* Brian Patrick Kennedy's *The Irish Kennedys: The Story of the "Rebellious O'Kennedys";* Peter O'Connor's *Beyond the Mist: What Irish Mythology Can Teach Us About Ourselves;* Lenon's "The Kennedy Sept, Part III," the *Irish Independent;* Kevin Whelan's *Fellowship of Freedom: The United Irishmen and 1798;* Macken's *The Silent People;* the *Illustrated London News,* July 6, 1850: Reese's *A Fairewell to Famine;* Nathaniel Hawthorne's *The English Notebooks;* Landry Preteseille's "Gone to Look for America"; Davis's *The Kennedy Clan: Dynasty and Disaster, 1948–1984;* "Papers Relative to the Emigration to the British Provinces in North America"; "Report of the Committee of Internal Health on the Asiatic Cholera

(Boston, 1849)"; Handlin's *Boston's Immigrants 1790–1880*; and Collier and Horowitz's *The Kennedys: An American Drama*.

In addition, the author consulted the following documents: Glynn's *Manual for Irish Genealogy*; The Historical Research Center's *Family Name History: Fitzgerald*; Irish Department of Foreign Affairs' *Folklore in Ireland*; Irish Genealogical Society International's *Families in Ireland from the 11th to the End of the 16th Century*; John Fitzgerald Kennedy Trust's *Dunbrody: Rebirth of an Emigrant Ship, 1845–2001*; and O'Dowd's *John F. Kennedy Junior's Irish Legacy*.

The author conducted interviews with Sean Carberry, Michael Coffey, Tim Pat Coogan, Patrick Cronin, Linda Degh, Micky Furlong, Terry Golway, Patrick Grenan, Patricia Hardy, Robert Haydon Jones, Malachy McCourt, Pat McKenna, Terry Moran, Cormac O'Grada, Daithi O'Hogan, Fintan O'Toole, Richard Andrew Pierce, Pat Quilty, Peter Quinn, Robert Scally, John Scanlon, Jay Tunney, and Kevin Whelan.

2. JOHN FRANCIS FITZGERALD: FAVORITE SON

Published sources include Thomas H. O'Connor's *The Boston Irish: A Political History*; Handlin's *Boston Immigrants 1790–1880*; Davis's *The Kennedy Clan: Dynasty and Disaster, 1948–1884*; Coffey and Golway's *The Irish in America*; Ryan's *A Journey Through Boston Irish History*; O'Donovan-Rossa's *Rossa's Recollections 1838 to 1898*; Ainley's *Boston Mahatma: Martin Lomasney*; Goodwin's *The Fitzgeralds and the Kennedys: An American Saga*; McCormick's *The Hell-Fire Club*; Hashimoto's "Blather, 1998"; Beatty's *The Rascal King: The Life and Times of John Michael Curley, 1874–1958*; and Lowen's *Narcissism: Denial of the True Self*.

The author conducted interviews in America with Michael Coffey, Terry Golway, Patricia Hardy, Robert Haydon Jones, Malachy McCourt, Terry Moran, Peter Quinn, Robert Scally, John Scanlon, and Jay Tunney. In Ireland, the author spoke with Tim Pat Coogan, Patrick Cronin, Patrick Grenan, Pat McKenna, Cormac O'Grada, Daithi O'Hogan, Fintan O'Toole, Pat Quilty, and Kevin Whelan.

3. JOSEPH PATRICK KENNEDY: SPEAKING THE LANGUAGE OF HIS AGE

The author drew mainly on the following published sources: Beschloss's *Kennedy and Roosevelt: The Uneasy Alliance*; Kessler's *The Sins of the Father*; Collier and Horowitz's *The Kennedys: An American Drama*; Goodwin's *The Fitzgeralds and the Kennedys: An American Saga*; Koskoff's *Joseph P. Kennedy: A Life and Times*; Krock's *Memoirs: Sixty Years on the Firing Line*; Hersh's *The Dark Side of Camelot*; Roosevelt's *My Parents: A Differing View*; Wills's *The Kennedy Imprisonment: A Meditation on Power*; Leamer's *The Kennedy Men: 1901–1963* and *The Kennedy Women: The Saga of an American Family*; Clinch's *The Kennedy Neurosis: A Psychological Portrait of an American Dynasty*; Whalen's *The Founding Father*; Madsen's *Gloria and Joe: The Star-Crossed Love Affair of Gloria Swanson and Joe Kennedy*; Rose Kennedy's *Times to Remember*; Krock's bylined article in *The New York Times*, December 8, 1927, Arthur Krock Papers, Princeton University; Smith's *Hostage to Fortune: The Letters of Joseph P. Kennedy*; Higham's *Rose: The Life and Times of Rose Fitzgerald Kennedy*; Plaice's, "The British Fifth Column That Never Was," *BBC History Magazine*, December 2000; Amelan's "Appeasement, Anyone?" *Jerusalem Post*, February 4, 2001; Rose's *The Cliveden Set: Portrait of an Exclusive Fraternity*; Joseph P. Kennedy diaries in Smith, *Hostage to*

Fortune: The Letters of Joseph P. Kennedy; William Manchester's *The Last Lion: Alone: 1932–1940;* Nigel Hamilton's *JFK: Reckless Youth;* Joseph P., Kennedy's diplomatic memoirs in Smith, *Hostage to Fortune: The Letters of Joseph P. Kennedy;* Lewis B. Lyons's article in *The Boston Globe,* November 10, 1940; Gore Vidal's article "Eleanor" in *The New York Review of Books,* November 18, 1971.

4. KATHLEEN KENNEDY: THROWING CAUTION TO THE WIND

The description of the glass-roofed vault of St. Pancras Station is drawn from Trachtenberg and Hyman's *Architecture: From Prehistory to Post-Modernism.* They write: "The skeletal transparency of the ferrovitreous vault added a futuristic, magic dimension to the stunning space, especially as the vault was made to spring from the platform level where the passengers stood."

In addition, the author relied on the following published sources: Smith's *Hostage to Fortune: The Letters of Joseph P. Kennedy;* Leamer's *The Kennedy Women: The Saga of an American Family;* McTaggart's *Kathleen Kennedy: Her Life and Times;* Collier and Horowitz's *The Kennedys: An American Drama;* "Kathleen Kennedy, 24, to Wed British Lord," *Boston Herald,* May 4, 1944; "Fitz Backs Granddaughter's Choice but Bogs Down on Wedding Details," *Boston Herald,* May 5, 1944; "Mrs. Kennedy in Hospital Here; Good Condition," *The Boston Globe,* May 5, 1944; "Kennedy Daughter Weds in London," *The Boston Globe,* May 6, 1944; Rose Kennedy's *Times to Remember;* "Mrs. Kennedy Leaves Boston by Plane," *The Boston Globe,* May 6, 1944, "War Bars Cable to Kennedys as Daughter Is Wed in London," *Boston Herald,* May 7, 1944; Nigel Hamilton's *JFK: Reckless Youth;* Goodwin's *The Fitzgeralds and the Kennedys: An American Saga;* Whalen's *The Founding Father: The Story of Joseph P. Kennedy;* "Earl Killed in Plane Crash," *Boston American,* May 14, 1948; Klein's *All Too Human;* Gibson and Schwarz's *Rose Kennedy and Her Family: The Third Generation.*

5. JOHN FITZGERALD KENNEDY: THE ROAD TO DALLAS

The quotes attributed to President Kennedy come from Dave Powers, one of the President's closest aides, who was a primary source for this chapter. Powers accompanied the President most of the time during the last two days of his life and was a witness to the President's frolic in the White House swimming pool with Fiddle and Faddle and the assassination in Dallas. The author interviewed Powers in April 1997.

The author also interviewed Jay Tunney, Helen O'Donnell, Sue Erikson Bloland, Hamilton Brown, Paul "Red" Fay, Lyndal L. Shaneyfelt, and Anthony Sherman.

Published sources for this chapter: Clinch's *The Kennedy Neurosis: A Psychological Portrait of an American Dynasty;* Thomas Reeves's *A Question of Character: A Life of John F. Kennedy;* Manchester's *The Death of the President;* Beschloss's *The Crisis Years* and *Kennedy v. Khrushchev;* William Latham's "The Dark Side of the American Dream," *Rolling Stone,* August 5, 1982; Richard Reeves's *President Kennedy: Profile of Power;* Bryant's *Dog Days at the White House: The Outrageous Memoirs of the Presidential Kennel Keeper;* Lawford's *The Peter Lawford Story;* Giglio's *The Presidency of John F. Kennedy;* Race's article in *The New York Times,* July 29, 2002; Hersh's *The Dark Side of Camelot;* Lewis H. Lapham's "Edward Kennedy and the Romance of Death," *Harper's,* December 1979; "JFK and the Mobsters' Moll," *Time,* December 29, 1975; Davis's *The Kennedy Clan; The Warren Commission Report;* MacNeil's *The*

Way We Were: 1963—The Year Kennedy Was Shot; "Revealed: How Irish-Americans Held the Power in John F. Kennedy's White House, *The* (London) *Sunday Times,* May 26, 2002; White's *In Search of America;* Collier and Horowitz's *The Kennedys: An American Drama.*

6. WILLIAM KENNEDY SMITH: TWILIGHT OF THE GODS

Interviews were conducted with Floyd Abrams, Barbara Gamarekian, Barry Krischer, Pat McKenna, Ellen Roberts, Mark Scheiner, Kevin Selvig, Christine Stapleton, David Pecker, and Mike Edmonson.

The author relied heavily on sworn statements, depositions, and other official documents in the 1991 William Kennedy Smith rape trial. Among them: *Deposition of Patrick H. Barry; Deposition of Stephen P. Barry;* David H. Bludworth's *Petition for Writ of Prohibition; Statements of Patricia Bowman* to the Palm Beach Police Department; *Statement of Michele Cassone; Deposition of Chuck Desiderio; Statement of Chuck Desiderio; Statement of Dr. Lynn Gulledge; Deposition of Dr. Lynn Gulledge;* Warren D. Holmes's Letter to Sergeant Keith A. Robinson; *Deposition of Edward M. Kennedy; Deposition of Patrick J. Kennedy;* Landmark Preservation Commission's *1095 North Ocean Boulevard: Designation Report; Statement of Lisa Lattes; Deposition of Lisa J. Lattes; Statement of Anne Mercer; Deposition of Leonard Mercer;* Herbert J. Miller Jr.'s Letter to State Attorney David H. Bludworth; New Mexico Board of Examiners' *Application for Approval to Practice as a Resident Physician: William K. Smith;* Office of the State Attorney's "Senator Edward Kennedy Chronology"; *Statement of Lieutenant Thomas M. Perry; Statement of Detective Christine E. Rigolo; Deposition of Detective Christine E. Rigolo; Statement of Stephen Michael Scott; Deposition of Amanda Smith;* and *Deposition of Jean K. Smith.*

The author drew on the following articles: Fox Butterfield, "Views of the Kennedy House: Poignant Past, Busy Present," *The New York Times,* April 8, 1991; Alan McConagha, "Kennedy Media Control Slipping," *Washington Times,* April 11, 1991; "Who's Who in the Palm Beach Rape Case," *The Palm Beach Post,* April 14, 1991; "The Soul of the Kennedys," *Washington Times,* April 18, 1991; "Hints of Favoritism Still Swirl Around '84 Kennedy Probe," *The Palm Beach Post,* April 21, 1991; Tim Pallesen, "Pro-Kennedy Charges Again Haunt State Attorney," *The Palm Beach Post,* April 21, 1991; " 'New York Times' Regrets Action in Kennedy Rape Case," Associated Press, April 26, 1991; Jodi Mailander, "Gumshoes Seek Tale of Sleaze to Discredit Kennedy Accuser," *The Palm Beach Post,* April 28, 1991; "Naming the Victim," *Newsweek,* April 29, 1991; Lance Morrow, "The Trouble with Teddy," *Time,* April 29, 1991; John Donnelly and Dave von Drehle, "Kennedy Kin Faces Rape Count," *The Miami Herald,* May 10, 1991; Mary Jordan, "Willy Smith, the 'Independent' Kennedy, Anonymous No More," *The Washington Post,* May 10, 1991; Mary Jordan, "The Prosecutor Never Rests: Moira Lasch, Building the Case Against William Kennedy Smith," *The Washington Post,* October 30, 1991; Karen Goldberg and Joe Dimaola, "Lawyers: Acquittal Probable," Fort Lauderdale *Sun-Sentinel,* May 16, 1991; "Spotlight on the Senator: What Did Teddy Know?" *Newsweek,* May 27, 1991; Margaret Carlson, "When in Doubt, Obfuscate," *Time,* May 27, 1991; Margie Kacoha, "Miller a Longtime Lawyer for Kennedys," *Palm Beach Daily News,* June 9, 1991; David Zeman, "Smith Switches Attorneys in Rape Defense," *The Miami Herald,* June 25, 1991;

David Zeman, "Smith Defense: Alleged Victim Resents Men," *The Miami Herald,*
August 10, 1991; "Maid Disputes Kennedy Friend's Story," *The Miami Herald,* June
26, 1991; David Zeman, "Witness Disputes Kennedy," *The Miami Herald,* July 17,
1991; Timothy Clifford, "Smith Rape Defense to Focus on Woman's Sexual History,"
Newsday, July 19, 1991; Christine Stapleton, "Evidence of Similar Crimes Can Devastate a Defense," *The Palm Beach Post,* July 24, 1991; Christine Stapleton, "Smith As-
sault Statements Similar," *The Palm Beach Post,* July 24, 1991; Christine Stapleton,
"Smith Attorney: Woman Is Mentally Ill," *The Palm Beach Post,* August 10, 1991; Chris-
tine Stapleton, "Doctor Backs Story Claiming '88 Rape Try by Smith," *The Palm Beach
Post,* August 22, 1991; Val Ellicott and Christine Stapleton, "Kennedy Lawyer Tried to
Contact '88 Accuser," *The Palm Beach Post,* August 10, 1991; Joe Treen, "Maximum
Moira," *People,* August 12, 1991; E. J. Dionne, "Changes for Kennedy: Friends See Toll
from Palm Beach Incident," *The Washington Post,* August 28, 1991; "Psychologist Says
Smith, Accuser Have Serious Emotional Problems," Associated Press in *The Palm
Beach Post,* October 6, 1991; Diane White, "Willie's Lawyers Dress Down Accuser,"
New York Daily News, November 10, 1991; Val Ellicott, " 'Will' Smith Strikes a Pose at
Photographers' Request," *The Palm Beach Post,* November 11, 1991; Pope Brock, "Hot
on the Trial," *People,* December 16, 1991; David Hiltbrand, "Picks & Pans," *People,* De-
cember 23, 1991; Joe Treen, "The Most Famous Woman Never Seen," *People,* Decem-
ber 23, 1991; Dominick Dunne, "The Verdict," *Vanity Fair,* March 1992; Frank
Cerabino, "Twists, Tangles in Kennedy Case," *The Palm Beach Post,* April 14, 1992.

Books included Ash's *Private Palm Beach: Tropical Style;* Clymer's *Edward M.
Kennedy: A Biography;* Gibson and Schwarz's *The Kennedys: The Third Generation* and
Rose Kennedy and Her Family; and Leamer's *The Kennedy Women: The Saga of an
American Family.*

7. JOHN FITZGERALD KENNEDY JR.: CUT FROM THE SAME CLOTH

The scene of Carolyn Bessette Kennedy's assignation in Greenwich Village was described by a close personal friend and business associate of Carolyn's boyfriend, who
was in the apartment when she came to call. The author interviewed this source, who
requested anonymity, in April 2002.

The scene of the meeting among Lauren Bessette, her sister Carolyn, and JFK
Jr. was described by Lauren to a friend, who conveyed it to the author shortly after
the fatal plane crash.

Many of the sources drawn upon in this chapter are the same as those in the
introduction.

The author drew on the following articles: Edward Kennedy, Eulogy for John F.
Kennedy Jr. in *New York Post,* Saturday, July 24, 1999; Caryn James, "Generating
Significance to Apply to Celebrity," *The New York Times,* July 24, 1999; "Special
Report: John F. Kennedy Jr., 1960–1999," *Time,* July 26, 1999; "Remembering John
F. Kennedy Jr.," *People,* August 2, 1999; "Special Report: Ask Not . . . ," *Time,* August
2, 1999; "Lost in the Night," *People,* August 2, 1999; "Prince of the City," *New York,*
August 2, 1999; "Hour of Loss," *People,* August 9, 1999; Evgenia Peretz, "The Private
Princess," *Vanity Fair,* September 1999; "To Have and to Hold," *People,* July 24, 2000;
Rick Marin, "Men Are Crazy for Women Who Are, Too," *The New York Times,* Feb-
ruary 12, 2001; "Farewell Issue," *George,* May 2001.

EPILOGUE: THE FALL OF THE HOUSE OF KENNEDY

The scene of Carolyn's friend removing her stash of cocaine from her refrigerator comes from a source who was present and who requested anonymity.

In addition, interviews were conducted by the author with Dr. Bob Arnot, Dr. Michael Baden, Captain Greg Brown, Captain Sam DeBow, Dr. Richard Evans, Sergeant William Freeman, Captain Mark Helmkamp, Captain Burt Marsh, Jocelyn Stern, Candace Trunzo, Roy Wachtel, and Leon Wagner.

The scene of Rose Schlossberg sticking her tongue out at the media was witnessed by the author.

The author drew on the following articles: Julian Brouwer, "We Need Caroline: Plea to JFK's Girl Over Family Crisis," *Sunday Mirror,* August 25, 2002; "The Fading Lure of Camelot," *The Economist,* August 31, 2002; "Magical History Tour: A Busload of Kennedys Pay Homage to the Past—Their Own—on a Summer Road Trip," *People,* September 2, 2002; Bob Dart, "Kennedy Mystique Enlivens Maryland Races," *The Palm Beach Post,* September 8, 2002; Dave Espo, "Campaign Notebook: Republicans Concerned About Gekas Re-election in Pennsylvania," Associated Press, September 9, 2002; "Inside Track," *Boston Herald,* September 11, 2002; Jeff Barker, "For Shriver, Kennedy Ties Not Enough in 8th District; Voters Saw Van Hollen as Stronger vs. Morella," *Baltimore Sun,* September 12, 2002; Page Six: "Kennedy's Loss Tolls Darkly," *New York Post,* September 13, 2002; Dave Boyer, "Shriver's Loss Suggests Kennedy Dynasty Fades; Still, Liberal Followers Say the Younger Generation Can Look to Having a Role in Politics," *Washington Times,* September 15, 2002; Francis X. Clines, "In Maryland, a Blowout Becomes a Nail-Biter," *The New York Times,* September 15, 2002.

INDEX